Commercial Real Estate Restructuring Revolution

Commercial Real Estate Restructuring Revolution

Strategies, Tranche Warfare, and Prospects for Recovery

STEPHEN B. MEISTER

WILEY

John Wiley & Sons, Inc.

Published by John Wiley & Sons, Inc., Hoboken, New Jersey.

Published simultaneously in Canada.

For general information on our other products and services or for technical support, please contact our Customer Care Department within the United States at (800) 762-2974, outside the United States at (317) 572-3993 or fax (317) 572-4002.

Wiley also publishes its books in a variety of electronic formats. Some content that appears in print may not be available in electronic books. For more information about Wiley products, visit our web site at www.wiley.com.

Library of Congress Cataloging-in-Publication Data:
Meister, Stephen B.
    Commercial real estate restructuring revolution : strategies, tranche warfare, and prospects for recovery / Stephen B. Meister.
        p. cm.——(Wiley finance series)
    Includes index.
        ISBN 978-0-470-62683-2 (cloth); 978-0-470-94430-1 (ebk); 978-0-470-94429-5 (ebk)
    1. Commercial real estate–United States.   I. Title.
    HD1393.58.U6M45 2010
    333.33'870973–dc22

                                                                                2010032274

10 9 8 7 6 5 4 3 2 1

To my wife and partner, Melissa,
who endured many weekends and several holidays with
a husband in absentia so that this book could be written.

Contents

Preface

Owners of office and apartment buildings, and retail and hotel properties, draw upon both consumers and businesses as their customers. The businesses that occupy our office buildings and book our hotels, and our retailers, in turn, depend largely upon consumers, whose spending accounts for over 70 percent of our gross domestic product. One way or the other, commercial real estate is dependent upon consumers.

The financial health of U.S. consumers was decimated by the bursting of the housing bubble, while American businesses, particularly small businesses, were ravaged by the abrupt curtailment of credit following on its heels. The credit freeze itself was triggered by the subprime mortgage crisis.

To understand where our commercial real estate markets are headed, we must gauge the health *and future prospects* of U.S. consumers. This, in turn, requires an understanding of the subprime mortgage crisis, the building and bursting of the U.S. housing bubble, and where the housing sector is headed—matters covered in Chapters 1 and 2. Consumer purchasing power and sentiment are largely driven by the relative health of the housing and equities markets.

During the first half of the 20th century, the U.S. home ownership rate hovered in a tight range—roughly 45 to 48 percent. After the end of World War II, however, the percentage of home ownership began a steady climb, reaching 55 percent in 1950 and from there up to 66.2 percent at the turn of the millennium. By 2004–2005, the U.S. home ownership rate had skyrocketed to 69 percent.

The stunning post–World War II increase in U.S. home ownership rates—going from about 47 percent to 69 percent (representing a 47 percent increase in the home ownership rate)—was not brought about by laissez-faire market forces, but rather by aggressive government intervention designed and driven by a liberal vanguard so blinded by the political correctness of marching toward the American Dream for America's minorities that they could not foresee the devastating consequences to both the supposed beneficiaries of their intervention, as well as to all other Americans (and really, people the world over). Regrettably, however, good intentions are not enough; as Oscar Wilde said, "All bad poetry springs from genuine feeling." And as the late neoconservative publisher, Irving Kristol, added, "The same can be said for bad politics."

Empowered by the powerful influence of Congress over the government-sponsored enterprises and the corrupt influence of mortgage lenders like Angelo Mozilo's Countrywide Financial over Congress and Fannie and Freddie; assisted by mortgage originators, who, courtesy of Wall Street's securitization prowess, retained no stake in the loans they originated and therefore no reason to underwrite them soundly, and the appraisers they controlled; aided and abetted by an oligopoly of credit raters who, protected by our government from the pressures of free-market competition, had fallen asleep at the switch; and enabled by the swollen supply of cheap and easy money put into place in the years preceding the bursting of the housing bubble by the Greenspan Fed, there was no stopping the mainstream-media-praised racial lending quotas established under our affordable home ownership mandate. The results, given the scale of the U.S. housing market, were nothing less than cataclysmic.

Trillions of dollars were loaned to homebuyers who put little or no money down on homes they purchased, and to existing homeowners who used their appreciating homes like ATM machines by taking ever larger cash-out refinancing loans. In both cases, the borrowers lacked the income and other assets necessary to repay those loans.

A massive housing bubble resulted from trillions of dollars in government-subsidized and mandated affordable housing loans. That bubble began imploding in 2006, as unfit borrowers, many of whom were granted loans well beyond their means to repay, started defaulting in droves.

In order to comprehend the impact of the collapse of the housing markets on commercial real estate ("CRE"), Chapter 3 traces the history of the CRE capital markets, so that the reader has an understanding of the required structures and concepts before delving into more detailed aspects of CRE financing in later chapters. I explain the composition of modern complex CRE debt stacks, including securitized mortgage loans and junior loans, now known as mezzanine loans, and recurring issues such as maturity defaults, value declines, and extension rights.

At the end of 2008, nominal investments in U.S. commercial real estate totaled $6.4 trillion, composed of $2.9 trillion of equity investments and $3.5 trillion in debt. CRE assets are held by a diverse group of investors—individual entrepreneurs, including multigenerational "real estate families," publicly traded and private real estate investment trusts (REITS), real estate private equity firms, hedge funds, banks and savings and loan associations, privately held real estate holding companies, publicly traded and private businesses, not-for-profit corporations, foreign, federal, state and local governments, and a whole plethora of foreign investors, including foreign individuals, banks, and sovereign wealth funds.

In Chapter 4, I address CRE values, which are a function of both underlying fundamentals and the yields demanded by CRE investors—capitalization (cap) rates. This chapter explains why increases in market cap rates, more than eroding market fundamentals, are responsible for CRE value reductions. A corollary of this observation is that once rental and vacancy rates return to their prerecession levels, CRE values will likely still lie behind their prerecession levels due to increased cap rates.

In Chapter 5, I describe a process that began unfolding in the last two quarters of 2009 and that will continue to unfold for the next five to eight years, as several hundreds of billions of dollars of CRE loans mature annually in that period. While lender reactions have varied—even within the participants owning a single loan—one consistent lender-driven theme has already emerged: putting off the day of reckoning until a better market arrives.

The deferral of lender loss-taking can take different forms. Where the real property is encumbered by a single mortgage loan (i.e., there are no mezzanine loans or junior lenders), the decision about what to do at maturity—from the lender side—is simplified in that one lender makes that decision, at least where that single mortgage loan is not owned by multiple participants or securitized. In such a case, assuming the loan is partly underwater (i.e., the loan balance exceeds the property value), the lender has essentially four options:

1. Sell the loan at a discount to a third party.
2. Take a discounted payoff (DPO) from the borrower (or sell the loan to a borrower affiliate at a discount, the economic equivalent of a DPO).
3. Take back the property either by way of a deed in lieu of foreclosure or through the prosecution of foreclosure proceeding (whether judicial or nonjudicial).
4. Enter into a modification and extension of the loan with the borrower, usually involving three elements—an increase in term, an increase in interest rate, and a cash payment from the borrower, some of which may be applied to reduce the principal balance of the loan and the balance of which may be held as reserves for future costs not otherwise fundable from property cash flow.

In Chapter 6, I discuss the intramural battles among lenders in complex debt stacks, colloquially referred to as "tranche warfare." As CRE debt maturities and payment defaults hit on individual properties or portfolios encumbered by commercial mortgage-backed securities (CMBS) or whole mortgage loans coupled with hierarchical mezzanine debt stacks, tranche warfare has erupted between subordinate and senior lenders, as well as between lenders and borrowers.

No better example of the "tranche warfare" phenomenon is presented than by what happened on David Lichtenstein's massive 2007 Extended Stay Hotels acquisition. In June of 2007, developer David Lichtenstein purchased for $8 billion the more than 75,000-unit Extended Stay Hotel (ESH) portfolio—an enormous portfolio of some 683 extended stay hotel properties located in 44 states and Canada—from Blackstone (not to be confused with BlackRock, the co-investor in Peter Cooper Village/Stuyvesant Town). Blackstone had purchased the ESH portfolio (then 475 hotel properties) for less than $2 billion in March 2004, three years before it sold the expanded 683-hotel chain to Lichtenstein. In 2004, the ESH portfolio traded for $4.2 million per hotel property while just three years later it traded for $11.7 million per hotel property—a nearly threefold price increase in just three years. The Bank of America and the other original lenders attempted to take the hotel properties back from Lichtenstein in a "transfer-in-lieu-of-UCC-foreclosure" transaction that would have wiped out $2.6 billion in junior mezzanine lenders. I represented one of these mezzanine lenders and obtained a temporary restraining order blocking that transaction. As a result, Lichtenstein put the entire portfolio into bankruptcy. Eventually, Centerbridge, Paulson and Blackstone bought the portfolio out of bankruptcy for $3.88 billion—about $5.7 million per hotel property.

As the CRE crisis has deepened, a host of hedge funds, real estate private equity investors, publicly traded and private REITs, and foreign and domestic investors have sought to buy distressed commercial real estate. Unfortunately, the distressed CRE owner is rarely in a position, alone, to convey title at a market price. Given the 40–60 percent decline in CRE values since the height of the market, and the far greater leverage levels offered in the frothy refinancing markets CRE investors tapped into during the 2003–2008 period, it is a rare CRE asset that is not leveraged beyond its current value. As a result, CRE investors must resort to indirect methods of acquiring commercial real properties—buying a "loan to own" or a short-sale by the deed holder with the consent of the lenders. I discuss these acquisition strategies in Chapter 7.

CRE investors anxious to acquire overleveraged properties have taken to purchasing either at or below par, depending on the situation, one or more mortgages or mezzanine loans encumbering the target property and thereafter foreclosing against the collateral. In states where mortgage foreclosures must take the form of court proceedings, strategic buyers of "loans to own" will often purchase both the first mortgage and senior mezzanine loan, so they can avail themselves of the streamlined (nonjudicial) UCC foreclosure proceeding available to the foreclosing mezzanine lender. The trick is identifying and buying the loan or participation in the control position.

Once a lender, whether the whole loan owner itself or the servicer for a CMBS loan, determines that the loan is underwater—that the CRE asset has a market value less than the balance due on the loan—a series of obvious economic motivations set in. These economic motivations have spawned two recurring themes in lender-borrower conflicts: funding cessations and extension fights. I discuss both these trends in Chapter 8.

For one thing, the lender does not want to get in any deeper—it does not want to advance any more money. Second, if the property is income-producing, the lender is loathe to allow net cash flow (even after debt service) to leak to junior stakeholders (whether junior mezzanine lenders or equity participants in the borrower). Such excess net cash flow, from the perspective of the senior lender, ought to be applied toward reduction of the principal balance of the senior loan—thereby reducing the senior lender's eventual loss—instead of going to any subordinate stakeholder. However, typical loan documents do not permit the senior lender (prior to maturity, including an extended maturity date) to trap all net cash flow available after servicing the senior debt interest, provided the borrower is not in default.

I discuss key bankruptcy considerations for CRE assets in Chapter 9. Bankruptcy filings are infrequent, relatively speaking, for commercial real estate. For one thing, the vast majority of CRE assets are held by single-purpose entities (SPEs). These SPEs generally do not directly employ management or building personnel, who, more often, are employed by a separate management company, even if that management company is controlled by the same principals who own the SPE. In consequence, the majority of CRE-owning SPEs are not operating companies in the true sense of that term, but rather are dedicated legal vehicles for maintaining CRE ownership in an isolated format, offering protection (via liability immunization) to the SPE's equity holders and their other assets (including other CRE assets).

As a result, commercial real estate–owning SPEs are not well suited to classic bankruptcy reorganization, which contemplates a leaner going concern exiting the bankruptcy process, though bankruptcy reorganization can be used to force the deleveraging of an overleveraged CRE asset through a cram down (debt restructuring).

There are, of course, exceptions to this generalization. CRE assets held by public and private real estate investment trusts and hotel chains, for example, do present true operating companies capable of benefiting from the bankruptcy reorganization process. Recent examples of CRE-based going concerns that have entered the bankruptcy process include Extended Stay Hotels and shopping mall giant General Growth Properties. In addition, while debt cram downs sometimes do occur within the context of Chapter 11 reorganization, the ubiquitous nonrecourse carve-out guaranty—making a principal, fund, or holding company liable for the loan in the event of a bankruptcy filing—make such cram downs relatively rare.

The multifamily sector, discussed in Chapter 10, presents unique considerations not affecting other CRE asset classes. First, multifamily lending is the only category of CRE asset lending supported by government-subsidized loans—multifamily properties are financed by Fannie Mae and Freddie Mac. Second, the multifamily sector is the only CRE asset class subject to price controls, the most severe restriction on the free market possible, short of a government takeover. For these two reasons, the multifamily sector presents both risks and benefits not found in other CRE asset classes.

According to its website, "Fannie Mae provides multifamily financing for affordable and market-rate rental housing. We operate nationally, in all multifamily markets and under all economic conditions. Every day, Fannie Mae delivers economical, flexible, and tailored financing for investors. In 2008 Fannie Mae invested over $35.5 billion in the multifamily affordable housing market. Eighty-nine percent of the homes and rental housing financed by Fannie Mae lenders are affordable to families at or below the median income of their communities." Likewise, Freddie Mac boasts that its "multifamily division supports the acquisition, refinance, rehabilitation and construction of apartment communities across America."

Fannie and Freddie dominated the multifamily lending market in 2009. According to the Co-Star Group, a commercial real estate information company, Fannie Mae and Freddie Mac overwhelmed private-sector multifamily financing in 2009: "The two federal government sponsored entities financed 81% of multifamily activity based on Freddie Mac's accounting. Their combined activity totaled $36.4 billion. Fannie Mae, through its lender and housing partners, provided $19.8 billion in debt financing for the multifamily rental housing market in 2009."

While the vast majority of the approximately 17 million rental apartments in the United States are priced by the free market, some major U.S. cities (like New York, the District of Columbia, and San Francisco), as well as some smaller towns in New York, California, New Jersey, and Maryland, have chosen to fix rents through rent control laws. Few legislative efforts in our history have proved as misguided or resulted in more damage than our rent control laws, though it remains to be seen whether Obamacare gives rent control a run for its money on the worst-legislative-idea-ever list.

Oddly enough, universal condemnation of rent control has been advanced by economists on both the right (Nobel Prize winners Milton Friedman and Friedrich Hayek, for example) and on the left (Nobel laureate Gunnar Myrdal, an architect of the Swedish Labor Party's welfare state). In fact, Myrdal said, "Rent control has in certain Western countries constituted, maybe, the worst example of poor planning by governments lacking courage and vision." Another Swedish socialist and economist, Assar Lindbeck, bluntly put it that "in many cases rent control appears to be the most efficient technique presently known to destroy a city—except for bombing."

As with any price control, rent control—by mandating prices below the level dictated by a free market—inevitably creates a shortage of the price-controlled commodity—here housing. Said differently, in a price-coordinated or free market economy, suppliers furnish more of a given commodity as the price goes up while buyers do the reverse—buy more as prices go down. The market price, always in a state of flux, tentatively sets where buyers' and sellers' desires are optimized, resulting in the most efficient allocation of scarce resources (with alternative uses) possible.

Since the core function of any economic system is the allocation of scarce resources with alternative competing uses, housing (a commodity like any other) must nevertheless be allocated—only with price control, the market can no longer perform that function. In a rent-controlled housing market, cronyism, succession rights, gamesmanship, and luck replace price as the resource allocator. In the end, no serious economist quarrels with the notion that rent control results in a reduction in both the quality and quantity of housing, and to boot creates crushing inequities to market newcomers.

In New York City, for example, while rent control laws have kept rents down for a fortunate few—long-standing in-place tenants—it has increased the rents for others—themselves often low-income renters—and on balance have driven rents up on average. By protecting in-place tenants, older (often dilapidated) tenement buildings from the turn of-the-century dot the city's streetscape. They would have been replaced with new, larger apartment buildings absent rent control laws. The result has been a constriction in the city's housing supply. Prices of free-market apartments are driven up and new entrants to the market are forced into overcrowded conditions (often three or four roommates per apartment), while older rent-stabilized empty nesters whose children have grown up and moved out continue to hoard three- and four-bedroom below-market rent-controlled units.

No place is more notorious than New York City for the cronyism infecting the allocation of below-market rent-controlled apartments. Stories about the wealthy elite occupying vastly below-market rent-regulated apartments abound. Actors Mia Farrow and Dick Cavett, for example, held rent-regulated apartments in New York City.

As for cronyism, nothing can match Congressman Charles Rangel's four rent-stabilized apartments in Harlem's Lenox Terrace. Imagine a public servant hoarding four different below-market rent-regulated apartments in a city with the lowest vacancy rates and greatest housing shortage of any major U.S. city. That's what rent control enables.

In 2007, Rangel paid about $4,000 per month for all four apartments, easily half the market rate, and one of them was located on a different floor than the others and used solely as an office, even though rent-stabilized apartments in New York City must be used solely as primary residences. Worse, Rangel took a homestead tax break on his Washington, D.C. house during the same years he occupied his four Manhattan rent-stabilized apartments, thus simultaneously claiming a primary residence in two different cities (while he was the chief tax-law writer).

In Chapter 11, I explain how government inflicts us with a disease and then rushes to our aid with a supposed cure. The "affordable housing crisis" was really brought about by earlier misguided governmental actions. Regrettably, the cures the government has offered in response to the disease of its own making are even worse than the disease itself.

Named after the 18th-century Baron Munchausen, the psychological disorder Munchausen syndrome describes someone who intentionally harms himself in order to gain medical attention and sympathy. In a different form of this awful syndrome—called Munchausen by proxy—the afflicted individual, a parent, secretly harms his or her child, so that the child is hospitalized and treated, thereby achieving the clandestine object of the mentally ill parent—self-aggrandizement for his or her excellent caregiving. In extreme cases, afflicted parents have poisoned their children in order to be lavished with praise for their ensuing dedication to the care and welfare of the poisoned child.

Munchausen by proxy offers an instructive analogy to various governmental actions. Examples abound in which government initially takes some action that causes great harm to society and then later responds with some (supposed) legislative "cure" for the societal ill brought about by the original ill-advised governmental intervention. Though the examples are legion, for our purposes, a good starting place is the congressional reaction to the so-called affordable home ownership crisis—a situation that, though hardly qualifying as a crisis at all, was brought about largely by earlier misguided governmental actions.

Land cost is a very substantial component cost of all housing—be it multifamily rental housing or individual homes. Laws and regulations reducing the yield of land—the square footage of gross building area that may be built upon a lot (whether by bulk or zoning restrictions or overlaying conservation restrictions, which curtail building footprints)—drive the price of housing up. So do rent control laws, because they inhibit the demolition and redevelopment of more efficient housing accommodations.

This inability to see the true long-term costs of governmental policies and who bears them is one of the greatest shortcomings of our political system. Although, in Chapter 11, I use Nantucket as a handy example, this story repeats itself in thousands of communities throughout the United States. In fact, wherever housing is exorbitantly priced, development-thwarting (and/or rent control) regulations are likely to be found. While affluent communities from Puget Sound to Nantucket concern themselves with recreating endangered habitats for earthworms and other species of "special concern," without regard to the costs imposed by that effort, I tend to doubt these lowly creatures generated as much concern among those in charge of inner city planning in the Detroit neighborhoods about to be bulldozed.

In this way local governments throughout the United States created pockets where home ownership (and for that matter, rental housing as well) was no longer affordable. They did this by taxing home buyers and using the proceeds to buy and place undeveloped lands in permanent protected trust and by enacting a labyrinth of common sense-defying zoning restrictions and conservation rules, many of which became powerful weapons in the hands of "Not-In-My-Back-Yard" neighbors or not-for-profit collectives funded by NIMBY neighbors.

Our federal government then came to the rescue—governmental Munchausen by proxy—via forced lending to low down-payment minority buyers (the Community Reinvestment Act) and explicit quotas on Fannie and Freddie buying those low down-payment mortgage loans. Local government created the affordability crisis—the disease—and our federal government came to the rescue with the cure—subprime mortgage loans. Unfortunately, the cure turned out to be far worse than the disease.

This analysis raises a critical threshold question—should government concern itself (at all) with the form of ownership of its citizens' housing? Said differently, isn't the proper role of government ensuring the decency and quality of housing and not whether it is owned by the housed citizen or the landlord? Governments have a place making sure their citizens' housing accommodations are safe, well equipped, sanitary, heated, perhaps air conditioned in some areas, and free of vermin and pests, but why should our government concern itself with a citizen's decision whether to own or rent housing?

In Chapter 12, I discuss the Obama administration's efforts to combat the housing crisis and why they have been worse than tragic failures—they have only compounded the crisis, as the White House insists on printing more and more subprime paper. The administration's efforts at financial reform are really nothing more than a power grab and do little to mitigate the risks of a repeat crisis. In order to get "reform" passed without even mentioning the real culprits—Fannie and Freddie—Obama waged and won a propaganda war against business.

The Obama administration's multiple past attempts to fix housing have been both frighteningly expensive and miserable failures. First, through his Home Affordable Modification Program (HAMP), Obama tried to pay both delinquent homeowners and their banks to modify defaulted loans—an attempt to stop foreclosures (and the resulting resetting of housing prices). It failed miserably.

Next—call it HAMP 2.0—Obama tried to pay the banks holding second mortgages—the piggyback home equity lines—thinking they were getting in the way of the modifications. That failed too.

He attacked the demand side of the equation as well, hoping to stimulate buying—only at the lower end, of course—in an apparent realization that his attempts to stop foreclosures would not work. Through the First Time Home Buyer's tax credit, we ended up paying $8,000 apiece to 1.5 million people who would have bought homes anyway, borrowing sales from the future, inviting billions in taxpayer fraud, and chasing out of the market middle and upper price bracket buyers who waited in the wings, astutely fearful of a double dip in housing prices once the unsustainable government supports fell away.

It all failed. We got 10 percent of the 4 million modifications Obama promised us; handouts to first-time homebuyers resulted in billions of dollars being paid to those who would have eventually bought houses anyway; and foreclosures, while delayed, continued to stack up in the legal pipeline. Housing prices will remain flat for years, or, more likely, double dip in foreclosure-rich regions, as the foreclosed homes finally hit the market.

Meanwhile, to stimulate demand for purchases and refinancings, we've pumped $1.4 trillion into the mortgage market (through Fed and Treasury purchases of mortgage-backed securities), taking rates to the lowest level in decades. Yet neither has occurred in a meaningful way: Middle- and upper-market buyers continue to wait in the wings for the bottom that has yet to come, while overleveraged homeowners found themselves unable to refinance.

In Obama's desperate last-ditch effort to help housing—call it ObamaHome 5.0—instead of subsidizing delinquent homeowners, this program benefits homeowners who are underwater on their mortgages but continue to pay.

Obama has subsidized upper-income homeowners (folks owing mortgage balances up to $729,750) by paying their banks if they reduce the principal balance to 97.5 percent of the home's value and payments to "affordable" levels—31 percent of the homeowners' income. For homeowners who owe second mortgage loans, the balance need only be reduced to 115 percent of the home's value. Obama will pay billions of taxpayer dollars to the principal-forgiving banks—from 10 to 21 cents per dollar of principal forgiven, depending upon the overall percentage of principal forgiven.

Even so, banks would never take the principal hit, unless they were getting cashed out on the unforgiven principal balance. After all, the redefault rate on Obama's prior modifications has been abysmal. And the amounts at stake are huge: One in four homeowners is underwater—around $2.75 trillion of loans.

So the administration declared that the Federal Housing Administration would insure refinancings of qualifying underwater loans. Where first and second mortgages are reduced to 115 percent of the home's value, Obama will use additional TARP money to insure the portion of the reduced principal balance exceeding the 97.5 percent FHA limit.

Mind you, the FHA is now insuring one in three home mortgage loans, up from just over three in one hundred in 2005. Plus, it's running at one-quarter of the required minimum capital reserves, before taking into account the additional loans insured under this new program. Lenders will seize the one-time chance to shed their riskiest nondelinquent mortgages by laying them off on the taxpayers. It's a bailout of lenders who've refused to do short sales or work things out with borrowers.

And it will never end up costing the taxpayer only the incentives paid up front to get those lenders to reduce principal balances. The real bill will come down the road when the FHA-insured refinancings default, and the homes are foreclosed and sold for less than the new loan balance. And it still can't stop home prices from falling.

In normal times, 15 million homes would turn over during the three-year period 2010 to 2012. But the market will also have to absorb likely another 10 million foreclosed homes over the same period—which means we need to draw in two new buyers for every three we would normally have to find. Only a price drop will attract those additional buyers. Housing values will have to drop further.

All Obama's efforts can't stop this inevitable free-market adjustment; at best, he'll delay it—at the price of shifting the risk of hundreds of billions in losses on underwater loans from lenders to taxpayers.

Maybe he sees that as a worthwhile price for kicking the can down the road. (With elections coming up in November, 2010, maybe that's the plan.) But it's not worth it for the rest of us. The sooner we take the pain, the better off we'll be.

In Chapter 13, I assess blame for the financial crisis. Doing so is not as complicated as it is often made out to be. Far more complex is the task of concealing the true causes and politicizing the process of fault attribution.

The financial contagion that set off the financial crisis was subprime (and Alt-A) mortgages. Given the success of the RMBS market, Wall Street began bundling up commercial real estate mortgage loans to back collateralized debt obligations. Thanks to a robust CMBS market, commercial real estate owners found themselves awash in money. Whole-loan lenders were forced to lend to second-tier commercial properties as CMBS loans pushed rates lower. Cap rates were driven to new lows and CRE prices skyrocketed. A widespread failure to appreciate risk in both residential and commercial real estate permeated the marketplace.

As $1.4 trillion of commercial real debt comes due over the five-year period 2010 to 2014, several trends will emerge. CRE lenders who seek to put off taking loan impairments will come under increasing pressure. Many will prefer to sell their notes and collateral as "loans to own" to opportunistic real estate owner-operators—frequently real estate private equity firms and publicly traded REITS—who will then commence or continue the foreclosure process.

Mezzanine UCC foreclosure sales, where available, will become the preferred enforcement mechanism due to their ease, speed, and low cost structure. Where borrower workouts occur, they will frequently be forced into short-term extensions where additional equity is posted, and little or no net cash flow is leaked to the borrower or underwater junior lenders.

Where extensions occur and junior lenders are deprived of cash flow, or where one lender in a multilender debt stack seeks to take over the property from the borrower and wipe out junior lenders, tranche warfare will be waged.

All this will play out over the next five years, much of it in our courts. Fortunes will be made and lost. Regrettably, due to delays in residential foreclosures brought about by Obama's policies, much of the CRE losses will occur simultaneously with a double dip in housing. This will place our banks, particularly our regional banks, with high concentrations of CRE exposure, often to lower tier whole-loan collateral, under increasing and sometimes insurmountable financial pressure.

It remains to be seen whether our politicians will demonstrate the political will to bail out the hundreds more banks that will inevitably fail as residential and commercial real estate foreclosures peak in unison.

Here is my scorecard for those at fault for the housing crisis:

Congress, past administrations, the GSEs, and the liberal mainstream media:	70%
Wall Street and mortgage loan originators:	15%
Rating agencies:	10%
Greenspan Fed:	5%

In Chapter 14, I discuss the centerpieces any genuine financial reform effort must address:

- The failed policy underlying the housing bubble—pushing home ownership rates
- Fannie and Freddie
- The Federal Housing Administration
- The Community Reinvestment Act

In Chapter 15, I discuss other areas in need of financial reform including:

- Raising capital reserves for banks and lowering leverage limits for investment banks
- Instituting across-the-board risk retention requirements for both residential and commercial real estate loans
- Compensation reform for residential and commercial real estate loan originators
- Putting credit default swaps and interest rate swaps and caps under control of a clearinghouse
- Finally breaking the control of residential and commercial real estate lenders over appraisers
- Using our tried and true bankruptcy laws instead of creating an altogether new and dangerous class of "too big to fail" rules
- Expanding whistleblower laws to cover political malfeasance
- Slashing federal spending and adopting across-the-board tax cuts

Excluding the current recession, the 10 since WWII have lasted on average 11 months—the longest lasting 16 months. At 32 months and counting, this one appears radically different. That has prompted pundits to ask, "What's different this time?" Many have answered: President Obama's *economic* policies.

But pundits are missing one crucial piece of the puzzle—Obama's *housing* policies. They have stunted the spending of tens of millions of consumers who continue to pay high interest rates on unsecured mortgage balances, which, absent those policies, would have been compromised and written off long ago.

Obama's housing policies have greatly reduced consumer spending—as a vast population of consumers has been denied lower housing costs as a result. Also, because these consumers continue to be shackled to homes they cannot sell—their mortgage balances exceed current home values—they are unable to relocate to other areas of the country offering better job opportunities.

Consumer spending accounts for 70 percent of GDP, and we are trapped now in a vicious negative feedback loop. Though housing got us here, it now is alternately effect and cause of our economic woes. Without jobs, housing continues to falter; and with housing faltering, consumers don't spend, so businesses are afraid to expand and hire.

At the height of the bubble, affordable home ownership policies pushed the homeownership rate to 69 percent. Today, due to foreclosures, it has fallen back to 66 percent. Given a population of 310 million, that means that 205 million live in homes they own.

Previously 1 in 5 and now, due to foreclosures, still more than 1 in 4 households are underwater. Their mortgage debt exceeds the value of their house. Likely 60 to 70 million consumers live in houses whose owners have no recoupable net equity after brokerage commissions and closing costs.

Millions of consumers are paying far more in housing costs than they would had they lost homes to foreclosures, given their banks deeds in lieu of foreclosures, or closed short sales—and then rented or even repurchased comparable housing at reduced market prices and interest rates.

This population of negative or zero-equity homeowners cannot realize the benefits of vastly lowered housing costs brought about by market declines in housing prices and interest rates, because they are trapped paying loans they took out before the bubble burst.

Pundits speak of the "moral hazard" created by our bailout mania. We hear about "strategic defaults" by homeowners who have the money to continue to pay their mortgages but choose not to. But what about the reverse—strapped homeowners hanging on longer than they normally would?

Creditors experience collection problems all the time. They work through a process of rational compromise based on market realities. Free markets clear away uncollectible debt and collateral is sold. And it normally happens quickly.

But Obama's modification program, by giving underwater homeowners false hope, has delayed free-market clearing processes. They believe that if they just hang on and keep paying interest, even on the portion of the debt exceeding the value of their house, Obama will rescue them.

But Obama's program failed. While he promised 3 to 4 million modifications, he has produced less than 10 percent of those, and even more program dropouts. Yet the failure of Obama's program does not stop people from continuing to hope . . . and pay.

The program also gives banks false hope. They won't take short sales or accept deeds in lieu of foreclosure and have delayed foreclosure proceedings because they, too, hold out false hope for bailout-subsidized modifications. And, because Obama has been a vocal critic of banks that don't work out modifications, they fear regulatory reprisal if they take back the homes.

While the program has delayed inevitable free-market clearing processes by giving false hope to lenders and borrowers alike, 60 to 70 million consumers with no recoupable home equity have depleted their savings and continued to pay housing costs far higher than they needed to, in a desperate effort to preserve "their home equity." But they lost their equity long ago—that happened when the bubble burst.

By delaying free-market clearing processes, Obama's housing policies have siphoned off into our banking sector vast amounts of consumer spending power that otherwise would benefit other sectors of the economy.

If households containing 60 to 70 million consumers continue to pay $500, $750, or even $1,000 per month in above-market housing costs as a result of Obama's program, that means that by killing the program we would see a stealth stimulus of tens of billions of dollars annually. The vast majority of those cost savings would get spent on dinners out, vacations, cars, furniture, clothing, and electronics—a recurring stimulus at negative cost to the taxpayers (we would be spared the current giveaways).

Also, by keeping underwater homeowners in their homes longer, the program prevents the unemployed from relocating to find employment. Although unemployment rates remain high throughout the country, rates vary widely. In June, North Dakota had an unemployment rate of only 3.6 percent while Nevadans suffered with 14.2 percent. By delaying market clearing processes, jobless homeowners in regions with high unemployment rates cannot relocate to regions offering more jobs. They continue paying interest on their unsecured mortgage balances because they can't possibly sell their houses for what they owe.

That means much of the extended unemployment benefits are going directly into the pockets of lenders who hold unsecured debts they refuse to write down, as jobless homeowners use their benefits to pay interest on unsecured loan balances, instead of relocating to seek job opportunities.

Free-market clearing process can be delayed but not avoided—Obama's housing policies only kick the can down the road. But we pay for that dearly in the form of reduced consumer spending, depleted consumer savings (which means future increases in savings and reductions in spending), slower growth, and greater unemployment.

Regrettably, HAMP is not the only Obama policy thwarting recovery. Obama's out-of-control spending has brought our publicly held national debt from $5.4 trillion on August 1, 2008 to $8.8 trillion by August 1, 2010. While it took the first 232 years of our country's existence—1776 to 2008—to accumulate $5.4 trillion in publicly held national debt, under Obama, we accumulated another $3.4 trillion in the following two years. That means we went from accumulating $1 trillion of public debt every 43.3 years to accumulating $1 trillion of public debt every seven months—an apocalyptic debt trajectory that threatens all Americans.

And at $142 billion per month the public debt is accumulating seven and a half times faster than our economy is growing ($3.4 trillion divided by 24 months) as of the second quarter of 2010. Far worse, though, are our unfunded entitlement liabilities for Social Security, Medicare, and prescription drugs. These unfunded liabilities total a mind-bending $109 trillion. Together, our national debt and unfunded entitlement liabilities come to nearly $400,000 per citizen (not per taxpayer). The United States, the greatest borrower in the world, is insolvent.

In 2010, President Obama spent nearly 25 percent of U.S. gross domestic product. But when one adds in state and local spending (including sales and real estate taxes), total government spending is more like half of all U.S. economic output (depending on the state). No economy can withstand such a high level of economic output being siphoned off by punitive taxation for too long. Much of this government spending, of course, is being financed with borrowed dollars. The Congressional Budget Office estimates that in 2011 the federal deficit will be 10.3 percent. That's not that far from the Greek deficit, which is estimated to be 13.6 percent. CBO estimated that the portion of our national debt held by the public would more than double from 40 percent in 2008 to 90 percent by 2020.

Most of our state governments are insolvent with California leading the charge. The states are going broke because public sector unions are bribing "management"—elected officials—with millions in campaign contributions. We cannot afford to go on granting our police officers, firefighters, and teachers gigantic defined benefit pensions (versus the defined contribution pensions more popular in the private sector) based on a huge percentage of their last few years' work including overtime.

Career politicians who have never run a business, never refrained from paying themselves in order to make a payroll, or ever really created a single job in their lives may think they can tax the private sector into oblivion—and equalize wealth no matter what the losses are in terms of overall prosperity—but they can't.

Back in 1993, Hoover Institute scholar and economist W. Kurt Hauser published a paper making a remarkable assertion: Federal tax revenues since World War II have always been equal to approximately 19.5 percent of GDP, regardless of wide fluctuations in the top marginal tax rate. Said in reverse, individual and corporate taxpayers somehow always find a way of not paying more than 20 percent of gross economic output to the federal government. Whether that's done by tax cheating, the economy going underground (which is what happened in Greece), or by clever tax avoidance techniques, the empirical data over many decades reveal what is now known as "Hauser's Law" because of its inviolate nature.

No matter how high the highest marginal tax bracket has been, the Feds have never collected more than 20 percent of GDP. Einstein taught us that matter can approach but never reach the speed of light, and Hauser taught us that the federal tax receipts can approach but never reach 20 percent of gross domestic product.

What this means is that unless federal spending is brought below the Hausian limit (20 percent), federal spending will of necessity be funded out of borrowed funds. But deficit spending cannot go on forever. Given that public debt is now accumulating more than seven times faster than the economy is growing, the public debt will eventually reach proportions not tolerable to the lending community. Lending will be curtailed and the government's cost of borrowing will skyrocket.

Sooner or later the massive federal spending will stop—the only question is, will it stop before it's too late for the United States to recover? Tragically, profligate federal spending and the prospect of the vastly increased taxes that must necessarily follow, far from stimulating the economy, ensure economic stagnation.

As the private sector is crowded out and punitively taxed into abandoning or deferring expansion plans, job growth is stultified. And of course jobs are exactly what we need to break the vicious negative feedback loop in which we now find ourselves. People lose their jobs, can't find new ones, and go into default on their home mortgages. That triggers bank losses, reductions of capital reserves, and less bank lending and more bank failures. And that in turn triggers lower rents and higher vacancy rates at apartment buildings (people without jobs can't pay rent), office buildings (job growth directly affects office vacancy and rental rates as each office worker takes up about 200 square feet), and retail projects (as retailers depend on consumers). With businesses hurt by the weakened consumer and restricted credit, more businesses fail and we see more job losses.

The problem of stagnant job growth caused by profligate spending and taxation is particularly pernicious in the current recession because now, unlike prior recessions, nearly half of the 8 million unemployed have been unemployed for a long time. The long-term unemployed eventually burn through their savings or simply give up hope, and mortgage defaults follow.

The only way to break this tragic negative feedback loop is to slash government spending, disenfranchise public unions—I suggest flat out illegalizing the unionization of any federal, state, or local governmental workers—and cut marginal tax rates across the board. Doing that would unleash the awesome power of free market capitalism. Businesses would prosper and the job growth engine would begin firing on all cylinders.

On July 4, 1776, when our Founding Fathers signed the Declaration of Independence, they explained to the world the justifications for their actions. The oppressions of King George were so numerous and so punitive, revolution was their only course. In listing their grievances, the signers of the Declaration had this to say about the king's expansion of government and taxation: "He has erected a multitude of New Offices, and sent hither swarms of Officers to harass our people and eat out their substance."

The similarities of the present situation to the circumstances leading to our War of Independence do not end there. Cries of "taxation without representation!" led to the iconic Boston Tea Party, which now bears the name of a newly emerging and powerful grassroots movement.

While it is easy to say that in the present day all voters get a vote and therefore there is no taxation without representation, the statement rings hollow, because nearly half of all American taxpayers pay no tax whatsoever (or get checks in a disguised welfare/redistribution system). Those tax-filers are entirely decoupled from bearing any responsibility for our federal government and in consequence have no earthly reason to vote for politicians who seek to restrain federal spending.

Worse, with so many tax-filers freeloading, there is little political profit in trying to get voted in by the real taxpayers. In the end, the real job of a politician is to get reelected, and the easiest path to reelection is to promise more spending to the freeloaders.

So there really is taxation without representation, as any politician in favor of big government who captures even the even the smallest percentage of the real taxpayers is bound to get elected when he or she adds in 100 percent of the votes of the freeloaders. This has prompted some to propose that we grant an exception to the one person, one vote principle by granting voting rights that reflect tax burdens.

In an April 20, 2010, op-ed article appearing in *Investor's Business Daily*, Walter Williams, economics professor at George Mason University, proposed that each citizen get one vote plus one additional vote for every

$20,000 of federal tax he or she pays. It would be fascinating to see how many adherents the neo-Keynesians would lose upon the passage of law making that fundamental change to our voting rights.

However it is done, we must break the spend-and-tax mentality and the conspiracy between politicians and public unions. Perhaps we should grant Wall Street–style bonuses to all federal lawmakers for delivering a balanced budget. We could give everyone in the Oval Office and every senator and congressman a million-dollar bonus if the budget is balanced, and we would still save hundreds of billions of dollars.

When that good work is done we must slash marginal rates across the board. With those steps taken, ironically, federal revenues will increase; but we must use the surplus tax receipts to amortize our vast debts in order to restore growth and prosperity. We must not let well-intentioned but misguided notions of economic justice destroy our country and economy.

As Winston Churchill said more than a half century ago, "The inherent vice of capitalism is the unequal sharing of blessings; the inherent virtue of socialism is the equal sharing of miseries."

Stephen B. Meister
August 16, 2010

Acknowledgments

Great thanks to my brother-in-law, Michael Mogavero, CFA, for countless fact checking and edits, and most of all for being able to make sense of Fannie and Freddie's otherwise indecipherable financial statements. Thanks go out as well to my assistants Tara Gremillion and Gissel Arias for keeping this project organized; my colleagues Stephen Lerner, for his help on bankruptcy matters, and CPAs Mark Bosswick and Grace Singer, for their help on financial accounting standards; my associates Stacey Ashby and Kevin Fritz, for cite and fact checking; and family members Jason Meister, for market data, and Gerard Meister and Ellen Meister, for general editing.

CHAPTER 1

The Housing Bubble

Owners of U.S. commercial real estate, comprising principally office build-ings, multifamily rental properties, retail properties, and the hotel and hospitality sector, draw upon both consumers and businesses as their cus-tomers. The businesses that occupy our office buildings and book our hotels, and our retailers, in turn, depend largely upon consumers, whose spending accounts for over 70 percent[1] of our gross domestic product. One way or the other, U.S. commercial real estate is dependent upon the U.S. consumer.

Consumer spending was decimated by the bursting of the housing bubble, which began unfolding in 2006, while American businesses, par-ticularly small businesses, were ravaged by the abrupt and unprecedented curtailment of credit following on its heels. The credit freeze itself was trig-gered by the subprime mortgage crisis.

The sudden seizure of our credit markets in August 2008 was preceded by the sale of Merrill Lynch to Bank of America,[2] was followed by the Lehman bankruptcy and then–Treasury Secretary Paulson seizing government-sponsored enterprises Fannie Mae and Freddie Mac and placing them under federal conservatorship.[3]

To understand where our commercial real estate markets are headed, we must gauge the health *and future prospects* of the U.S. consumer. This, in turn, requires an understanding of the subprime mortgage crisis, the building and bursting of the U.S. housing bubble, and where the housing sector is headed. Consumer purchasing power and sentiment are driven in large measure by the relative health of the housing and equities markets.

The systemic risk to our banking sector created by trillions of dollars worth of defaulted securitized subprime (and later prime) residential mortgages spread like a wind-fueled brushfire throughout our worldwide banking system, and as well to the myriad other investors attracted to diverse pools of U.S. home mortgages. Real estate private equity firms, life insurance companies, public and corporate pension funds, and hedge funds, to name a few—really, a cadre of investors, which had become, by virtue of the securitization process, a shadow mortgage banking system unto itself—were drawn to home mortgages, then thought to be a bullet-proof asset class.

THE U.S. AFFORDABLE HOME OWNERSHIP MANDATE

To understand the subprime mortgage crisis, we must roll back the clock. For the first four decades of the twentieth century—prior to the onset of World War II—the percentage of home ownership in the United States hovered in a tight range—43.6 percent to 47.8 percent, a spread of only 4.2 percent.[4] Discounting the 1940 figure as an aberrational low brought about by the Great Depression, the range tightens further—45.6 percent to 47.8 percent—a spread of a mere 2.2 percent over a span of four decades. (See Figure 1.1.)

After the end of World War II, however, a dramatic change took place. The percentage of home ownership jumped to 55 percent in 1950 and then began a steady climb from there up to 66.2 percent at the turn of the millennium. By 2004–2005, the U.S. home ownership rate had skyrocketed to over 69 percent.

The stunning post–World War II increase in U.S. home ownership rates—going from about 47 percent to 69 percent (representing a 47 percent increase in the home ownership rate)—was not brought about by laissez-faire market forces, but rather by aggressive government intervention designed and driven by a liberal vanguard so blinded by the political correctness of marching toward the American Dream for America's minorities that they could not foresee the devastating consequences to both the

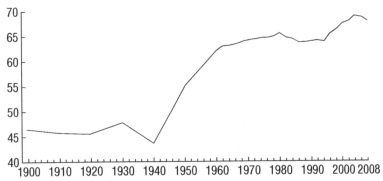

FIGURE 1.1   U.S. Homeownership Rates, 1900–2008 (in percent)
Source: U.S. Census Bureau

supposed beneficiaries of their intervention, as well as to all other Americans (and really, people the world over). Regrettably, however, good intentions are not enough; as Oscar Wilde said, "all bad poetry springs from genuine feeling." And as the late neoconservative publisher Irving Kristol added, "the same can be said for bad politics."

Empowered by the influence of Congress over the government-sponsored enterprises and that of the banking sector over Congress and Fannie and Freddie; assisted by mortgage originators who, courtesy of Wall Street's securitization prowess, retained no stake in the loans they originated and therefore had no reason to underwrite them soundly, and by the appraisers they controlled; aided and abetted by an oligopoly of credit raters who, protected by our government from the pressures of free-market competition, had fallen asleep at the switch; and enabled by the swollen supply of cheap and easy money put into place in the years preceding the bursting of the housing bubble by the Greenspan Fed, there was no stopping the mainstream-media–praised racial lending quotas established under our affordable home ownership mandate. The results, given the scale of the U.S. housing market, were nothing less than cataclysmic.

THE BIRTH OF THE GOVERNMENT-SPONSORED ENTERPRISES

Initially the government intervention was relatively tame and not racially driven. Starting with the G.I. Bill,[5] which provided home loans to returning soldiers, and the Federal National Mortgage Association or "Fannie Mae" as it is now commonly called, the federal government undertook a consistent policy of promoting home ownership, primarily through subsidizing home mortgage loans and making them easily and readily available, and secondarily via tax policy by making home mortgage interest deductible.[6]

Fannie Mae was chartered in 1938 by Franklin Delano Roosevelt as a governmental agency in the wake of the Great Depression. In 1968, it was converted by Lyndon Johnson to a private stockholder-owned (but government-sponsored) enterprise or GSE,[7] in order to remove its activity from the balance sheet of the federal budget.

Fannie Mae was formed as part of the New Deal to promote liquidity in the mortgage market by providing a robust and efficient secondary mortgage market—a market where home mortgage loan originators could come to sell their mortgage paper and replenish their capital in order to redeploy it and originate more loans.

Even though conceived during the severe financial stresses of the Great Depression, Fannie Mae purchased conforming mortgage loans with sensible down payment requirements. Initially, Fannie's down payment requirement was 20 percent.[8] Fast forwarding to the present, the down payment requirement imposed by the Federal Housing Administration, an arm of the U.S. Department of Housing and Urban Development, which issues explicit government-backed mortgage insurance,[9] was reduced to an astonishing 3.5 percent,[10] nearly one-seventh of the original mandate.

Although there have been very low (including 0 percent) down payment programs, beginning with the Veteran's Administration as early as 1944, these programs were used far more broadly after 2000. The big change came with the greater use of second-lien home purchase loans (sometimes called piggyback loans) beginning in 2002, which let more borrowers put no money down to buy a house.[11]

THE U.S. AFFORDABLE HOME OWNERSHIP MANDATE IS RADICALIZED AND RACIALIZED

A radicalization of the federal policy of promoting home ownership took place during the 15-year period preceding the bursting of the housing bubble—1992 to 2007—initially led by the efforts of the Clinton Administration, most notably then–Attorney General Janet Reno, and thereafter by leading liberal congressmen and senators, whose campaign coffers were stuffed with contributions from Fannie Mae and its sister agency, Freddie Mac They included Senate Banking Committee Chairman Christopher Dodd and House Financial Services Committee Chairman Barney Frank. Some Republicans as well fell prey to the irresistible lure of housing subsidies, including President George W. Bush, who signed into law the American Dream Downpayment Act in 2003.

Besides the Clinton Administration, Senator Dodd, Congressman Frank, and their liberal minions, another key player in the liberal left vanguard pushing for ever higher home ownership rates among American minorities was the since disgraced liberal advocacy group, ACORN (Association of Community Organizations for Reform Now).[12]

In 1992, under intense lobbying pressure from ACORN, Congress passed the Federal Housing Enterprises Financial Safety and Soundness Act, also known as the GSE Act.[13] Forced to comply with the GSE Act's "affordable housing" mandate—a mandate pushed through by ACORN—Fannie Mae and Freddie Mac now own or are responsible for (via securitization) a jaw-dropping $5.5 trillion of residential mortgages, roughly half of all U.S. residential mortgages (by dollar value, but more than half in number of mortgages).

THE COMMUNITY REINVESTMENT ACT

Congress had bought into ACORN's goal of pressuring the GSEs—Fannie and Freddie—into purchasing home mortgage loans with a heavy emphasis on mortgages made to low-income minority borrowers looking to purchase homes with razor-thin down payments. These "affordable housing" loans were in turn made by the banks under an earlier law—the Community Reinvestment Act of 1977, an act of Congress signed into law by President Carter, designed to stop the alleged bank practice known as "redlining" (the supposed discriminatory credit practices against minority, low-income, inner city neighborhoods).

The CRA's mandate merely admonished "each appropriate Federal financial supervisory agency to use its authority when examining financial institutions to encourage such institutions to help meet the credit needs of the local communities in which they are chartered consistent with the safe and sound operation of such institutions." It was easy for aggressive liberal lawmakers to twist loan disapproval rate statistics to the end of converting the CRA's seemingly benign mandate into a radicalized and racialized monster.

As Mark Twain quipped over a century and a half ago, "facts are stubborn, but statistics are more pliable." Distorting loan denial rate statistics was easy, and the liberal mainstream media did whatever it could to help move the process along.

As Hoover Institution (Stanford University) economist and author Thomas Sowell compellingly explains in his book, *The Housing Boom and Bust*, instead of reporting that the vast majority of mortgage applications submitted by both blacks and whites were approved, as was the case, the mainstream media only reported the differences in rejection rates. Whenever possible, rationale differences in loan applicants' qualifications were ignored.

The trivial differences in approval rates among the races were explained by sound underwriting standards. If a certain percentage of African Americans or Hispanics of a given income level were denied mortgages while a higher percentage of whites in that same income bracket were granted their applications, other relevant factors like the amount of cash being put down or the overall cash assets of the applicant were ignored.

And, as Mr. Sowell aptly hypothesized, if 99 percent of loan applications by whites were granted while 98 percent of blacks' applications were granted, though it would be technically true in such a case to say that blacks suffered twice the rejection rate as whites, such an observation hardly presents a clear picture of what was really happening—that the great majority of all loan applications by both whites and blacks were approved.

Although actual approval rates were not quite that high, Mr. Sowell's point—that rejection rate statistics were being used to distort the true picture—is irrefutable. In any event, as Mr. Sowell noted, Asians had a higher mortgage approval rate than did whites, a statistic conveniently ignored by both the mainstream media and our lawmakers.

The whole notion that banks intentionally refused to make loans to African Americans or Hispanics simply because of the color of their skin and not because of some reasonably grounded fear that applicants of any race with inadequate assets, income, or credit histories would not be able to pay back the loans they sought, in and of itself should have raised the hair on the backs of our necks.

Why would the very same executives whom President Obama now describes as "fat cat bankers" refuse to turn a profit from the interest paid by putative borrowers simply because of the color of their skin? When exactly did the "fat cat bankers" lose their capitalist urges? Was their racism so strong that mortgage bankers were prepared to pay for it in millions of dollars of lost profits (which would then go to their nonracist competitors), even after spending millions of advertising dollars in order to attract borrowers?

Astute commercial trial lawyers look for simple economic motivations to explain human behavior. Isn't a far more plausible and simpler theory that these bankers had sound, objective reasons for denying the few loans they did in fact deny, or for granting such applications and charging higher interest rates to make up for the higher default rates to applicants (of any race) with poor credit characteristics?

This irrational insistence on seeing racism in what was nothing more than sound underwriting criteria consistently applied is explained by what another Hoover Institute scholar, Shelby Steele, referred to in a December 30, 2009 *Wall Street Journal* article as an American sophistication—"the sophistication of seeing what isn't there rather than what is"—likening the process to the parable of the emperor's new clothes.

As related by Mr. Steele, "[t]he emperor was told by his swindling tailors that people who could not see his new clothes were stupid and incompetent. So when his new clothes arrived and he could not see them, he put them on anyway so that no one would think him stupid and incompetent. And when he appeared before his people in these new clothes, they too—not wanting to appear stupid and incompetent—exclaimed [at] the beauty of his wardrobe. It was finally a mere child who said: 'The emperor has no clothes.' "

Not seeing racism in loan rejections, even though there was none, was thus forbidden by an embedded cultural taboo denouncing a failure to see racism everywhere. And those who failed to see racism in loan rejection rates were themselves branded racists. Political correctness, and the ostracism faced by those who violated its strictures, commanded that we see racism that did not exist.

People who professed not to see the emperor's (nonexistent) clothes were quickly branded fools by the political class. When Barney Frank was taken to task by Bill O'Reilly for lauding the fiscal soundness of Fannie and Freddie Mac just two months before then–Treasury Secretary Paulson seized them both to prevent their imminent bankruptcy, Mr. Frank responded by telling Mr. O'Reilly he was "stupid." Mr. O'Reilly, it seemed, did not see the emperor's clothes.

Spawned by the civil rights movement of the 1960s led by Dr. Martin Luther King, the Community Reinvestment Act—or at least the perversion of it that took root during the Clinton era—was itself predicated on another perversion, one twisting the principles for which Dr. King stood.

Contrast what President John F. Kennedy had to say about equal opportunity in 1963 to what has been done in the last 15 years in the name of the Community Reinvestment Act. President Kennedy said that Congress should "make a commitment to the proposition that race has no place in American life *or law*" (emphasis is the author's). In 1964, Senator Hubert Humphrey, a principal sponsor of the Civil Rights Act of that year, bristled at what he called the "nightmarish propaganda" then being espoused by the law's detractors, who argued that the Civil Rights Act would permit preferential treatment because of race or racial imbalance.

In short, sometime between 1964, when the Civil Rights Act was enacted, and the mid-1990s, when Clinton Administration Attorney General Janet Reno began her vicious campaign compelling banks—supposedly guilty of discriminatory redlining practices—to make low down payment loans to minorities regardless of tarnished credit histories, the civil rights movement had been hideously transformed from one supporting a policy requiring that all citizens be treated equally, as Dr. King demanded, to one mandating that they intentionally be treated unequally.

The answer to *de facto* racism had become *de jure* racism. It is no wonder that *Claremont Review of Books* editor William Voegeli called this perverse transformation of our civil rights laws "one of the most audacious bait and switch operations in American political history."[14]

RACIALLY BASED LENDING QUOTAS ARE IMPOSED IN THE NAME OF THE CRA

Extensive federal controls over the varied aspects of banking operations such as acquisitions (for example, of stock brokerage and insurance businesses), were openly applied by regulators to reward banks that met, and to punish those that did not meet, the racially driven CRA lending quotas. Eventually the federal government imposed outright quotas on private mortgage lending.

In 1996, HUD set an explicit target commanding that 42 percent of the loans bought by Fannie and Freddie in the secondary market be to people with incomes below the median in the area. Eventually the target was raised to 50 percent in 2000 and to 52 percent in 2005.[15]

As Mr. Sowell noted, Clinton Administration Attorney General Janet Reno brought costly-to-defend actions backed by the Department of Justice merely for a bank (Chevy Chase Federal Savings Bank) not having a branch in a minority neighborhood she wanted to see one in, even where there was no evidence of racially discriminating lending practices by such bank whatsoever.[16] The Federal Reserve Board refused to approve a bank's (Shawmut National Corp.) proposed acquisition of another bank (New Dartmouth Bank) due to unproven charges of racial bias in the acquirer's mortgage lending practices.[17] Given the expense of defending government lawsuits aimed at ensuring bank compliance with racial lending quotas, and the arguably even greater costs stemming from regulatory blocks on bank acquisitions and mergers, the banks yielded. Eventually, racially based lending quotas became baked into our mortgage lending system.

So eager was Congress to appease activist community organizer groups like ACORN that the latter effectively wrote federal policy under the CRA and GSE acts. These community advocacy groups, with the backing of Congress, set the goal: the percentages of minority borrower/low income/low down payment mortgages purchased by the GSEs, Fannie and Freddie. Naturally, sound underwriting standards were cast aside in order to meet these racially based lending quotas. Congress ordered the GSEs to lower down payment requirements and to disregard credit blots over a year old.

Republicans are not without some blame in this tragedy, as many in their ranks fell prey to the irresistible political pull of the vote-getting affordable housing agenda. For example, on December 16, 2003, President Bush signed into law the American Dream Downpayment Act of 2003, apparently lured into the fold by the economic activity President Bush thought this act would engender in the post–9/11 environment.[18]

Unlike voting shares of corporate stock, where shareholders cast a number of votes proportionate to their investments in the collective (the corporation), in a democratic republic's one person, one vote system, it is far more politically strategic to err on the side of overburdening the "wealthy," since the other voters are so much more numerous.

Racial lending quotas and the watered-down underwriting standards they spawned; former Federal Reserve Chairman Alan Greenspan's very low Federal Funds Rate, held in place for an extended period following the dot-com crash, the 9/11 attacks, and the Enron scandal; the triangle of corruption and influence peddling that emerged among lawmakers, top executives at Fannie and Freddie, and their counterparts at private mortgage lenders; mortgage originators retaining no skin in the game thanks to the securitization efforts of Wall Street, bank-controlled appraisers, and asleep-at-the-switch credit rating agencies, all made for a perfect storm in housing.

All the vast firepower of the formidable GSEs, under the control of congressmen and senators (some of whom had received preferential loans from private sector lender Countrywide Financial), supplied with a nearly inexhaustible cache of ammunition, as Greenspan's monetary policies caused our money supply to swell to unprecedented levels, was unleashed in all its fury and without restraint.

A TRIANGLE OF INFLUENCE PEDDLING AND CORRUPTION—LAWMAKERS, FANNIE AND FREDDIE EXECUTIVES, AND PRIVATE MORTGAGE LENDER EXECUTIVES

Not content with the mere tripling of these toxic low down payment mortgage loans, Congressman Frank (along with 13 other congressmen including California Congresswoman Maxine Waters) co-sponsored a bill (HR 1852) in 2007 (thankfully never passed by the Senate), which would have reduced the down payment requirement to zero.[19]

The triangle of lawmakers, GSE executives, and bank executives became a hotbed of corruption and influence peddling. Senate Banking Committee Chairman Christopher Dodd, Senate Finance Committee Chairman Kent Conrad, and former Fannie Mae CEO (and former Obama VP vetter) Jim Johnson received special low-rate mortgage loans from Countrywide Financial through a program personally overseen by Countrywide's chairman and CEO, Angelo Mozilo, known as the "Friends of Angelo" program.

Senator Dodd received a $75,000 reduction in mortgage payments from Countrywide at below-market rates on his Washington, D.C. and Connecticut homes. Clinton Jones III, senior counsel of the House Financial Services Subcommittee on Housing and Community Opportunity, was singled out for special treatment. Jones became state director for federal residential-mortgage bundler Freddie Mac and was thereafter hired to serve on the House Financial Services Committee.

Alphonso Jackson, acting secretary of the Department of Housing and Urban Development, received a discounted mortgage loan for himself and sought one for his daughter. In 2003, using VIP loans for nearly

$1 million apiece, Franklin Raines, the since disgraced chairman and CEO of Fannie Mae from 1999 to 2004, twice refinanced his seven-bedroom home.[20]

Under intense pressure, both Democrats and Republicans on the House Oversight and Governmental Reform Committee issued a congressional subpoena on October 23, 2009, demanding documents relating to charges of Countrywide's efforts at influence peddling at all levels of government.[21] The fallout from that investigation, if it is ever concluded, remains to be seen.

As I explained in a *New York Post* Op-Ed piece, Democrats claim their sweeping financial-sector reforms will guard against the kind of problems that triggered the recent economic meltdown. But if they *really* wanted to do that, they would have focused on how so many U.S. officials were simply bought off by Angelo Mozilo.

Rep. Darrell Issa (R-Calif.), ranking member of the House Committee on Oversight and Governmental Reform, has demanded just such a review—and, for the sake of the nation, he should get one.

In July 2010, Rep. Issa wrote to Alfred Pollard, general counsel to the Federal Housing Finance Agency, which oversees Fannie Mae and Freddie Mac, asking for a probe of "VIP" mortgage loans given to Fannie and Freddie executives by Countrywide Financial Corporation.

The documents Rep. Issa subpoenaed strongly suggest that, through a VIP loan program at Countrywide for "Friends of Angelo," Mozilo helped spur officials to keep up Fannie and Freddie's multitrillion-dollar mortgage-spending spree and, especially, buying Countrywide's junk mortgages. Special account executives were hired to administer the "FOA" loan program. Their business cards contained the designation "VIP Loan Program," so that the VIPs who received these discounted loans would know they were being given special treatment. Thousands of dollars were saved by each VIP borrower, and each had to have known it.

Beyond Dodd, Conrad, Jones, Jackson, and Raines, the more than 44,000 documents subpoenaed by Issa showed that the corruption in the system ran even deeper. They show that a staggering 153 VIP loans were extended to the quasi-governmental employees who decided what loans Fannie would buy with the taxpayers' money. Another 20 VIP loans were made to Freddie Mac executives.

Mozilo's seemingly systematic efforts to sway lawmakers, a cabinet member, White House staff, and the executives at Fannie and Freddie appear to have paid off. In 2007, Countrywide alone originated 23 percent of a massive volume of Fannie and Freddie's mortgage purchases. In that year alone, Mozilo made more than $140 million. VIP borrower and Fannie CEO Jim Johnson signed a strategic agreement with Countrywide granting

Fannie exclusive access to Countrywide's junk loans. Mozilo, in effect, had managed to make the United States and Countrywide joint ventures in the most prodigious—dangerous—subprime-mortgage operation in our country's history.

Mozilo also seems to have stifled numerous bills in Congress aimed at reform—despite warnings by Republicans that a failure to rein in Fannie and Freddie posed grave dangers to taxpayers. When Sen. Richard Shelby (R-Ala.) pushed for a comprehensive fix, Dodd successfully threatened a filibuster.

Meanwhile, despite ethical codes governing Congress, the Executive Branch, and Fannie and Freddie, which ban the acceptance of gifts or discounts, influential "Friends of Angelo" accepted their discounted loans.

If House Leader Nancy Pelosi really were interested in reform and in "draining the swamp," she'd have launched a probe long ago. She didn't. Even worse, multiple VIP loan recipient Dodd served as sponsor of the financial-reform law, which made no effort to deal with Fannie and Freddie, even though to date they've received $148 billion in taxpayer bailouts—with no end in sight.

President Obama and his fellow Democrats singled out Wall Street in their massive reform package. They should have looked in the mirror first.

Executives at the GSEs also profited handsomely and at one time cooked Fannie's books to perpetuate their unearned compensation levels. A study jointly conducted by the Securities and Exchange Commission and the Office of Federal Housing Enterprise Oversight found that Fannie executives had engaged in "extensive financial fraud" over the six-year period 1998–2004 and arranged a settlement of $400 million, which, in typical government fashion, was paid by Fannie Mae and therefore penalized the victims of the fraud perpetrated by the book-cooking executives—Fannie's shareholders. Further investigation of and efforts to bring about disgorgement of tens of millions of dollars of "ill gotten" compensation received by then–Fannie CEO Franklin Raines and CFO Timothy Howard have continued to languish for years.[22]

LAWMAKER LAPDOGS OBEY THEIR MASTERS

As criticism of Fannie and Freddie heated up in 2003, Congressman Frank responded in his typical fashion: "Critics conjure up the possibility of serious financial losses to the Treasury, which I do not see."[23] In response to $11 billion of book-cooking irregularities being reported by the Office of Federal Housing Enterprise Oversight in 2007, President Bush called for a "robust reform package" to be put in place for the GSEs. Senator Dodd responded by saying that President Bush should "immediately reconsider his ill-advised" recommendation.[24]

Back in 2004, when the Franklin Raines scandal broke, Dodd called Fannie and Freddie "one of the great success stories of all times," urging "caution" in restricting their activities. As late as July 2008, just two short months before the insolvent mortgage giants were seized and placed into federal conservatorship by Treasury Secretary Paulson, Dodd continued his unflinching support for the GSEs, saying even then, on the eve of disaster, that they were "on a sound footing."[25]

In 2003, California Congresswoman Maxine Waters said, "We do not have a crisis at Freddie Mac, and in particular at Fannie Mae, under the outstanding leadership of Mr. Franklin Raines." Ms. Waters added that regulatory reforms at the GSEs "must be done in a manner so as not to impede their affordable housing mission, a mission that has seen innovation flourish from desktop underwriting to 100 percent loans."[26]

What Ms. Waters was referring to, of course, was the replacement of old-school 30-year, self-amortizing, fixed-rate mortgage loans with innovative interest-only "option ARMS"[27] the private lenders needed to put in place to justify the riskier loans (with their higher anticipated default rates) required to be made in order to fill the racial lending quotas imposed under the CRA. Said differently, Ms. Waters insisted that reform not stop the precise lending practices that ended up causing the subprime mortgage crisis and housing bubble.

As recently as Christmas Eve 2009, Jane Hamsher, editor of liberal website Firedoglake, and Grover Norquist, head of the conservative group, Americans for Tax Reform—sent a joint letter to Attorney General Eric Holder, demanding that he investigate Obama's White House Chief of Staff Rahm Emanuel. Emanuel was appointed to the board of Freddie Mac by President Clinton in 2000 and served there for 14 months.[28]

According to a story broken by the *Chicago Tribune*, the Office of Federal Enterprise Housing Oversight, the same Congressional oversight office that charged Fannie CEO Raines with cooking Fannie's books in order to line his own pockets, issued a report finding that, during Emanuel's tenure as a Freddie Mac board member, a plan was put in place by "the executives and the board to use accounting tricks to show shareholders they were reaping massive profits even as they continued down a path of risky investments."[29] The profits were then used to justify the executives' big bonuses, as well as compensation to outside board members, including Emanuel.

When Emanuel left the board to enter Congress in 2002, he qualified for $380,000 in stock and options and $20,000 cash. It seems Emanuel made as much as $400,000 for attending about six Freddie Mac board meetings. Not bad for a man who makes a $172,000 salary as the White House Chief of Staff.

Worse, charges were levied by Hamsher and Norquist that Emanuel had used his powerful position as White House Chief of Staff to prevent the filling of the vacant Freddie Mac Inspector General post in a stonewalling effort to force the running of the 10-year statute of limitations on Emanuel's alleged corruption before charges could be brought against him.

The demand for Holder's investigation of Emanuel's alleged corruption came on the heels of the White House approving $42 million in Wall Street–style year-end bonuses for the top 11 executives at Fannie and Freddie, including a stunning $6 million apiece for the CEOs of Fannie and Freddie. That's a pretty good chunk of change to be given to individuals who, given the federal conservatorship imposed on the GSEs and the hundreds of billions of dollars they will receive in taxpayer subsidies, are really just government bureaucrats who have no mission in life other than to "democratize credit," or said differently, lose taxpayer money—and a lot of it.

Wall Street–style year-end bonuses were lavished on the top GSE executives by Obama, despite his incessant ravings that he would not allow "fat cat bankers" to continue to be paid millions in unjust compensation—that was why, after all, he had appointed Kenneth Feinberg in the first place. A $6 million bonus for losing $5 to $20 billion per quarter is pretty good work if you can get it. Where is Ken Feinberg when you need him?

It would seem that when it comes to running a big company, the White House feels the need to pay big bonuses to attract top talent, the same plaintive cry the major banks laid at Pay Czar Feinberg's feet. (Apparently, losing that much money takes a lot of talent.) Unless a company is giving away taxpayer money to meet government-imposed racial lending quotas, it would seem attracting executive talent is not much of a concern for Obama appointees.

FHA MORTGAGE INSURANCE

The GSEs and the liquidity they provided to the secondary mortgage market was not the only tool in the government's arsenal. In addition, the Federal Housing Administration, a department of HUD, issues default insurance to private mortgage lenders insuring them against losses up to 100 percent of the loan amount.

Although the FHA insured just three out of 100 residential mortgages as recently as 2006, due to substantial pullback of private lending in the residential arena following the subprime mortgage crisis, the FHA's market share quickly swelled to nearly one out of every three mortgage loans made by the first quarter of 2010. This should not be confused with the overall rate of mortgage loans currently being made or insured by U.S. taxpayers, which stands at 96.5 percent—nearly the entire home mortgage market—as of May 2010.

While I was waiting to go on air at Fox Business News Channel on Thursday, November 12, 2009, for an interview with FBN anchors Dave Asman and Liz Claman to discuss "Cracks in the Foundation of the Fed's Housing Fix," FBN cut to a live feed from HUD's Washington, D.C. headquarters, where HUD Secretary Shaun Donovan was explaining why we should not be worried that the FHA's capital reserves had fallen to razor-thin levels. In fact, the FHA's capital reserves had fallen to barely more than one-quarter of the minimums mandated by Congress for the FHA's book, which as of September 2009 included $685 billion of mortgage loans.[30]

SO, HERE'S WHAT HAPPENED

A crushing tsunami of shoddily underwritten mortgage loans overtook us. Mortgage lenders readily complied by flooding the secondary mortgage market with trillions of dollars of the high loan-to-value mortgage loans to minority borrowers mandated by Congress and the GSEs. Wall Street did its part, as well, providing the financial engineering (the slicing and dicing) and distribution channels necessary to enable Fannie, Freddie, and Ginnie Mae residential mortgage-backed securities to work their way onto the balance sheets of investors throughout our shadow banking system worldwide. As a result, the percentage of home mortgage loans made to borrowers putting up a down payment of 5 percent or less more than tripled from 9 percent in 1991 to 27 percent in 1995, eventually reaching a staggering 29 percent in 2007.[31]

CHAPTER 2

The Bubble Implodes

The art of economics consists in looking not merely at the immediate but at the longer effects of any act or policy; it consists in tracing the consequences of that policy not merely for one group but for all groups.

—Henry Hazlitt

As I demonstrate in this chapter, the reaction of Democratic lawmakers and the Obama administration has only delayed the inevitable day of reckoning and compounded the crisis by turning the federal government into the subprime mortgage lender of last resort.

Whether due to the well-meaning, albeit delusional, efforts of an ideologically driven radical left, or through an orgy of self-dealing and influence peddling, the end result was a massive tidal wave of subprime (and ALT-A)[1] loans written per congressional racial quotas to vastly watered-down underwriting standards. This staggeringly complex and radical government intervention spawned a housing bubble of titanic proportions.

That massive housing bubble began imploding in 2006, as unfit borrowers, many of whom were granted loans well beyond their means to repay, started defaulting in droves. The serious delinquency rate on the GSEs' subprime loan portfolio is about seven times the rate for other loans, as Figure 2.1 demonstrates.

THE PRIVATE SECTOR'S ROLE

In order to fuel this frenzy of quota-driven residential lending, Fannie, Freddie, and sister government-sponsored enterprise (GSE) the Government National Mortgage Association, or as it is commonly known, Ginnie Mae, securitized the home mortgages they purchased in the secondary market (or insured). These mortgages, originated by banks and other mortgage lenders,

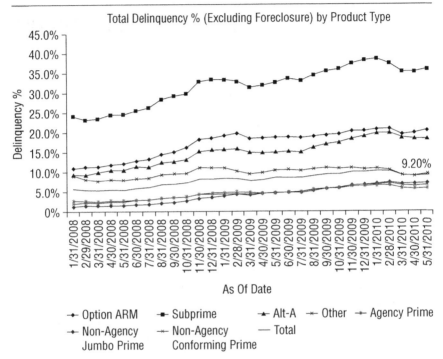

Total Delinquencies increased from April to May
Total Delinquencies (excluding Foreclosures) = 9.20%
Month over Month Increase of 2.3%, Year over Year Increase of 7.9%

FIGURE 2.1   Total Delinquencies Increased from April to May
Source: Lender Processing Services

were purchased (or insured) by the GSEs and securitized—bundled into diverse pools of mortgages, the ownership of which was transferred[2] to a single corporation, which would then issue diverse investors scattered across the country (if not the globe) collateralized debt obligations backed by the pool of mortgages.

Given that U.S. housing, when measured on a national basis, had never materially declined in value for the 76 years preceding 2007,[3] and given the (apparent) risk diversification offered by the securitization process, Wall Street obliged the GSEs with a fervor characteristic of private free enterprise. It was no wonder residential mortgage-backed securities were thought by investors worldwide to be bulletproof.

What Wall Street and the residential mortgage-backed security (RMBS) investors all had missed, however—at least initially—was the free-market tampering brought about by the unprecedented, radical, and racial lending quotas imposed under the auspices of the Community Reinvestment Act, a process initiated by the Clinton administration and bought to unprecedented heights by ACORN, Mozilo, and Frank, Dodd, Waters, and their minions.

That massive government intervention had dramatically altered the historic (and stable) 47/53 balance between homeowners and renters until it hit an unsustainable, near 70/30 relationship—a radical and experimental government intervention into the free market, driven by an unstoppable new paradigm, political correctness.

This terribly gone awry and reckless government intervention required the extension of trillions of dollars of credit to woefully unfit borrowers with little or no down payments and frighteningly low FICO[4] scores, using watered-down underwriting standards euphemistically known as "no doc/ no income check" loans and MAI[5] (known in the trade as "made as instructed") appraisals—all in order to meet the racial lending quotas imposed under the auspices of the Community Reinvestment Act.

While Wall Street's securitization prowess worked to spread the contagion, other private sector participants facilitated the making of toxic loans. Mortgage originators, stripped of any skin in the game once their loans were bought by the GSEs or securitized as private-label RMBS, compromised underwriting standards and in some cases committed outright fraud.

Appraisers, controlled by banks and other loan originators, were also willing participants, signing off, as they often did, on overly optimistic appraisals.

An oligopoly of protected credit rating agencies—Standard and Poor's, Moody's, and Fitch—were asleep at the switch and regularly issued high-grade ratings to subprime-backed RMBS, until the market started to crash, at which point they downgraded RMBS *en masse*.

But the foundation of the crisis was laid by the GSEs—they provided the demand behind all of this risky financial activity. If they had not made massive purchases of subprime loans in the secondary market—including a large share of private-label RMBS—the crisis would never have occurred.

Lastly, the Greenspan Fed, of course, cannot completely escape blame, as its low rate and monetary easing provided the needed liquidity.

THE BURSTING OF THE BUBBLE

When it all came tumbling down, the effects were both global in scope and cataclysmic in intensity. Trillions of dollars of toxic subprime loans were found on the balance sheets of banks, private equity firms, life insurance companies, hedge funds, and corporate and state pension funds the world over. The system collapsed.

Today, there are some 56 million residential mortgages in the United States totaling nearly $11 trillion. As it now stands, about 31 million mortgages amounting to some $5.5 trillion are owned or guaranteed by the U.S. taxpayer (via Fannie and Freddie). By now, $1 trillion more likely are guaranteed by the taxpayers via mortgage insurance issued by the Federal Housing Administration, whose reserves, as a result of the surge in defaults, are now at roughly one-quarter the congressionally mandated minimum level.

Private investment in the residential mortgage-backed securities market fell to nearly zero (though it began to rebound in 2010), and the FHA's market share has skyrocketed. As of May 2010, nearly all U.S. residential mortgage loans were being bought or insured by the U.S. taxpayer via Fannie, Freddie, or the FHA.

By the writing of this book, Fannie and Freddie have received $148 billion in direct taxpayer subsidies. Fannie's losses alone for Q3 2009 were nearly $20 billion, more than 16 times the losses sustained by General Motors for the same period. Freddie Mac's losses for the same period were about $5 billion.[6]

As of December 2009, the Case Schiller Index claimed about a 28 percent value loss in U.S. homes from the peak.[7] While there is evidence of a recent leveling off, suggesting that we may be past the nadir, these data must be considered in light of historically low mortgage rates, a cash-for-clunkers-like borrowing of future sales via the first-time home buyers' tax credit, and the temporary damming back of foreclosures (thus far) achieved by the Obama administration.

THE POLITICAL BLAME GAME

As recently as July 2008, only two months before Fannie and Freddie were seized by Treasury Secretary Paulson and placed under federal conservatorship, Barney Frank said of the GSEs, "They are fundamentally sound, not in danger of going under." Dodd echoed Frank's remarks at the same time.

Imagine what would happen if a stock analyst in the private sector reported that a company was "fundamentally sound" and "not in danger of going under,"[8] customers bought stock in the company based on that report, and just two months later the company was placed in emergency conservatorship due to its then imminent bankruptcy. That analyst would have been fired—on the spot. What's more, his or her career would be over.

But what happens when that sort of flagrant incompetence—or worse, corrupt conduct—happens in government? The incompetent politician just blames the other guy and moves on. In fact, the incompetent politician's career likely skyrockets if he or she can lay blame at someone else's feet in an effective and compelling manner.

Instead of begging for mercy, as he would have if he worked for a living in the private sector, Frank took the offensive. In a 2007 interview with the *Financial Times* of London, Frank said that "the financial crisis demonstrates the serious negative consequences of too little regulation" and that "bad decisions were made by people in the private sector."[9]

Frank was right. The bad decision made in the private sector was not standing up to Frank and other economically illiterate politicians by refusing to accept racial lending quotas. In 2008, Frank said, "Thanks to a conservative philosophy that says the market knows best . . . we are in a worldwide crisis now because of excessive deregulation."[10] Later, Frank (together with Richard Shelby, Republican senator from Alabama) was put in charge of fashioning the "too big to fail rules"—apparently a role Frank earned for the prescience he showed in predicting the housing crisis.

When the credit markets seized in response to the subprime mortgage crisis in August 2008, Barack Obama deftly shifted the entire focus of the election debate from "get out of Iraq and into Afghanistan" to "Bush and the Republicans are to blame for the economic crisis because of their belief in free markets and deregulation." Few would argue with the proposition that Obama won the election based on his successfully blaming Bush and the Republicans for the economic crisis by asserting that deregulation was the cause of our woes.

By the summer of 2009, a sort of political statute of limitations had begun to set in, with unemployment rates continuing to skyrocket. Shrewdly, Obama revised his blame-game strategy. Since Obama was now the regulator-in-chief, he no longer stood to gain by blaming the crisis on incompetent regulation over the banks.

Instead, Obama argued, due to a lack of regulatory *authority*, banks were able to and did make risky loans—and that was the cause of our problems, not inadequate regulation from the Oval Office. By October 2009, with unemployment rates still continuing to climb, and the Obama (really Pelosi-Reid) stimulus bill having produced no jobs, Obama revised his blame strategy a third time. In this iteration, Obama explained that unemployment rates were still climbing not because banks had loaned too much money (that was the cause back in the summer), but rather, just the opposite, because the banks wouldn't lend enough money, and as a result businesses (particularly small businesses) could not grow and create jobs.

THE PAULSON SEIZURE

On September 6, 2008, just days before Lehman would file bankruptcy, then–Secretary of the Treasury Henry Paulson seized both Fannie and Freddie, placing them into a federal conservatorship. We were right back where we started 70 years earlier—in 1938—when FDR had formed Fannie as a federal agency. Seventy percent home ownership and we go backward 70 years—kind of has a ring to it, don't you think?

In what can only be regarded as an exquisite irony, less than two months previously, Congressman Frank, who became the ranking member of the House Financial Services Committee in 2003 and its chair in 2007,[11] said of Fannie, "Things look good going forward," thus contributing to millions of dollars in further GSE stockholder losses as hapless investors foolishly paid heed to Frank's false ramblings.

THE CURRENT STATE OF AFFAIRS

At the writing of this book, nearly one in four homeowners is underwater, and one in seven is delinquent. With unemployment rates having steadily skyrocketed since Mr. Obama took office—eventually breaching the psychological 10 percent barrier, and with real unemployment rates (including the underemployed and those who have given up looking for a job) closer to 17 percent—the housing crisis is not yet behind us. (See Figure 2.2.)

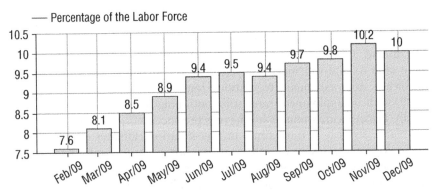

— Percentage of the Labor Force

FIGURE 2.2 United States Unemployment Rate
Source: Bureau of Labor Statistics

Perhaps worse than the systemic risk and temporary seizure of the credit markets will be the toll on human lives—millions of foreclosures and the attendant blight and community devastation. There were 1.7 million foreclosure filings in 2008 and over 2 million in 2009.[12] Likely there have been more than 5 million foreclosure filings since the onset of the recession in 2007 through the end of 2009.[13] However, only 2.2 million homes were actually repossessed by the end of 2009. There was thus a built-in backlog (or shadow inventory) of approximately 3 million homes at the end of 2009.

Given the millions of underwater homeowners still current on their mortgages and no end in sight to the high unemployment rates, millions more foreclosures in 2010, 2011, and 2012 are inevitable.

How's that for the law of reversed effect? Intent on helping minorities, the relentless liberal push to increase home ownership rates from 47 percent to 69 percent only ended up wreaking havoc on the lives of the very people they intended to help—the unfortunate millions of low-income minorities who were offered if not talked into abandoning renting in order to pursue the American dream by purchasing homes they could not afford. Both they and the rest of the world would have been better off—far better off—had the intended beneficiaries remained as they were before their liberal protectors had come to their rescue—as renters (which is exactly where, inevitably, most of them–and others–will end up).

THE CURRENT REACTION

Exactly as Henry Hazlitt warned, massive government intervention had the undesirable (and unintended, though not unforeseeable) effect of overallocating our scarce resources to the subsidized sector—here, housing. By way of government intervention, home builders were effectively asked to build millions of homes that never would have been built were the free markets allowed to operate efficiently without unnecessary (and hazardous) government intervention. As of the first quarter of 2009, a staggering 19,000,000 housing units were sitting vacant.[14]

That means that due to the massive federal subsidies, building materials were used to build millions of houses we did not need instead of the factories and nursing homes we did (and still do) need.

In substantial part because investors have bought and rented many of the foreclosed homes, additional pressure has been brought to bear on the apartment rental sector, such that rental vacancy rates increased to 8 percent in 2009.[15] According to the Congressional Oversight Panel's February 2010 report on commercial real estate, the number of rental apartments in the United States totals about 17.35 million. Thus, of the 19 million vacant housing units, only 1.4 million are rental apartments (8 percent of 17.35 million).

This is a stunning anomaly. Rental apartment units are built "on spec," while homes are built "to order" off signed contracts, for the most part. The rental apartment sector, being built on "spec," should account for a far higher percentage of the total vacant housing units.[16]

The 2000 U.S. Census estimates 114.8 million American households in 2010. If there are 115 million households and 19.1 million vacant dwellings, that suggests a staggering 16.6 percent oversupply in number of housing units. To the extent these houses were ever occupied, the former occupants have consolidated with other households as adult children have moved in with parents and other domestic partnerships have formed due to rising unemployment rates, a condition likely to continue for at least another half decade.

Thanks to the radicalization and racialization of the affordable housing mandate, we built millions of homes we don't need (and didn't build facilities we did and still do need), and it will take many years of population and GDP growth to absorb this vacant housing inventory. In the meantime, we can look forward to the blight to our neighborhoods caused by vacant houses.

The single overarching purpose of any economic system is to assure an efficient allocation of scarce resources. The Soviet Union failed because central planners could not possibly cope with the impossible burden of ordering the production of the millions of different goods and services to be produced by the gigantic Soviet economy—from the number of sweaters knitted to the amount of wheat grown in the Ukraine. Soviets either starved or went cold—the right mix was never achieved.

Although the U.S. economy is still predominantly a free market one, where market prices (and not government bureaucrats) drive the allocation of our scarce resources, radical government intervention—as in the case of housing—distorts the allocation of these resources. By using government-sponsored enterprises (Fannie and Freddie) and FHA insurance to flood the mortgage market with trillions of dollars of nearly zero down-payment loans, our federal government subsidized the housing sector and prompted the private sector (home builders) to construct millions more homes than we really needed. All the scarce resources deployed in the construction of those millions of unneeded homes (for example, lumber) could have been deployed in the construction of other products or facilities we really needed, or could have been left unused.

Ironically, the "global citizens" who call for "sustainability" when it comes to energy production (renewable energy sources) and halting global deforestation somehow fail to see that various progressive social agendas, such as an affordable housing mandate taken to the extremes to which it was taken in the United States since the mid-1990s, results in the unsustainable (and unnecessary) consumption of the earth's scarce resources.

Instead of waxing the hair off his chest, actor Harrison Ford would have been better off demanding the closure of Fannie and Freddie to protest deforestation. So too Al Gore should have sought the closure of the GSEs—had we not pumped trillions of dollars into our mortgage markets, those 19 million vacant homes would never have been built, thousands of acres of forest would have been spared, and our greenhouse gas emissions would be much lower than they now are (since trees consume carbon dioxide and emit oxygen). As Mr. Hazlitt admonished over a half century ago, when adopting public policy, we must consider the long-term consequences of our policies on all groups.

Despite all this, we still anxiously pore over each set of home building numbers released, looking for signs of recovery in the beleaguered home building sector.

President Obama responded (I would suggest via abdication) with a slew of social spending initiatives, including the Pelosi-Reid $787 billion stimulus bill, further TARP (the Troubled Asset Relief Program) expenditures (originally commenced by Bush and Paulson to staunch the flow of blood),[17] but most remarkable of all, by having the government ensure that new subprime mortgage loans continue to be made even though the private sector now refuses to make these loans.

It may be hard to believe, but despite this unprecedented debacle, and despite getting elected on a platform of fixing the economic mess allegedly created by President Bush and other Republicans, President Obama has doubled down on this failed strategy—through a new generation of government-sponsored subprime mortgage loans. Mr. Obama has specifically acted to make further subprime loans with taxpayer funds, even after the subprime mortgage crisis unfolded.

How, you ask? First, through Obama's $75 billion Home Affordable Modification Program (HAMP), we are once again demanding that our banks—and Fannie and Freddie—abandon sensible underwriting standards by modifying and extending defaulted mortgages. In fact, we are paying our banks to do so.

On November 29, 2009, the *Wall Street Journal* carried a story headed "New Push on Mortgage Relief," detailing Mr. Obama's dissatisfaction with the efforts by our banks and how he intends to push them to make more modifications. Second, Obama's first-time homebuyer's tax credit has been used to create down-payment funds for a new generation of no-skin-in-the-game minority buyers.

With an FHA down payment requirement of only 3.5 percent, a $200,000 home can be bought with as little as $7,000 down. But what about the home buyer who has no money and can't wait to receive the $8,000 "tax credit"—really a check from the Treasury? No problem; in the spring of 2009, Mr. Obama rolled out a separate $35 billion program to invest in state Housing Finance Agency bonds. These taxpayer funds were used in part by the HFAs to make bridge loans to advance the $8,000 first-time home buyer's tax credit to folks who wanted to buy a home but didn't have two nickels to rub together.

In late November 2009, Fannie announced its "First Look" program. Under this initiative, foreclosed homes taken in by Fannie are exclusively offered for the first 15 days only to two categories of buyers—the defaulted homeowner in occupancy and third-party buyers who use HFA or other public financing.

In other words, the policy attempts to ensure that if the present occupant does leave the home, it goes to a minority buyer (minorities often use HFA assistance). The idea behind this initiative is to prevent well-heeled investors from buying the foreclosed homes before the protected classes of no-money-down minority buyers—the HFA borrowers—have a chance to buy.

Most alarming of all, Obama has converted the FHA into the subprime lender of last resort, as the FHA's market share has risen a stunning twelve-fold, going from 3 percent in 2006 to one-third of all residential mortgages being made in early 2010.

In April 2010, Obama announced a daring new program. Instead of subsidizing delinquent homeowners, this program benefits homeowners who are underwater on their mortgages but continue to pay.

Obama promised to subsidize upper-income homeowners (folks owing mortgage balances up to $729,750) by paying their banks if they reduce the principal balance to 97.5 percent of the home's value and payments to "affordable" levels—31 percent of the homeowner's income. For home-owners who owe second mortgage loans, the balance need only be reduced to 115 percent of the home's value. Obama will pay billions of taxpayer dollars to the principal-forgiving banks—from 10 to 21 cents per dollar of principal forgiven, depending upon the overall percentage of principal forgiven.

Even so, banks would never take the principal hit, unless they were getting cashed out on the unforgiven principal balance. After all, the redefault rate on Obama's prior modifications has been abysmal. And the amounts at stake are huge: One in four homeowners is underwater—around $2.75 trillion of loans.

Where first and second mortgages are reduced to 115 percent of the home's value, Obama will use additional TARP money to insure the portion of the reduced principal balance exceeding the 97.5 percent HFA limit.

In short, we are using taxpayer funds to create a new generation of soon-to-go-into default subprime loans. In fact, we are making sure private banks can reverse–cherry pick their riskiest loans and get them off their books and onto the taxpayers.'

By so doing, we will reintroduce into our financial arteries a second generation of the very same toxic subprime loans that nearly destroyed our banking sector in the first place.

Indeed, I would argue that "Subprime 2.0" will be even more toxic than the original generation. The first time around, subprime loans were originated at razor-thin equity levels, often as low as 3 percent. Today, under Obama's Home Affordable Refinancing Program, GSE-owned loans are being refinanced even when the mortgage debt exceeds the home value by as much as 25 percent—that means a homeowner who owes $500,000 on a home worth $400,000 can get refinanced by Fannie or Freddie. A homeowner who refinances such a loan under a customary 30-year amortization schedule would have to pay that loan for 12 years in order to pay down the loan to the $400,000 refinancing-date value (absent price appreciation, which now seems very far off). The same can be said of HFA-insured loans, which, thanks to Obama's new program, will include loan-to-value ratios as high as 115 percent (15 percent negative equity).

To compound matters, 12 of 50 states have "nonrecourse" laws immunizing homeowners from deficiency liability with respect to purchase money home mortgage loans.[18] Included among the 12 "nonrecourse" states are three of the four states most adversely affected by the bursting of the housing bubble—California, Florida, and Arizona. In sum, we are systematically "retoxifying" rather than "detoxifying" the U.S. residential mortgage market.

THE MORAL HAZARD

The moral hazard for mortgage lenders, arising from our bail-out mania, is reaching epic proportions, as recently evidenced by two attention-getting decisions by New York State Justice Jeffery Skinner. Judge Skinner canceled a $292,500 mortgage debt owed to a federally subsidized[19] bank based solely on the judge's unhappiness with the way the bank handled the mortgage modification negotiations.[20] In a later decision, Judge Skinner not only canceled a borrower's mortgage debt, he ordered the bank to pay the borrower $100,000 to boot. In a similar vein, some legislators have pushed, thus far unsuccessfully, for laws enabling bankruptcy judges to modify mortgage loans by reducing principal balances.[21]

The moral hazard works on the lender side of the equation as well. While the big four banks—Wells Fargo, Citibank, JP Morgan Chase, and Bank of America—own only 8 percent of first mortgages (because they sold off to the GSEs or via private-label RMBS securitization most of the first mortgages they originated), they hold 42 percent of the home equity lines of credit (or piggyback second mortgages).[22] Obama's efforts to modify mortgages and stave off foreclosures has been an abysmal failure because principal reductions are needed but have not been happening.

Ironically, while the RMBS first mortgage holders are willing to make principal reduction concessions (they have lost the money represented by the portion of their loan balances exceeding current home values whether their books show that loss or not), the holders of the piggyback loans are insisting that some portion of their loans survive the restructuring process. Of course, not one dollar of a second mortgage loan should survive a first mortgage holder being asked to take one dollar off the principal balance. But the second mortgage holders are not reviewing appraisal reports, they are looking at the Congressional Panel Oversight reports and resisting modifications that properly wipe them out in the hope that one day they will get another bailout.

OBAMA'S HOME AFFORDABLE MODIFICATION PROGRAM FAILS

Under Obama's Home Affordable Modification Program, now aggressively being pursued by both the GSEs and private banks, subsidies (paid with taxpayer funds) are doled out to mortgage lenders as part of a mortgage modification mandate designed to stave off foreclosures. In April 2009, President Obama, under pressure from the big four banks, Bank of America, Wells Fargo, Citibank, and JP Morgan Chase, amended HAMP to allow the mortgage modification subsidy payments to go to the holders of home equity lines of credit—or HELOCs as they are called—in addition to holders of first mortgages.

Though the big banks hold 42 percent of the HELOCS and only 8 percent of the first mortgages, they act as servicer for both first and second mortgage loans (even where they have parted with the first mortgage). As a result, and with President Obama's support, these TARP-funded banks are trashing private contracts by negotiating and structuring modifications of both first mortgages and HELOCs, and receiving federal subsidies for modifying their out-of-the-money HELOCs (which otherwise would be wiped out altogether in bankruptcy or by foreclosure), even while simultaneously insisting (as servicers) that the RMBS first mortgage investors take a principal write-down.

While the Obama administration touts HAMP as accomplishing a necessary deleveraging, no real deleveraging is occurring whatsoever—other than by sleight of hand, and in all events the program is an abject failure. The delinquent mortgage debts of those homeowners who were unable to resist the temptation of turning their homes into ATM machines by taking out piggyback home equity lines of credit (the proceeds of which enabled them to live above their means) are being cleaved into two parts—one borne by the delinquent homeowner (at least for the time being) and the other being funded by HAMP subsidies and thereby becoming part of the national debt (and increasing the "shadow mortgages" owed by the 67 million taxpayers who actually pay taxes).

While the administration recently laid claim to achieving their November 2009 goal of 500,000 modifications, nearly all of these modifications are so-called trial modifications. And nearly all of them never take hold and become permanent, as these hopelessly underwater (newly minted subprime) borrowers realize there is simply no point in continuing. In fact, in June 2010, over 400,000 HAMP enrollees just gave up and voluntarily exited the program.

According to a lawsuit filed by former Fannie executive Caroline Herron in June 2010, Fannie, which was hired by President Obama to administer HAMP, is intentionally signing up "trial modifications" with hundreds of thousands of ineligible borrowers because the United States will pay bonuses to Fannie executives based on their trial modifications, whether or not they ever become permanent.[23]

As Fannie Mae noted in its Third Quarter 2009 Results, "[t]he Making Home Affordable Program will likely have a material adverse effect on our business, results of operations, and financial condition, including our net worth." Said differently, the HAMP program, by modifying hopelessly underwater mortgage loans, is only converting private mortgage debt to public national debt, and, in conjunction with the First Time Home Buyer's Credit and Fannie's First Look program, is minting a new class of subprime borrowers. In so doing, our current policies are only putting off the day of reckoning and thereby clogging the clearing process, as foreclosures (or short sales) are put off in the desperate hope that by the time the day of reckoning arrives the houses will have appreciated in value.

THE GSE BAILOUT

Despite Fannie's and Freddie's insolvency and the mind-numbing rate of their losses, in November 2009 the Obama administration refused to allow Goldman Sachs and Warren Buffett to purchase for $3 billion low income housing tax credits (LIHTCs) from Fannie—really limited partnership interests in money-losing low-income rental housing projects. As a result, these LIHTC credits will never be sold and will expire worthless.

There is little doubt that this decision (by which Fannie lost the opportunity to receive a $3 billion cash injection from private parties) was motivated entirely by the supposed political backlash to the opposite decision—no matter how much good business sense a sale of Fannie's otherwise worthless LIHTC investments made. Having placed the GSEs in a federal conservatorship, the federal government is now openly making decisions for the GSEs based not on the effects of those decisions on the GSEs' business (and therefore its stakeholders), as a real board of directors would be bound to do, but based on the supposed effects on U.S. Treasury receipts.

CHINA AS GSE BONDHOLDER

According to the U.S. Treasury, as of June 2009, China held $1.5 trillion of U.S. securities, including $757 billion of long-term Treasury debt and $454 billion of long-term government agency debt (Fannie and Freddie). (See Table 2.1.) By December of 2009, China held $894.8 billion of U.S. Treasury bonds.[24]

According to the U.S. Treasury, as of June 2008, China held $1.2 trillion of U.S. securities, including $522 billion of long-term Treasury debt and $527 billion of long-term government agency debt (Fannie and Freddie).

Did the Obama administration consider the increased losses it will have to underwrite on those bonds in the long term as a result of turning away Goldman Sachs and Buffett? What's next, telling TARP-subsidized banks that they cannot raise mortgage rates, because mortgage interest is tax deductible and the rate raise will reduce Treasury revenues?

The financial Armageddon brought about by the housing bust—itself a product of government-imposed racial lending quotas, which pushed U.S. home ownership rates to unsustainable levels by extending trillions of dollars of credit to unfit no-skin-in-the game borrowers—is far from over. In fact, the administration's responsive steps (really missteps), aimed at putting off the day of reckoning, have only ensured that the inescapable correction will be even more painful—and coincide with a second tsunami of commercial real estate foreclosures.

TABLE 2.1 Top Three Foreign Holders of U.S. Securities as of June 30, 2009 ($ billions)

Type of Security	Total	Treasury	LT Government Agency	LT Corporate	LT Equities	Short Term
China	1,462	757	454	15	76	160
Japan	1,270	646	219	154	182	69
United Kingdom	812	54	16	441	278	23
World Total	10,393	2,602	1,197	2,498	2,246	1,150
Change in China's Holdings over June 2008	257	235	−73	−11	−24	130
China's Holdings as a Percent of World Total %	14.1	29.1	37.9	0.1	3.4	13.9

Source: U.S. Treasury Department, Preliminary Report on Foreign Portfolio Holdings of U.S. Securities as of June 30, 2009, February 2010
Note: LT securities are those with no stated maturity date (such as equities) or with an original term to maturity date of more than one year. Short-term securities have a maturity period of less than one year

U.S. taxpayers now fund, for all practical purposes, our entire home mortgage market. Home sales were artificially propped up (especially at the low end) by the First Time Home Buyer's Credit, which expired on April 30, 2010 (but with contracts closing thereafter). The inevitable flood of further foreclosures—millions of homes—is temporarily being dammed back by HAMP. But none of these government actions is sustainable in the long term.

A MERRY CHRISTMAS FOR THE GSEs

When Secretary Paulson seized the insolvent mortgage giants back in September 2008, a $200 billion cap on taxpayer subsidies was imposed. That cap was doubled with congressional approval to $400 billion in May 2009.[25]

On Christmas Eve, 2009, without warning or explanation, the administration killed the cap entirely—by executive order—without congressional approval and in a mere "status update" on the GSEs. Why the breathtaking hike in maximum taxpayer subsidies to infinity? Why the cloak and dagger methodology? Why no press conference?

Well, no one (outside the administration) knows for sure. But here's my guess. With a national debt of $13 trillion and climbing, the United States needs to roll about $2.5 trillion of debt in 2010 and 2011; we have a good three-quarter trillion in underwater commercial real estate debt coming due during that same period and there are about $7 trillion in corporate bonds rolling during the same 24 months. That's a combined debt roll of well over 11 trillion in 2010 and 2011. Problem is, we are not out of the woods on residential mortgage-backed securities—not by a long shot.

My guess is that Obama's financial wizards finally figured out that the GSE bailout will top $400 billion. They also figured out why HAMP has turned out to be such a loser—the modifications just won't stick without massive principal reductions. Worse, Obama's advisors realized that in order to bring to bear the firepower necessary to modify a meaningful share of the defaulted mortgages in the $5.5 trillion loan portfolio owned or guaranteed by Fannie and Freddie (half of all mortgages by dollar volume, but more than half in number of mortgages), Obama would have to buy back possibly trillions of dollars worth of mortgages.

That's because only $1.5 trillion of mortgages (as whole loans or RMBS) are owned outright by Fannie and Freddie. The remaining $4.5 trillion worth have been securitized—Fannie and Freddie have sold them but remain responsible for them and must buy them back, out of the RMBS pools, in order for them to be modified. That takes a really big checkbook.

Obama's advisors also realized that the banks are going to cut loose millions more foreclosures in 2010 and 2011—not a good thing when you are rolling $11 trillion of public and private debt and looking forward to reelection. So, what to do?

One solution—apparently Obama's—was to pull a fast one on Congress (and on the American people) by killing entirely the Fannie/Freddie $400 billion subsidy cap.

WHAT WILL HAPPEN?

The only way out of the housing mess is to let the free market seek its own level and to mitigate future losses by hastening the overall economic recovery by fostering job growth—people, after all, pay their mortgages with wages. This in turn can only happen by unburdening private free enterprise and unleashing the formidable power of free-market capitalism. But that's not happening—4 million jobs have been lost since Obama took office—as profligate spending, and the prospect of trillions of dollars in increased taxes and medical insurance costs looming on the horizon (thanks to Obamacare), all work in unison to beat down business and thwart job growth.

Given the radical level of government intervention in housing, the racial lending quotas imposed by liberal lawmakers under the auspices of the Community Reinvestment Act, the resultant orgy of federally subsidized lending, the cooking of the books by GSE executives, and the bribery and influence peddling surrounding the GSEs, it's remarkable that Dodd's financial reform bill fails to even mention Fannie and Freddie.

While there is no arguing that securitizers, loan originators, appraisers, and credit rating agencies could and should be made to conduct themselves in a more responsible manner through thoughtful and targeted reform, a future crisis cannot be averted without reigning in the GSEs and the FHA.

The housing crisis was principally caused by excessive government intervention *in* the free markets, not by too little government regulation *of* free markets. Outright welfare checks are one thing. The recipient spends the money and we are done. But with CRA racial lending quotas, we give the gift that keeps on giving, as the recipients of the subsidy default on their subsidized loans.

After taking office, President Obama continued campaigning as he spoke of "mopping up" for his predecessor. But the water on the floor was spilled primarily by his liberal cohorts and by him (as a senator, Obama recorded the second highest amount of Fannie contributions of any lawmaker), and in any event he was not mopping up anything—rather, he was only spilling more water. But as White House Chief of Staff Rahm Emanuel has commented, "Never let a crisis go to waste."[26]

Sometime in 2010 or 2011 these various unsustainable actions of the Obama administration will come crashing down of their own weight, as the free market simply will not be denied. We need to take our medicine and the longer we put it off, the worse it will be.

Sooner rather than later the market will find an unsubsidized price level and millions of Americans will lose their homes to foreclosure—likely 8–12 million families before it's over. This tidal wave of foreclosures, and the realization that we have minted Subprime 2.0, will take a heavy toll on the economy (and job picture) in general, but in particular on the already beleaguered commercial real estate market, whose debt maturities are fast approaching and whose troubles thus far have been largely concealed from the general public, courtesy of near-zero base interest rates.

CHAPTER 3

Capital Markets Supporting U.S. Commercial Real Estate

This chapter traces the history of the commercial real estate capital markets, so that the reader has an understanding of the required structures and concepts. I explain the composition of modern complex CRE debt stacks including securitized mortgage loans and junior loans, now known as mezzanine loans, and the basic principles underlying maturity defaults, value declines, and extension rights.

SCOPE OF THE U.S. COMMERCIAL REAL ESTATE MARKET

At the end of 2008, investments in U.S. commercial real estate (CRE) totaled $6.4 trillion, composed of $2.9 trillion of equity investments and $3.5 trillion in debt.[1] The asset classes comprising commercial real estate include multifamily apartment buildings, office buildings, shopping malls and other retail facilities, hotel and hospitality properties, warehouse buildings, and manufacturing and flex or research and development space. Often individual properties are developed as mixed-use projects, such as apartment or office buildings containing ground-floor retail space and combined hotel and residential condominium projects. Most commercial real estate properties are occupied by multiple tenants, though some are net leased to single users. In other words, every building that's not a single or two-, three-, or four-family house or condominium apartment qualifies as commercial real estate.

U.S. commercial real estate assets are held by a diverse group of investors—individual entrepreneurs, including multigenerational "real estate families," publicly traded and private real estate investment trusts (REITS), real estate private equity firms, hedge funds, banks and savings and loan associations, privately held real estate holding companies, publicly traded and private businesses, not-for-profit corporations, foreign, federal, state, and local governments, and a whole plethora of foreign investors, including foreign individuals, banks, and sovereign wealth funds.

CRE LEVERAGE

As a practical matter, nearly all U.S. commercial real estate investors, no matter into what category they fit, lever their acquisitions by using the mortgage markets. Some avail themselves of additional leverage by using both the mortgage market and the subordinated debt market, and many utilize the maximum leverage offered by resorting to equity capital markets in addition to institutional senior and subordinated debt markets. These three capital markets—the senior or mortgage debt market, the subordinated debt market, and the equity market—have undergone radical changes since the mid 1990s.

Historical CRE Capital Markets

During the 1950s, 1960s, and 1970s—the age of famed New York City CRE investor Harry Helmsley—the CRE investor's financing options were severely limited. Banks would make (and hold until maturity) relatively low-leverage 60–70 percent loan-to-value first-mortgage loans.

Cash-strapped CRE investors had available to them "high-temperature hard money" loans as well. The hard money lenders would take second mortgages to secure their loans, and most CRE investors regarded these hard money loans as temporary "bridge loans" to be replaced by lower rate first mortgage refinancings as soon as the asset could be "repositioned"—its tenants and rents upgraded per the investor's development scheme.

Equity markets were not well formed, being for the most part populated by noninstitutional investors. Equity was raised by passing the hat around to "friends and family." In those years—long before the advent of the limited liability company and before enactment of the "at risk" limitations imposed by the Tax Reform Act of 1986—limited partnerships were the legal enterprise of choice for CRE owners, offering as they did pass-through or conduit tax status so that both general and limited partners could avail themselves of the excess "paper" losses (then deductible against ordinary non-real estate–related losses) allowed by the accelerated depreciation rules then governing CRE.

In the 1980s greater leverage was made available when our savings and loan associations discovered CRE loans. Looking backward at the suburbanization of America and the related proliferation of malls and suburban office buildings, the S&Ls jumped in with both feet. Older inner city rental apartment buildings were "converted" by the thousands to condominiums in the golden age of the "condo converter." Equity capital raises were augmented (and somewhat institutionalized) by tax syndications—the sale of limited partnership interests (in the era preceding the Tax Reform Act of 1986) by mom and pop broker-dealers operating under a variety of private offering exemptions (for example, Rule 146), providing exemption from registration under the Securities Act of 1933.

The resultant increase in leverage drove CRE prices upward and eventually resulted in the S&L crisis of the late 1980s and early 1990s, following the CRE value declines resulting from enactment of the Tax Reform Act of 1986 and the concomitant loss of CRE's theretofore tax-favored status. Reminiscent of the current "too big to fail" debate, the S&L Crisis would forever change our regulatory landscape. It resulted in the enactment of the Federal Institutions Reform, Recovery and Enforcement Act of 1989 (FIRREA), which in turn spawned the following changes:

- The Federal Home Loan Bank Board (FHLBB) and the Federal Savings and Loan Insurance Corporation (FSLIC) were abolished.
- The Office of Thrift Supervision (OTS), a bureau of the Treasury Department, was created to charter, regulate, examine, and supervise savings institutions.
- The Federal Housing Finance Board (FHFB) was created as an independent agency to oversee the 12 federal home loan banks (also called district banks).
- The Savings Association and Insurance Fund (SAIF) replaced the FSLIC as an ongoing insurance fund for thrift institutions (like the FDIC, the FSLIC was a permanent corporation that insured savings and loan accounts up to $100,000). SAIF is administered by the Federal Deposit Insurance Corp.
- The Resolution Trust Corporation (RTC) was established to dispose of failed thrift institutions taken over by regulators after January 1, 1989.
- Ironically, both Fannie Mae and Freddie Mac were given additional responsibility to support mortgages for low- and moderate-income families.

Ultimately 747 savings and loan associations and thrifts failed. Together with non-S&L but related bank failures, the FDIC and RTC supervised the failure and/or liquidation of some 1,600 banking institutions. The total cost of the S&L Crisis is estimated to have run approximately $160 billion, of which $124 billion was funded directly by the taxpayer. In short, the S&L Crisis looks like child's play compared to our current crises, the taxpayer-funded costs of which will be measured in trillions, not billions.

Modern CRE Capital Markets

Following the recession of 1990–1991, which many economists attribute at least in part to the S&L Crisis, our CRE capital markets started to undergo rapid and radical change, as Wall Street took notice and eventually securitized the CRE capital markets. CRE mortgages were pooled and placed into trusts or corporations. Bonds, with varying maturities, priorities, and risk profiles, but all secured by those diversified mortgage pools, were issued to a vast array of investors the world over, including but not limited to banks. A shadow banking system emerged as the role of the portfolio lender diminished. Banks and a host of other institutions became eager "loan originators," ready to make huge fees with no risk as the loans they underwrote were sold and taken off their books quickly and efficiently by the securitization process.

Subordinated debt markets—offering "mezzanine loans"—seemed to develop overnight. Lured by the promise of higher yields, a host of banks, hedge funds, REITS, and real estate private equity firms clamored to make the higher yield mezzanine loans. Many of the these mezzanine lenders, including Lehman Brothers, were themselves highly leveraged, using "repo lines"—akin to margin loans—in an effort to quickly reclaim their capital so that they could make more and more mezzanine loans.

Equity markets were also institutionalized. Many mezzanine lenders, not content with the higher yields appurtenant to mezzanine loans, reached for the even higher yields offered by "preferred equity investments"— unsecured equity investments used to purchase limited liability company membership interests structured in a manner reminiscent of preferred (corporate) stock, requiring that the return on and the return of their capital be paid ahead of common equity.

There can be little doubt that the securitization and related "institutionalization" of the CRE senior (CMBS),[2] subordinate (mezzanine) debt, and preferred equity markets drove CRE capitalization rates (cap rates) down and CRE values up in the boom years following the brief and shallow post-9/11 recession, as Figure 3.1 demonstrates.

To understand the risks now facing U.S. CRE, we need to understand in some depth the vast complexities and attendant confusion surrounding the legal instruments and structures employed in modern CRE capital markets.

SPECIAL-PURPOSE ENTERPRISES

Because of the contingent liabilities associated with real estate ownership, including "slip and fall" cases, floods and fires, and structural and

FIGURE 3.1 Monthly Average Historical Cap Rate
Source: Real Capital Analytics

design-related collapses and failures, the vast majority of commercial real estate assets are held in "single-purpose enterprises" (SPEs)—that is, each building or project is owned and held by a dedicated legal enterprise, which owns no other assets. Due to the availability of depreciation-driven noncash tax losses against some income tax liabilities (for those actively engaged in the real estate business), as well as the tax-exempt status of some CRE investors (e.g., sovereign wealth funds and public pension funds), the SPEs in turn are now almost universally organized as limited liability companies (LLCs). The LLC is generally not itself subject to income tax but is treated as "flow-through" enterprise for tax purposes, with the tax attributes of its operations being allocated to, and thereby suffered or enjoyed by, its members.

BANKRUPTCY REMOTENESS

Beyond the liability-limiting and tax-based objectives of CRE owners driving usage of the SPE format, since the advent of the commercial mortgage-backed securities (CMBS) debt market in the mid 1990s, lenders have increasingly required that the commercial real estate assets they finance be held by SPEs in order to achieve "bankruptcy remoteness." Bankruptcy remoteness—making it highly unlikely that ownership would voluntarily file a bankruptcy petition (or an owner's creditors would file for an involuntary bankruptcy petition)—is achieved through a variety of legal tools including so-called "SPE covenants" and the by now infamous springing nonrecourse guaranty.

SPE covenants, inserted by lenders into loan agreements, compel the CRE-owning SPE borrower to own no other assets besides the CRE property being financed, and frequently require the SPE to pay its trade payables in a timely manner, so that there are fewer creditors capable of banding together to file an involuntary bankruptcy petition. In addition, most CMBS lenders took to inserting as one of the SPE covenants a clause requiring so-called "independent directors" whose votes were required prior to the SPE owners filing a voluntary bankruptcy petition. Independent director clauses have not, however, uniformly been enforced by the courts. A violation of any of these SPE covenants results in a default under the loan.

The last line of defense in bankruptcy remoteness is the springing non-recourse guaranty. Typically, CMBS (as well as other) lenders designate a nonrecourse carve-out guarantor—generally the lead individual principal, holding company, or fund (in the case of real estate private equity firms)—and require that guarantor to sign a guaranty, which "springs" to life only if one of the SPE covenants is violated, the borrower files a voluntary bankruptcy petition, or creditors of the borrower, in collusion with the borrower, file an involuntary petition, which the borrower fails or refuses to dismiss in a timely manner.

These nonrecourse carve-out, springing guarantees generally provide for the guarantor to be responsible for actual losses to the lender arising from the SPE covenant violations. The entire debt usually becomes recourse to the guarantor in the event a bankruptcy petition is filed (treating the note as if the guarantor had been the borrower), generally subject to some overarching ceiling or cap. These clever legal devices demonstrate that bankruptcy was regarded as anathema to lenders at the outset of their loans, but as we are now starting to see, many senior lenders are resorting to bankruptcy in order to wipe out junior lenders, and thus find themselves in the uncomfortable position of having to overcome their own bankruptcy remoteness provisions. More details on this interesting trend will be discussed later. For now, suffice it to say that between the self-imposed (liability-limiting and tax-motivated) reasons for using SPEs to hold CRE assets and lender-forced SPE usage, the vast majority of commercial real estate assets are now SPE owned and controlled.

CRE DEBT STACK COMPOSITIONS

Besides equity owners, the other stakeholders in commercial real estate assets—the debt holders—have seen a radical restructuring of their positions since the advent of CMBS lending. The loans used to finance and refinance commercial real estate have undergone major structural changes in the last 15 years. Many first mortgages are now "securitized"—not held or "portfolioed" by the lender. The golden age of the CRE second mortgage is over;[3] the "mezzanine loan" has taken its place—in spades.

In years past, a single SPE—back then typically a limited partnership—would own fee title to the real property, and if a greater percentage of financing were required than that available from the first (portfolio) mortgage lender, a second (or sometimes a "wraparound") mortgage was secured. In today's financing environment, the lender originating the first mortgage often securitizes the mortgage loan such that beneficial ownership thereof is scattered among a diverse group of investors, and the second mortgage is virtually extinct (except in residential markets), having been replaced with subordinate mezzanine loans—so-called because such loans are made to upper-tier holding companies, not to the mortgage borrower.

In the case of the now out-of-favor second mortgage loan, the borrower under both the first and second mortgage loans was one and the same enterprise—the property owner. Thus, both the first and second mortgage loans appeared on one balance sheet—that of the property-owning enterprise. But CRE financiers were quick to import financial innovations from other areas into CRE lending. Thus, the off-balance-sheet lending techniques that led to the Enron scandal found a home in the CRE lending via the mezzanine loan. Since the advent of CMBS lending in the 1990s, subordinate CRE loans have been made to an upstream parent of the property-owning enterprise, or in the case of multiple subordinate loans, multiple upstream holding companies. Each mezzanine loan thus requires a successive upstream holding company.

The mortgage loan is therefore made to the property-owning enterprise, and the mezzanine loan is made to its parent or holding company. While the mortgage loan is secured by a mortgage lien against the property, the mezzanine loan is secured by a pledge of the equity interests (typically limited liability company membership interests) that the mezzanine borrower (the holding company) owns in the mortgage (or senior) borrower. Since the property-owning enterprise, or mortgage borrower, holds title to the property subject to the lien of the mortgage, it is only the equity (if any) that the mortgage borrower has in the property (i.e., the value of the property in excess of the mortgage debt) that secures the mezzanine loan.

Real estate lawyers universally use organization charts or "org charts" to visualize these multi-enterprise "debt stacks" (so-called because with mezzanine loans the debts are most easily visualized as vertical stacks).

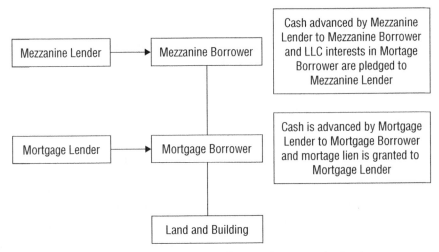

FIGURE 3.2   Typical Organization Chart for Simple CRE Debt Stock

Figure 3.2 shows a typical org chart for a simple single-mortgage, single-mezzanine loan, single-property deal.

As the CMBS market developed, mezzanine loans proliferated. Where once a second mortgage was the sign of a distressed or overleveraged owner, and a third mortgage was a true rarity, at the height of the market, mezzanine loans were stacked as many as 10 deep, as in the case of David Lichtenstein's since imploded 2007 acquisition of the Extended Stay Hotel chain.

In the Extended Stay Hotel acquisition (see Chapter 6), a securitized 18 tranche CMBS $4.1 billion mortgage loan was made, and behind it a series of 10 mezzanine loans aggregating another $3.3 billion was advanced by a plethora of hedge funds, private investors, and real estate private equity firms. To make things even more complex, 683 hotel properties were involved in the Extended Stay Hotel transaction. Thus for each one of those properties—all of which were held by individual SPEs—there are 11 levels of borrowers—a mortgage borrower and 10 successive upstream holding companies. That brings the total number of distinct borrowers into the many hundreds of enterprises. Moreover, some of the hotel properties were ground leased with the mortgages in such cases being leasehold mortgages. To boot, as stated above, the $4.1 billion first mortgage was securitized—having been cut up into 18 separate prioritized tranches. While it is impossible to depict the Extended Stay Hotel org chart, in concept a 10-deep mezz stack would appear as shown in Figure 3.3.

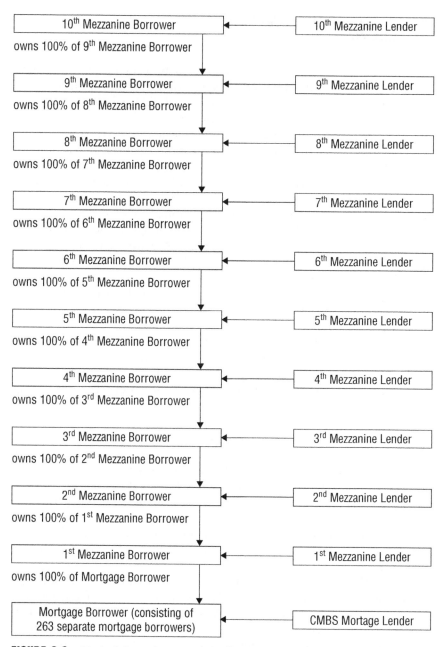

FIGURE 3.3 Typical Organization Chart for Complex CRE Debt Stock

THE MARKET FORMERLY KNOWN AS
THE CMBS MARKET

Unlike portfolioed loans, which continue to be held by the originating lender through maturity, many commercial real estate first mortgage loans originated since the mid 1990s were securitized (CMBS loans).

In a CMBS transaction, many single mortgage loans of varying size, property type, and location are pooled and transferred to a trustee, typically a major bank, which then holds title to the mortgage loans pursuant to an Indenture Trust Agreement for the benefit of the CMBS bondholders—the investors to whom interests in the CMBS pool of mortgage loans are sold. The trust issues a series of bonds that may vary in yield, duration, and payment priority. Nationally recognized rating agencies such as Fitch, Standard & Poor's, or Moody's assign credit ratings to the various bond classes ranging from investment grade (AAA/Aaa through BBB-/Baa3) to below investment grade (BB+/Ba1 through B-/B3), and an unrated class is subordinate to the lowest rated bond class.

Investors are able to choose which CMBS bonds to purchase based on the level of credit risk they wish to assume, the yield they desire (yields go up as risk goes up), and the duration (maturity) they seek. Each month the interest received from all of the pooled CMBS loans is paid to the bondholders, starting with those holding the highest rated bonds, until all accrued interest on those bonds is paid. Then interest is paid to the holders of the next highest rated bonds, and so on. The same thing occurs with principal as payments are received by the CMBS indenture trustee.

This sequential payment hierarchy, including the priority of paying operating expenses, real estate taxes, and mezzanine loan debt service, is generally referred to as the "cash waterfall" and is typically set forth in one or more cash management agreements or CMAs. If there is a shortfall in contractual loan payments from the borrowers or if loan collateral is liquidated and does not generate sufficient proceeds to meet payments on all bond classes, the investors in the most subordinate bond class will incur a loss with further losses impacting the more senior classes in reverse order of priority.

Often, the pools of CMBS loans are placed into a real estate mortgage investment conduit (REMIC). The REMIC is a creature of the Internal Revenue Code, which allows the trust to qualify as a pass-through enterprise not subject to tax at the trust level. Bondholders predicate their investment decisions on the assumption that the REMIC will not be subject to taxation at the trust level; consequently, strict compliance with REMIC tax regulations is essential.

CMBS became an attractive capital source for commercial mortgage lending because the bonds backed by a pool of loans were generally worth more than the sum of the value of the constituent whole loans. The enhanced liquidity and structure of CMBS attracted a broader range of investors to the commercial mortgage market. This apparent value creation effect allowed loans intended for securitization to be aggressively priced, benefiting borrowers (and driving up CRE values).

Sometimes the pool of CMBS mortgages was transferred to a corporation—itself an SPE—set up to hold the mortgages. The SPE corporation then issued bonds—obligations of the corporation itself—backed by the CMBS pool of mortgages. This CMBS structure is commonly called a collateralized debt obligation or CDO, and was frequently used as a vehicle to pool fixed income corporate securities backed by non–real estate assets. Whether the mortgage-backed securities were structured as a flow-through REMIC or a CDO, the bondholders flocked to them, thinking that the mortgage backing significantly reduced risk, and that the pooling of many different loans secured by different properties in different parts of the country significantly diversified whatever risk remained.

So popular were CMBS structures that CMBS loan originations rose meteorically from under $16 billion in 1995 to over $230 billion at the height of the CMBS market in 2007. Beginning in 2008, CMBS originations fell off a cliff and are now virtually nonexistent, except for TALF-funded loans and the residential (RMBS) mortgages purchased by Fannie and Freddie. (See Figure 3.4.)

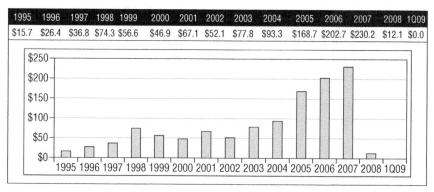

1995	1996	1997	1998	1999	2000	2001	2002	2003	2004	2005	2006	2007	2008	1Q09
$15.7	$26.4	$36.8	$74.3	$56.6	$46.9	$67.1	$52.1	$77.8	$93.3	$168.7	$202.7	$230.2	$12.1	$0.0

FIGURE 3.4   U.S. CMBS Issuance ($ billion)
Source: Commercial Mortgage Alert

MASTER AND SPECIAL SERVICERS AND THE HARD LOCKBOX

With the advent of CMBS lending, Wall Street needed to find a way to divorce the administration of the debt from the fragmented and diverse bondholders, and to ensure that such administration made its way into institutional hands. Enter the institutional primary or "master servicer." These administrators, in good times, would simply collect the interest and principal payments due the entire debt stack and pay those funds to those debt holders in the appropriate order of priority.

To ensure that the debt holders got their due, many CMBS loans required cash management agreements and the institution of a lockbox account—an account controlled by the master servicer into which tenants were instructed to pay or deposit all rent payments. Because the cash management agreements controlled all "top line" gross receipts, they had to provide for the payment not only of debt service among the stakeholders in the debt stack, but also of operating expenses, real estate taxes, management fees and, if there were any, profits to equity holders.

A typical cash management "waterfall" of funds requires that the master servicer first pay administrative costs of the servicer, then senior or first mortgage debt service, then taxes and operating expenses, thereafter mezzanine debt service, then management fees, and finally profits to equity holders.

If and when profits were ever reached, the internal provisions of the governing operating agreement of the top tier ownership enterprise (typically the holding company above the most junior mezzanine borrower) would govern the further distribution of those profits, first to preferred equity and then to common equity, often pursuant to a further "equity waterfall," which sometimes built in a "promote" or enhanced participation to the developer-sponsor as ever higher internal rates of return thresholds were achieved by preferred equity.

That's what happens when everything goes well. But when the things go poorly, Wall Street made sure a new player—the "Special Servicer" got involved. Various delinquency rates or other distress signs trigger a debt stack going into "special." As Figure 3.5 shows, the number of loans entering "special servicing" status has risen dramatically.

INTERCREDITOR AGREEMENTS

Due to the complexities presented by the number of stakeholders involved in CRE properties financed by complex debt stacks, these lenders have taken

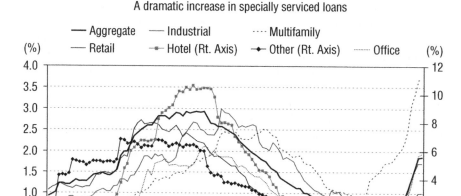

A dramatic increase in specially serviced loans

- Currently 1,363 loans ($12.9 billion) in special servicing versus 656 ($4.6 billion) one year ago
- Special servicing looks to become much more lucrative

FIGURE 3.5 A Dramatic Increase in Specially Serviced Loans
Source: Deutsche Bank

to entering into ever more complex agreements governing their intramural relationships. These agreements, to which the borrower is not a party (and which the borrower rarely if ever even lays eyes on), among other things, govern the limited rights of junior (mezzanine) lenders to commence enforcement (foreclosure) actions, and collection actions against guarantors (under both payment guaranties and springing nonrecourse guaranties). Typically intercreditor agreements afford junior lenders the right to cure borrower defaults under senior loans and to buy out senior loans at par (following a senior loan default) in order to enable junior lenders to protect their positions.

A particularly knotty problem addressed in some cases by the intercreditor agreement, and sometimes in other documents, is the determination of which of several participants in a single loan gets to decide whether and when to bring enforcement (foreclosure) actions. For example, in the case of securitized CMBS first mortgages, the CMBS bonds are typically tranched and prioritized. Thus a distress event may signal a loss for the junior bondholders but not the senior bondholders. In such cases, it makes sense for the junior tranche at risk to call the shots.

In reality, determining how deep the risk runs is easier said than done. Appraisal processes were employed by the securitized lending bar to make these determinations. As it turns out, the ability to control this process in and of itself has enormous value, as the lenders in the driver's seat are able to make deals with equity holders as to whether, when, and how to enforce, if at all. Similar problems exist within single mezzanine loans, as they are often "participated out" to multiple investors on a similar tranched and prioritized basis. The resultant intercreditor relationships became enormously complex. The Intercreditor Agreement in the Extended Stay financing, for example, ran 148 pages and was signed by 33 different parties.

Add to these complexities the fact that the borrower is forced to deal with first a master servicer and then a special servicer—and not any of the actual lenders—and it is not difficult to see just how inefficient, ineffective, and frustrating the workout process has become. Borrower principals often have no real decision maker to which to turn even if they have the ability and willingness to invest further equity.

PREFERRED EQUITY

It did not take long for mezzanine lenders to reach for higher yields. These same investors began making preferred equity investments. Instead of making loans secured by a pledge of LLC membership interests, they were issued preferred membership interests akin to preferred corporate stock having priority over "common equity" as to both the return of and on their initial cash investment. Often these preferred equity investments provided the "pref equity investor" overarching control rights on major decisions such as future sale or refinancings.

The $8 billion Extended Stay acquisition, for example, involved a consortium of preferred equity investors led by Ivan Kaufman's Arbor Realty Trust. Behind a $4.1 billion CMBS first mortgage and 10 tiered mezzanine loans aggregating $3.3 billion, the Extended Stay "pref equity" group invested several hundred million dollars more, thereby enabling developer David Lichtenstein to complete the $8 billion purchase with 98 percent leverage.

INTEREST RESERVES

A device frequently used by lenders during the boom years in an effort to enable them to advance ever-higher principal sums was the interest reserve.

CMBS lenders competing with one another by offering ever higher cash-out refinancings would underwrite CRE assets based on analysts' models, which projected future rent increases as leases turned over, and some low exit cap rate. The lenders would advance to a high percentage (a high LTV)[4] of that modeled "future value" by holding back a portion of their advance as an interest reserve. The theory was that the modeled future rents would be achieved before the interest reserve ran out. Sometimes, years of interest reserves would be built in to the underwriting.

In some ways, this method of underwriting to a future forecast value is similar to the negative amortization features built into the more exotic option arms made by residential lenders. In both cases, the lender was counting on future appreciation in its collateral rather than the borrowers' ability to pay to keep the loan safe. That bet proved to be a bad one for both residential and commercial lenders alike.

MATURITY DEFAULTS

While U.S. residential mortgages are typically made for 30-year terms (even if the rates are not fixed during the entirety of those long terms), CRE loans (mortgages and mezzanine loans) are typically made for much shorter terms. CRE terms have steadily declined as the debt markets became more complex and offered greater leverage rates.

Where once 10-year terms were common, typical CRE debt terms dropped to 5 years, and in the more recent loan vintages were underwritten as 2- or 3-year initial terms with one or more 1-year renewal options (almost universally subject to a debt yield or debt service coverage ratio test). In consequence, while near-zero, LIBOR-based, no-floor CRE debt stacks have enabled many owners to avoid payment defaults (and even to pocket cash while debt holders were vastly un- or undersecured), maturity defaults are not so easily overcome.

With no CMBS market and virtually no whole loan refinancing market, CRE owners facing debt maturities have few if any options (unlike home-owners, who benefit by a residential mortgage market almost entirely propped up by the U.S. taxpayer, courtesy of Fannie, Freddie, and FHA insurance). Unable to either refinance or sell (since a third-party buyer cannot obtain acquisition financing), CRE owners are left with no choice but to slug it out with their matured lenders.

It's no picnic for the lenders either, who realize that if they take in the property as "real estate owned" (REO), they are likely to hold onto it for a long time due to the lack of a CRE debt market. As Figure 3.6 shows, the volume of forthcoming CRE maturities is daunting.

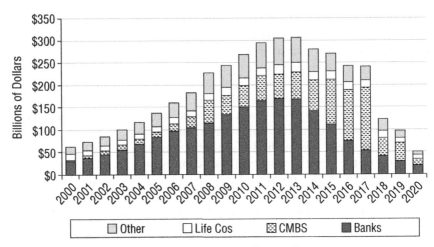

FIGURE 3.6   Commercial Mortgage Maturities by Lender Type

Major battles are ensuing between equity and debt stakeholders over loan term extension options. Where such options are contained in the loan documents and where they are absent, warfare among the various stakeholders—"tranche warfare"—often ensues. More on this later.

JUDICIAL, NONJUDICIAL, AND UCC FORECLOSURES

Mortgage loans are enforced by foreclosure proceedings—the public auction of the mortgaged property with the net proceeds being paid to the mortgage lender (and then other junior lienholders) before the surplus (equity), if any, is paid to the owner. Most CRE loans are nonrecourse to the borrower— that is, the lender is limited to looking to the real estate for repayment of the debt, absent the commission of "bad boy" nonrecourse carve-out events like misappropriation of rents, violation of SPE covenants, or the filing of a bankruptcy proceeding.

In some states, the mortgage foreclosure process is judicially supervised— it requires the foreclosing lender to commence a formal court proceeding and can take up to a year or longer to complete. In other states, the process is a quicker, nonjudicial one, whereby the lender simply follows a statutory procedure, advertises a public sale with the requisite advance notice, and is able to appoint a trustee who can sign a deed and convey title to the winning bidder (often the foreclosing lender, based on its credit bidding up to amount owed on the mortgage debt). Some states offer both judicial and nonjudicial procedures. (See Table 3.1.)

TABLE 3.1 Judicial and Nonjudicial Foreclosures

State	Judicial	Non-Judicial	Comments	Process Period (Days)	Sale Publication (Days)	Redemption Period (Days)	Sale/NTS
Alabama	●	●	○	49–74	21	365	Trustee
Alaska	●	●	○	105	65	365*	Trustee
Arizona	●	●	○	9 0+	41	30–180*	Trustee
Arkansas	●	●	○	70	30	365*	Trustee
California	●	●	○	117	21	365*	Trustee
Colorado	●	●	○	145	60	None	Trustee
Connecticut	●		○	62	NA	Court Decides	Court
Delaware	●		○	170–210	60–90	None	Sheriff
District of Columbia		●	○	47	18	None	Trustee
Florida	●		○	135	NA	None	Court
Georgia	●	●	○	37	32	None	Trustee
Hawaii	●	●	○	220	60	None	Trustee
Idaho	●	●	○	150	45	365	Trustee
Illinois	●		○	300	NA	90	Court
Indiana	●		○	261	120	None	Sheriff
Iowa	●	●	○	160	30	20	Sheriff
Kansas	●		○	130	21	365	Sheriff
Kentucky	●		○	147	NA	365	Court
Louisiana	●		○	180	NA	None	Sheriff
Maine	●		○	240	30	90	Court
Maryland	●	●	○	46	30	Court Decides	Court
Massachusetts	●	●	○	75	41	None	Court
Michigan	●	●		60	30	30–365	Sheriff
Minnesota	●	●	○	90–100	7	1825	Sheriff

(Continued)

49

TABLE 3.1 (Continued)

State	Judicial	Non-Judicial	Comments	Process Period (Days)	Sale Publication (Days)	Redemption Period (Days)	Sale/NTS
Mississippi		•	○	90	30	None	Trustee
Missouri		•	○	60	10	365	Trustee
Montana		•	○	150	50	None	Trustee
Nebraska	•		○	142	NA	None	Sheriff
Nevada		•	○	116	80	None	Trustee
New Hampshire		•	○	59	24	None	Trustee
New Jersey	•		○	270	NA	10	Sheriff
New Mexico	•		○	180	NA	30–270	Court
New York	•		○	445	NA	None	Court
North Carolina	•		○	110	25	None	Sheriff
North Dakota	•		○	150	NA	180–365	Sheriff
Ohio	•		○	217	NA	None	Sheriff
Oklahoma	•		○	186	NA	None	Sheriff
Oregon		•	○	150	30	180	Trustee
Pennsylvania	•		○	270	NA	None	Sheriff
Rhode Island		•	○	62	21	None	Trustee
South Carolina	•		○	150	NA	None	Court
South Dakota	•		○	150	23	30–365	Sheriff
Tennessee		•	○	40–45	20–25	730	Trustee
Texas		•	○	27	NA	None	Trustee
Utah		•	○	142	NA	Court Decides	Trustee
Vermont	•		○	95	NA	180–365	Court
Virginia		•	○	45	14–28	None	Trustee
Washington		•	○	135	90	None	Trustee
West Virginia		•	○	60–90	30–60	None	Trustee
Wisconsin	•		○	290	NA	365	Sheriff
Wyoming		•	○	60	25	90–365	Sheriff

*Judicial only.

In contrast to mortgage foreclosure proceedings, which are complex and burdensome, and which require judicial intervention, foreclosing against mezzanine loan collateral—usually LLC membership interests—is a far simpler, less costly, and quicker procedure. These proceedings are uniformly nonjudicial and are governed by the Uniform Commercial Code. UCC foreclosures involve simply notice and advertising a public auction of the mezzanine collateral—the LLC membership interests. The auctions often take place within 30 to 45 days and sometimes in as few as 10 days. Huge games of brinkmanship frequently erupt as junior mezzanine lenders are forced to protect by buying up the loans of foreclosing senior mezzanine lenders or face annihilation on auction day.

LENDER LIABILITY CLAIMS AND DEFENSES, AND DEBT NULLIFICATIONS

As the wall of CRE maturities hits—hundreds of billions of dollars worth per year, every year through 2017—CRE stakeholders will battle out foreclosures and loan modification/work out scenarios. Each side looks for whatever leverage it can assert. Competing debt holders vie for enforcement rights through appraisal mechanisms, and equity holders look to asset lender liability counterclaims and defenses whenever possible.

Add to this mix the moral hazard created by U.S. bailout mania, and the result is a highly unstable and unpredictable legal environment. Lenders, equity investors, and some judges wonder why some stakeholders are bailed out while others are not, especially when foreclosing lenders have been TARP subsidized. With securitized CMBS loans and even some syndicated loans, lead lenders often have far less skin in the game than do equity investors. Lenders who find themselves holding first mortgage loans having greater face amounts than the value of the underlying properties sometimes simply stop funding continuing construction loan commitments, preferring to take the legal risk of lender liability claims over the market risks associated with an escalating principal balance.

Our courts' dockets have been clogged with thousands of foreclosure actions, and even in states where mortgage foreclosure is nonjudicial, court dockets become clogged with proceedings seeking the appointment of temporary receivers. Borrowers have responded (and sometimes led) with lender liability suits based on alleged lender misconduct. Interlender disputes ("tranche warfare") break out, further contributing to the congestion of court dockets.

Add to this shrinking state budgets and state employee firings due to reduced tax revenues from recessionary conditions, and we have the makings of substantial delays. In one recent judicial foreclosure case I was defending in Florida with respect to a major South Florida office building, the judge commented that she was handling 6,000 cases involving 21,000 different litigants. This represents a multiyear backlog.

VALUE DECLINES

Given this massive proliferation of lending—in larger transactions like Extended Stay, the equivalent of 11 tiered loans on a single transaction, on top of hundreds of millions of dollars of preferred equity—the swollen money supplies held in place for so long by the Greenspan Fed, and the artificial stimulus provided to all sectors of the economy by flush U.S. consumers who cashed out of the ever rising equity in their homes during the boom years, via cash-out home refinancings and home equity lines of credit, it is not difficult to understand how commercial rents rose across all sectors—residential, office, industrial, and retail—while the yields demanded by CRE buyers (cap rates) dropped as more and more equity and debt dollars found themselves chasing a limited number of properties. Between 2002 and 2008, CRE cap rates, while ranging from sector to sector, plummeted from a blended average of 8.5 percent to just over 5 percent during this period, with cap rates in major markets, like New York City, dropping well below 5 percent.

In New York City, cap rates dipping below 3 percent were not uncommon for major office buildings at the height of the market. Today, as reality has set in and the CMBS market has dried up, blended cap rates in New York City have edged over 6 percent, and of course rents are down and vacancies are up. For example, in New York City's midtown market, vacancies in Class A buildings rose from 4.3 percent in the fourth quarter of 2007, to 9.9 percent in December 2009, while net effective rents in Class A buildings during that same period fell from $80.55 to $49.50 per rentable square foot.

A hypothetical 1,000,000-square-foot skyscraper in New York City, fully occupied and having average net effective rents of $30 per square foot in excess of operating costs and real estate taxes, might have fetched over $1,000 per square foot in 2007 or over $1 billion. In 2009, with a 10 percent vacancy rate and dropping rents, such a building might trade for $400 per square foot, or $400 million, a 60 percent decline in value. If such a building were either purchased or refinanced at the height of the market in 2007 to an aggregate 95 percent loan-to-value ratio, such a property might have a $650 million first mortgage and $300 million of tiered mezzanine loans, perhaps six separate $50 million mezzanine loans.

In such a case, the owner's cash equity ($50 million if he or she purchased in 2007) is lost, as is every single one of the six $50 million mezzanine loans—"vapor paper" as they are affectionately referred to. Further, nearly one-third—$200 million—of the first mortgage loan is lost as well—based on current values. Not a pretty picture, yet this scenario is not uncommon.

THE CRE BUBBLE BURSTS, WALL STREET CONSOLIDATES, AND TARP IS ROLLED OUT

Economically illiterate governmental policies imposing racial loan quotas on banks, forcing them to forego sound underwriting standards when it came to residential mortgage loans to the underprivileged, a swollen money supply held in place for too long by the Greenspan Fed, manifest corruption and influence peddling infecting the highest levels of government, Fannie and Freddie and some banking institutions, and complicit appraisers and credit rating agencies all worked in tandem to create an unprecedented housing bubble.

Before that bubble burst, U.S. consumers, representing better than 70 percent of our national GDP, went on a spending spree, using their ever appreciating house as an ATM machine via a seemingly bottomless pit of cash-out refinancings and piggyback home equity lines of credit, made possible through the magic of securitization and the distribution channels afforded by Wall Street. CRE rents soared and vacancies plummeted as U.S consumers pushed growth rates in all sectors of our economy.

Securitization of CRE first mortgage lending via an exploding CMBS market and the proliferation of theretofore unprecedented levels of multi-tiered subordinate financings of CRE assets via the newly minted mezzanine loan and preferred equity markets left CRE owners awash in money. Cap rates plummeted and prices soared.

Lenders, knowing they could not possibly underwrite their loans based on current rents, took to underwriting "interest reserves," bridging the asset to some future financially modeled date when, in theory, the liened asset could sustain the debt load they had placed against it. A separate CRE bubble was spawned.

In 2008 the subprime mortgage and credit crisis erupted with all its fury. The landscape would be forever changed—Bear Stearns, hours away from declaring bankruptcy, was sold to JPMorgan Chase in March. By September, Fannie and Freddie were seized and placed under federal conservatorship, and Lehman Brothers filed for bankruptcy and began liquidating.

Following the fall of Lehman, AIG was given massive capital injections from the U.S. Treasury; Wachovia nearly failed and was purchased by Wells Fargo; Washington Mutual failed and was bought by JPMorgan Chase; Bank of America, which purchased Countrywide Financial earlier in the year, purchased Merrill Lynch; and the last of the major Wall Street investments banks, Goldman Sachs and Morgan Stanley, along with charge card powerhouse American Express, converted into bank holding companies in order to survive.

Each of our four major banks—Bank of America, JP Morgan Chase, Wells Fargo, and Citibank—found themselves on the brink of disaster, eventually humbled and bailed out by U.S. taxpayers via TARP.

Although the massive federal interventions in the waning days of the Bush administration were successful in stemming the seizure of our credit markets altogether, the correction process in the housing market is far from over, and it has barely begun for CRE.

Fortunes will be made and lost in the process, new leaders will be minted (few would argue that President Obama got elected blaming the Republicans for the economic crisis), heads of industry and politics will be dethroned (already the CEOs of our automakers and banks have changed), new laws will be enacted (too big to fail and "financial reform"), and new decisional law will be made.

If we are thoughtful—and economically literate in our steps—the pain will be much shorter lived than if we continue our failed policies, which is precisely what we are now doing. But to come to the right decisions, we need a deeper understanding of what has transpired to date than our leaders for the most part have thus far demonstrated.

CHAPTER 4

CRE Values and Loan Defaults

Commercial real estate values are a function of both underlying funda-mentals and capitalization rates. This chapter explains why increases in market cap rates, more than eroding market fundamentals, are responsible for CRE value reductions. A corollary of this observation is that once rental and vacancy rates return to their prerecession levels, CRE values will likely still lag far behind their prerecession levels due to increased cap rates.

Rising cap rates and eroding market fundamentals, along with more stringent loan underwriting criteria, mean there will be maturity defaults in CRE loans of all types.

MARKET FUNDAMENTALS AND CAP RATES

Commercial real estate values are a function of both underlying market fundamentals and capitalization rates (cap rates). The underlying market fundamentals for the most part consist of rental values and vacancy rates. Cap rates reflect CRE investors' attitudes toward risk adjusted returns, and fluctuate wildly over time. The February 2010 Congressional Oversight Panel (COP) Report proffers the uncontroversial proposition that:

> *Commercial properties are generally income-producing assets, gen-erating rental or other income and having the potential for capital appreciation. Unlike residential property, the value of a commercial property depends largely on the amount of income that can be expected from the property.*[1]

With regard to CRE market fundamentals, the COP Report asserts that:

> *Increased vacancy rates, which now range from eight percent for multifamily housing to 18 percent for office buildings, and falling rents, which have declined 40 percent for office space and 33*

percent for retail space, have exerted a powerful downward pressure on the value of commercial properties.[2]

Based on the poorer fundamentals—increased vacancy rates and reduced rents—the COP Report suggests that "commercial property values have fallen more than 40 percent since the beginning of 2007."[3] However, there is another important factor at work that is now affecting CRE market values, apart from these market fundamentals.

Investors have adjusted the yields (investment returns) they now are demanding when purchasing CRE assets, presumably a reflection of their belief that CRE carries with it risks not sufficiently reflected in the investment returns demanded in the last cycle. This trend is demonstrated by Figure 4.1.

The powerful effects the increased risk-adjusted rates of return now being demanded by CRE buyers have on CRE values are easily demonstrated. Let's assume an office building generates $10 million of gross rents at a 40 percent profit margin, meaning that after real estate taxes and operating expenses, the building generates net operating cash flow of $4 million annually. In 2002, at an 8.5 percent cap rate, this translated into a value of about $47 million.

That same cash flow performance, however, at a 2007 cap rate of 5.1 percent, yielded a value of $78 million. Said another way, CRE investors

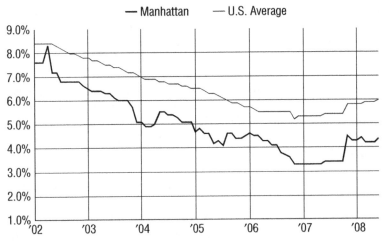

FIGURE 4.1　Monthly Average Historical Cap Rate

in 2007 were willing to pay $31 million more to buy the same cash flow stream in comparison to what they were willing to pay in 2002. That extra price represents an increase of nearly two-thirds in the price the 2007 investor was willing to pay for the same cash flow stream.

The sixty-four dollar question is: Where will cap rates settle? Will they move back to 2002 levels? Will they go even higher, or will they settle somewhere in between the 2002 and 2007 cap rate values? After rising through 2009, cap rates began falling once again, rather dramatically, in the first quarter of 2010, particularly in cities like New York, which attract foreign investors. That said, it is difficult to say where cap rates will end up simply because CRE trades, since the onset of the credit crisis, have been far and few between (due to the lack of a financing market).

In all events, it seems clear that blended national cap rates (cap rates tend to vary over CRE asset classes and locations) have moved from an average low of just over 5 percent to around 7 percent by the end of 2009 (lower for well-located assets and higher for others). Using a 7 percent cap rate as a benchmark, our hypothetical CRE asset, assuming it continued generating $4 million of free cash flow annually, will fetch roughly $57.1 million today versus $78.4 million at the height of the market. That's with no erosion in market fundamentals.

We now must factor in the erosion in market fundamentals observed by the COP Report. But before doing so, we need to understand how different classes of CRE assets reflect these eroding market fundamentals at differing rates of change. Hospitality properties have no long-term leases and as a result their performance immediately reflects lower occupancy levels and rates. Multifamily rental properties tend to be leased for terms ranging from 6 month to 2 years. In consequence, while their performances do not immediately reflect eroding fundamentals, they do so pretty quickly. Office buildings tend to be leased for terms ranging from 5 to 10 years, often with renewal options running beyond that.

These long-term leases present office building owners with frictional resistance to market changes both on the way up and on the way down. The rents in my law firm's Manhattan office building, for example, have dropped precipitously since 2008, yet my rents have not changed a dollar from the amounts set forth in my lease contract, which remains in effect for many more years. Of course, this frictional resistance to market changes is not without its limits. Tenants can and do go out of business or move to cheaper spaces before their leases term out, as a matter of survival. Some simply renegotiate their leases mid-term, arguing that absent reduced rents they will be forced to close down.

The retail sector presents long-term leases similar to those at office buildings, but anecdotal evidence suggests that retailers are more susceptible to bankruptcies and retail tenants are more prone to renegotiate leases mid-term. Therefore, CRE assets will likely show diminished performance based on eroding market fundamentals in the following order, with the first listed classes showing the most rapid erosion rates: hospitality, residential, retail, office.

In order to apply eroding market fundamentals to our hypothetical office building we need to make a few assumptions—the historic or frictional vacancy rate (departing the bull market), the amount of space under lease that termed out since the onset of the recession in late 2007, and the percentage of tenant failures. These factors will affect the degree to which downward rent and vacancy rate pressures have by now been reflected in the building's current cash flow performance.

While we can debate these matters endlessly, let's assume that our building was 95 percent occupied until the end of 2007 and that roughly 10 percent of the building "rolls" annually under staggered lease terms (i.e., average lease terms of 10 years). These assumptions would suggest that 25 percent of the building came up for renewal in the first two to three years of the recession. While the COP Report claims a 40 percent decline in office rents, we should not necessarily assume that new leases are entered into at 40 percent off the "coupon rate" set forth in the leases that termed out in the first two years of the recession. That's because the leases that termed out were entered into as much as 10 years earlier (long before the onset of the recession, and the inflationary escalations built into the leases likely did not keep pace with the growth in rents during the bull market). As an example, while the rents at my law firm's office building have dropped from nearly $80 per square foot at the height of the market to about $50 per square foot (about the 40 percent predicted by the COP Report), my firm's contract rate is still below the $50 market rate.

A more pronounced effect of down fundamentals is likely to be felt in terms of longer marketing periods (i.e., a substantially increased vacancy rate), more free rent in new leases (meaning reduced cash flow), and increased landlord contributions to tenant build-outs. The lease-up of rolling space will require the owner to reinvest millions of dollars (of additional equity or increased loan balances in the case of loans providing reserves for these functions) in brokerage commissions, legal fees, and tenant installation build-out costs.

Let's assume that the net effect from all of these factors is a reduction of our gross rent roll of 10 percent from $10 to $9 million. This will translate into a nearly dollar for dollar loss in free net cash flow since operating expenses are likely not reduced much by increased vacancy rates. (There will be some savings in cleaning costs and perhaps real estate taxes as the building's value drops, but the latter is likely to take a long time to be reflected). Let us assume that our net cash flow reduces by $800,000 from $4,000,000 to $3.2 million, a 20 percent reduction.

Applying the new market cap rate of 7 percent to the reduced $3.2 million cash flow yields a value of roughly $45,700,000 in comparison to a height-of-the market valuation of $78,400,000 ($4 million of cash flow applied to a 5.1 percent cap rate). While this analysis is hypothetical, some important and valid generalizations can be deduced from it.

First, the a $32.7 million value drop amounts to a 41.7 percent drop, as measured against the height-of-the-market value of $78.4 million, awfully close to the 40 percent drop in the market reported in the COP Report, suggesting that perhaps my assumptions are not at odds with the real world. Second, it is easy to see that about two-thirds of the value drop is not attributable to the decline in fundamentals (even though the authors of the COP Report attributed the value drop to declining fundamentals).

We know this by hypothetically looking at the value of our building once it regains its prerecession $4 million net cash flow performance (as will undoubtedly happen one day). At that point, assuming cap rates remain unchanged from their new level (assumed to be 7 percent), the building will then (with a $4 million net cash flow performance level) have a value of only $57.1 million. It can thus be said that $21.3 million ($78.4 million less $57.1 million) of its total value loss of $32.7 million ($78.4 million less $45.7 million) is attributable strictly to the cap rate adjustment (and not to declines in fundamentals). Said differently, the building will not regain its prerecession value even after market fundamentals have healed and returned to their prerecession values.

Indeed, in order to reestablish its height-of-the-market value of $78.4 million, our hypothetical building will have to establish not its prerecession cash flow of $4 million, but rather an enhanced cash flow of nearly $5.5 million ($5.5 million of net cash flow applied to a 7 percent cap rate yields our height-of-the-market value of $78.4 million). Said differently, our building must recover from a reduced $3.2 million net cash flow to an enhanced $5.5 million net cash flow before it can be said to have recovered fully (to its prerecession value), assuming no further change in cap rates.

This cash flow enhancement amounts to over 70 percent growth in net cash flow. Assuming a rather robust growth rate of 4 percent annually, this could take well more than a decade. While I am not suggesting that CRE assets must grow their net cash flow performance by 70 percent from their current levels until prerecession values are achieved, this analysis at least strongly suggests that prerecession values will not be reachieved once height-of-the-market fundamentals are restored, as is wrongly implied by reports (such as the COP Report), which at least suggest that the entire 40 percent or greater value drop is attributable solely (or even primarily) to eroding fundamentals. It is difficult to overstate the importance of cap rate increases.

This analytical framework is also helpful in that it hints at what I shall refer to as the "trend-sentiment" factor in determining cap rates. In rising markets, CRE buyers compete with one another to acquire properties, pushing prices to ever lower cap rates (higher prices) based on current net cash flows (whether calculated based on performance over the 12 or fewer months trailing the trade date or a snapshot of performance at the time of the trade, often called a "run rate" cash flow).

In essence, CRE buyers in a rising market are "buying the future." They rationalize accepting a paltry current return based on their belief that as leases roll over and higher rents are achieved, their rates of return will quickly increase. Conversely, in recessionary environments CRE buyers are unwilling to "buy the future" and may even see the future as yielding a worse, not better, return because height-of-the-market leases may be renewed at lower rents. This "trend-sentiment" tends to drive cap rates.

In all events, the question of when CRE markets will recover to their prerecession highs is largely a product of where cap rates are driven in future years, just as the current value drop was largely driven by cap rate increases (and not just eroding market fundamentals). Indeed, I would argue that the principal effect (on CRE values) of eroding or growing market fundamentals is the secondary effect those trends have on cap rates—that is, as we begin to rebuild higher rents and lower vacancy rates, CRE investor outlooks will improve and cap rates will likely drop somewhat. Indeed, this trend appears to have taken root in the first quarter of 2010.

Improving CRE market fundamentals will in turn be driven by overall improvements in GDP growth, unemployment rates, and by a recovery in our housing markets, since so much of the U.S. economy is driven by a healthy U.S. consumer. A healthy consumer means healthier retailers and other businesses, and lower unemployment rates means greater CRE occupancy levels.

Each new office worker, for example, occupies 200 additional square feet of space. These macroeconomic fundamentals are in turn driven by another sentiment-based factor—the perception of business owners regarding future spending, tax and regulatory burdens, and uncertainties. Predicting the recovery of the CRE markets therefore requires making predictions about future government policies, an endeavor more reliant on the skill set belonging to a political scientist than an economist.

CRE LOAN DEFAULTS—PRE- AND POSTMATURITY

As the COP Report noted, "between 2010 and 2014, about $1.4 trillion in commercial real estate loans will reach the end of their terms."[4] Many of the CRE loans now outstanding, particularly CMBS loans, are "no floor LIBOR[5] loans"—meaning these loans float at a fixed spread or margin above LIBOR rates with no minimum rate (no floor). Naturally, spreads (the percentage, expressed in basis points, to be added to LIBOR) enlarge with increasing risk, but it was not uncommon to see first mortgage spreads just above 100 basis points (1 percent) and blended average spreads throughout a debt stack ranging from 200 to 250 basis points (2–2.5 percent) over LIBOR.

In 2006, when 30-day LIBOR was over 5 percent, this yielded "stack-wide" blended cost of capital in the 7 percent to 8 percent range. But with the near-zero federal funds rate put into place in response to the subprime mortgage crisis and near seizure of our global credit markets, LIBOR sunk to and floated around 25 basis points (1/4 of 1 percent) throughout 2009. (See Figure 4.2.)

Because many CMBS and mezzanine loans had no interest rate floor, the near-zero LIBOR rates have put the blended cost of debt capital for much CRE well below 3 percent annually. Versus the 8 percent all-in rate in 2006, this means an interest savings on the order of $5 million annually

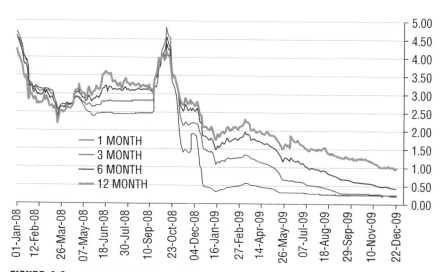

FIGURE 4.2 USD LIBOR Since 2008
Source: Kshitji Consultancy Services. www.kshitij.com/moneymkt/libor.shtml.

for every $100 million of debt. This vastly lowered cost of capital has covered up for a lot of sins—a lot of vacancies, rental defaults, retenanting costs, and reduced rental rates.

Unprecedented low LIBOR rates have saved many CRE projects from prematurity payment defaults. For example, at a typical first mortgage spread of 1.25 percent above 30-day LIBOR, a CMBS loan would have an effective rate of about 1.5 percent as of the end of 2009, compared with a rate of 6.5 percent assuming such a loan had been entered into when LIBOR was 5.25 percent. This 5 percent interest rate savings would translate into a cash savings of $3.1 million annually, assuming that our hypothetical office building took on 80 percent first mortgage financing of $62.7 million, based on its height-of-the-market value of $78.4 million.

Thus, while our hypothetical owner has sustained an $800,000 loss in net cash flow before debt service ($4 million to $3.2 million), the debt service has gone down from $3.76 million on $4 million of net cash flow (an opening debt service coverage ratio or DSCR of 1.06 to 1) to a stunning $940,000 (1.5 percent of $62.7 million, there being no amortization in most modern CRE loans) on net cash flow of $3.2 million (a current DSCR of 3.4 to 1). Thus, paradoxically, the owner's annual net operating income after debt service has actually gone up from $240,000 to $2,260,000. Likewise, the lender's coverage ratio has dramatically improved (from 1.06 to 1 to 3.4 to 1), despite a 20 percent erosion in net cash flow before debt service, based on declining market fundamentals.

Nevertheless, our hypothetical CMBS lender is deeply concerned. While its DSCR has dramatically improved, its loan-to-value (LTV) ratio has dramatically worsened. At loan opening, the LTV stood at 1.25 to 1 (a $78.4 million value against a $62.7 million loan, or a $15.4 million "equity cushion"). But the current LTV is .73 percent (a $45.7 million value against a $62.7 million loan, or negative equity of $17 million). Thus, while the borrower is current on interest payments, the lender is likely to face a loss of $17 million (or more) at maturity (and the owner's invested cash equity will be wiped out altogether).

It is easy to see how extraordinarily low LIBOR rates have covered up a lot of CRE woes and have delayed the onset of CRE foreclosures. But with $1.3 trillion in CRE loan maturities hitting through 2013 and $2.4 trillion hitting through 2018, it is also easy to see that this "calm before the storm" is about to pass.[6]

The problem gets even worse when one considers the current scarcity of credit and the consequent dearth of CRE trades. As a result of bank losses in both RMBS and CMBS (and whole CRE loans), the credit available to CRE transactions is enormously reduced, and underwriting standards have understandably tightened.

According to the COP Report, CRE loan underwriting standards now require LTVs of 60 to 65 percent.[7] Taking even the lower 65 percent LTV ratio and assuming there is no ready buyer willing to invest 35 percent equity ($16 million on a new value of $45.7 million), that means our hypothetical $62.7 million CMBS lender is facing the prospect of net refinancing proceeds of not quite $30 million (65 percent of 45.7 million) or less than half its $62.7 million loan balance (assuming there is any refinancing loan available at all). The CRE owner, faced with the prospect of investing $33 million fresh cash at maturity, is unlikely to comply, even assuming he or she has the ability to do so. That is why so many CRE owners and lenders face tough choices as the wall of CRE debt maturities hit.

For exactly these reasons, CRE lenders are loathe to allow leakage of excess net cash flow after debt service (as is now often the case, despite down market fundamentals, in the case of no-floor LIBOR loans). CRE lenders are thus doing all that they can to prevent cash flow leakage to junior stakeholders (both junior mezzanine loan and equity holders) prior to loan maturity, and they are mightily resisting extending those loans (including those that have extension options) without senior lenders trapping excess cash flow following loan extension.

Two complicating factors to this none too appealing analysis are (1) the prospect of substantially increased LIBOR rates in the future, and (2) counterparty defaults on credit default swaps. Given the unprecedented and profligate spending of the Obama administration, there is little question that, sooner or later, inflationary pressures will impel the Fed (and other central bankers) to raise their funds rates. When that happens, LIBOR will increase dramatically from its near-zero levels. In consequence, both unmatured and previously matured but extended CRE loans will come under severe risk for payment defaults. For this reason, many no-floor LIBOR loans require (or as modified and extended require) interest rate caps or swaps from solvent counterparties. These caps and swaps shift the interest rate risk (the risk of a rising LIBOR rate) to the counterparty issuing them, in exchange for the fee charged by the counterparty.

So long as the counterparty honors its obligation, the cap buyer/borrower is held harmless from interest rate rises above the cap or swap contract strike price (the LIBOR rate over which the counterparty bears the risk). At maturity, borrowers and lenders fight over how long to take out these derivative agreements. Caps and swaps get exponentially more expensive over time, since interest rate risks go up dramatically over time. Sometimes lenders succumb to borrowers' buying one-year caps or swaps, and require borrowers to reserve for future cap and swap costs. Whether the interest rate risk takes the form of actual rate hikes or vastly increased cap or swap costs, these costs will eventually force payment defaults.

As CRE loans mature and default, counterparties to CMBS credit default swaps (CDS) will be called upon to make payment. So too calls will be made upon LIBOR cap and swap counterparties when LIBOR rises. Thus beyond the direct impacts on bank capital levels affected by CRE loan losses, counterparty defaults on CDS and LIBOR caps and swaps may ripple through the global banking community. It is impossible to tell how severe these collateral effects will be.

CHAPTER 5

Putting Off the Day of Reckoning

Denial ain't just a river in Egypt.

—Mark Twain

In the last two quarters of 2009, the process we will see unfolding in commercial real estate for the next seven or eight years—several hundreds of billions of dollars of CRE loans maturing annually—began in earnest. While lender reactions have varied, even among the participants owning a single loan, one consistent lender-driven theme has already emerged: putting off the day of reckoning until a better market arrives.

DEFERRAL OF LENDER LOSS-TAKING

The deferral of lender loss-taking can take different forms. Where the real property is encumbered by a single mortgage loan (i.e., there are no mezzanine loans or junior lenders), the decision about what to do at maturity—from the lender side—is simplified in that one lender makes that decision, at least where that single mortgage loan is not owned by multiple participants or securitized. In such a case, assuming the loan is partly underwater (i.e., the loan balance exceeds the property value), the lender has essentially four options:

1. Sell the loan at a discount to a third party.
2. Take a discounted payoff (DPO) from the borrower (or sell the loan to a borrower affiliate at a discount, the economic equivalent of a DPO).
3. Take back the property either by way of a deed in lieu of foreclosure or through the prosecution of a foreclosure proceeding (whether judicial or nonjudicial).

4. Enter into a modification and extension of the loan with the borrower, usually involving three elements—an increase in term, an increase in interest rate, and a cash payment from the borrower, some of which may be applied to reduce the principal balance of the loan and the balance of which may be held as reserves for future costs not otherwise fundable from the property cash flow.[1]

The first two options, of course, require the lender to book the loss then and there. Except for institutions under severe regulatory pressures, banks, for the most part, and particularly the four major TARP-subsidized banks—Bank of America (which now includes Merrill Lynch and Countrywide), Wells Fargo (which now includes Wachovia), JP Morgan Chase (which now includes Washington Mutual), and Citibank—rarely took these routes (through the end of 2009), unless the discount was relatively minor (say 10–15 percent of principal amount). One exception to this general rule are some of the CRE loans acquired by Wells Fargo through its acquisition of Wachovia (more on this later).

The fourth option does not necessarily involve booking a loss (i.e., noting an impairment on the books and records of the lender), because the loan may be and remain technically current both before and after the extension and modification. Whether this option should involve booking a loss (noting a current impairment) is a whole different issue, which likely will be addressed by new rules to be promulgated by the gatekeeper of the prevailing accounting rules in the United States—GAAP (generally accepted accounting principles)—the Financial Accounting Standards Board (FASB).

For now, suffice it to say that lenders availing themselves of the extension and modification option—what many have called "extend and pretend"—are able, at least under current FASB pronouncements[2]—to defer noting an impairment to the value of the extended and modified loan under the theory that by the time the extended maturity date rolls around, the value of the property (whether through growth in rents or more favorable cap rates or both) will be sufficient (at that time) to repay the loan in full.[3]

Though the third option—taking the property back—may seem to require booking a current loss, that is not necessarily so. It is possible to structure a property take-back in such a manner as to keep the loan alive following the transfer of title. Where the borrower is cooperative and offers a deed in lieu of foreclosure, the lender will typically direct that the grantee named in the deed in lieu be a single-purpose enterprise (SPE) set up by the bank for that purpose as one of its subsidiaries.[4]

Sometimes, foreclosing banks contract with third-party property-holding companies to hold title subject to a nominee agreement indicating that they hold title for the benefit of the bank, which remains the beneficial (though not the titular) owner of the property. Either way, the bank can and often does choose to structure the legal documents so that the loan remains alive (without merging title and the mortgage lien). In such a case, although the bank would be required to show the property as "real estate owned," bank management and auditors may be persuaded to defer booking a loss until the property is sold, when one can definitively say what the property fetched.

Similarly, even where the borrower is not cooperative and the lender is forced to prosecute a foreclosure proceeding (whether judicial or nonjudicial), the court-appointed referee (in the case of a judicial foreclosure) or the lender-appointed trustee (in the case of a nonjudicial foreclosure) can execute the foreclosure deed in favor of a bank SPE[5] set up to "credit bid" at the foreclosure auction. (Since the foreclosing lender would only be paying itself, it is permitted to "credit bid" the amount of its mortgage debt at the foreclosure auction.) Thus, for the same reasons that apply in the case of a deed in lieu of foreclosure, the foreclosing lender may be able to put off the day of reckoning even when it takes back the property through a foreclosure sale and referee's or trustee's deed.

Of course, if the lender, after taking back the property, promptly sells it to a third party for less than the balance owed on the mortgage debt, then the full loss must be booked at that time. But few lenders have chosen to sell the CRE they have taken in as REO in the current market, though I think the trend is slowly reversing.

Significant complications arise in multitiered debt stacks, or where the property has been encumbered by a single mortgage loan but it has been securitized (a CMBS loan), and in consequence that single securitized loan is owned (beneficially) by numerous tranched and prioritized CMBS bondholders. In such cases, the senior and junior debt holders, unsurprisingly, have differing perspectives on property values, and it is often difficult, if not impossible, to arrive at any lender-wide consensus view. In such circumstances, intramural wars break out among lenders—"tranche warfare" (see Chapter 6).

All that said, as we move further along into the commercial real estate crisis, I think we will see banks and often CRE loan holders come under increasing pressure to sell loans at discounts and take their losses.

HARMFUL EFFECTS OF LENDER LOSS-DEFERRAL STRATEGIES

Apropos of Henry Hazlitt's admonition that the "art of economics [requires] looking not merely at the immediate but at the longer effects of any act or policy [and at] the consequences of that policy not merely for one group but for all groups," the loss-deferring strategies of CRE lenders must be examined not only for their immediate consequences to the loss-deferring lender but as well for the longer term consequences on others.

A strong case can be made that the lender loss-deferral strategies now being implemented by banks and other CRE lenders are bad for both the lender's stockholders (and bondholders), the property's occupants, the community in which the property is located, the lender's other borrower-customers, and for that matter, Americans at large. In fact, such strategies are really only good for one group—the lender's existing management; not surprisingly, the group responsible for adopting the loss-deferral strategy.

Lender loss-deferral strategies are bad for the stakeholders in the lender—its stockholders and bondholders—because there are far better yields available if the recoupable capital is deployed elsewhere (than in holding the property for a long term). If a CRE first mortgage lender who made a $500 million loan can currently recoup $400 million by selling the REO property now, but instead elects to hold onto that property for an extended period of many years (until that $500 million can be recouped), that "hold" is really a new investment decision, which must stand on its own.

For example, if it will take five more years to make back the $500 million loan balance, but the bank could return $600 million on a new and safe loan made with the $400 million of recoupable proceeds during the same period (a return of about 8 percent compounded annually), the bank (and its shareholders and bondholders) are $100 million better off selling the REO asset now and making the new loan. But the decision makers—management—often have vested personal interests in making it "appear" as if their prior underwriting decision did not result in a "loss." When management engages in such self-interested conduct, they are really breaching their fiduciary duties to their shareholders, but such breaches are not easily redressed because of the protection offered by the "business judgment rule."[6]

Others beside the bank's stock and bondholders are hurt by management's covering their keisters. The REO is inevitably managed by a third-party manager hired by the bank. Such managers have no vested interest in the asset and rarely look to the long term when making decisions or recommendations on improvements and repairs. Even if they did, there likely would be little appetite on the part of the bank to make long-term investments in equipment upgrades and the like given the bank's relatively short time horizon.

In short, the tenants of the REO property are likely to suffer as a bureaucratic bank officer, often in a distant city, and a third-party manager

, with no vested interest in the building decide on upgrades and building amenity packages. For the same reason, the community is likely to suffer when an important building is taken in as REO for an extended period. Often communities rely on major commercial properties and shopping centers to attract tenants and other commercial and sometimes cultural activities. So too, municipalities and taxing authorities may be adversely affected, as their tax bases are eroded.

In addition, other borrower-customers at the loss-deferring bank are adversely affected. We are seeing these adverse effects already. Banks are heavily regulated—most notably their ability to lend is limited by their capital levels. While selling the REO asset promptly would result in booking a loss and thereby lowering the bank's capital, so too the cash proceeds of the sale would be available for another loan.

Thus, management's decision to hold rather than sell the REO asset is in effect a decision to make a loan to a hypothetical borrower (the former borrower has been foreclosed). Said differently, by not selling the REO for, in our hypothetical example, $400 million currently, the bank is unable to loan that money to other customers—customers who need loans to expand their businesses (and thereby create more jobs).

In a sense, management is making a low-interest-rate loan to itself by holding onto the REO asset until it can be sold for a price that makes it "appear" as if they did not make a foolish decision in the past. This has the effect of curtailing credit and retarding a recovery in the job markets— something President Obama has been complaining about of late. Said differently, management's self-interested decision is forcing a misallocation of capital to CRE and away from some other sector in which it would do more good. Ironically, though, the Obama administration's policies are fostering rather than deterring the inefficient allocation of capital brought about by lender loss-deferral strategies. For one thing, TARP advances gave the banks the liquidity injections they needed to avoid being forced into selling REO assets. While one can argue that such injections were necessary to avoid a complete seizure of our credit markets, the same cannot be said for the appointment of pay czar Kenneth Feinberg. By targeting the "fat cat bankers" (unless they happen to work at Fannie Mae or Freddie Mac) and appointing a pay czar to curtail their bonuses unless and until they pay back their TARP funds, the administration's policies have fostered REO retention and therefore likewise incentivized banks against making new loans.

Because management wants to be able to pay bonuses, it is incentivized to pay back TARP funds as fast as possible. Already, most of these funds have been paid back. But in order to pay back the TARP funds, the banks were required to pass Treasury Secretary Geithner's stress tests. And in order to do that, banks were required to meet certain capital reserve ratios. How did they do that?

In two ways: First, by buying Treasuries (instead of using their funds to make new loans), the banks were able to avoid the requirement of additional capital reserves, because Treasuries are considered risk-free investments by federal regulations; second, by not selling REO and deferring the booking of losses, they were able to present fictitious representations of their capital positions (to the high side).

By attacking the fat cat bankers' bonuses—because it was politically expedient to do so—in tandem with the policy of not permitting the repayment of TARP absent meeting the stress tests, Obama got consequences he did not intend (but which were eminently foreseeable if only enough thought were put into policy making).

The president wanted to reduce executive bonuses. What he got was a reduction in executive bonuses AND a reduction in lending activity (and concomitantly a slowing of job creation). Unless and until the administration develops some minimal economic literacy, we are doomed to just these sorts of unintended and deleterious economic consequences from poorly thought out policies.

FASB 157-4

Though a full discussion about the heated debate concerning the mark-to-market accounting rules would be too great a detour, a brief word about this interesting issue and how it is now impacting CRE lenders is in order. Mark-to-market accounting, in this context, refers to the accounting standards requiring companies holding financial instruments on their balance sheets to mark them to market prices for similar instruments based on recent trades.

Mark-to-market accounting rules were made a part of GAAP by the FASB through the adoption of FAS 115 in May 1993 following on the heels of the Savings and Loan Crisis. FAS 115 called for varying accounting treatment depending upon how long the owning company intended to hold the debt securities, by categorizing such securities as either held-to-maturity securities, trading securities, or available-for-sale securities. This rule would normally allow (unsecuritized) loans intended to be held to maturity (portfolioed loans), to be carried at amortized cost less impairment (if an impairment event occurred).

In 2006, the FASB issued FAS 157 setting forth clarifications in making fair value measurements based on the reliability of market data inputs. Due to the success of the RMBS markets, trillions of dollars of these securities made their way onto the balance sheets of many financial institutions. Following the onset of the subprime mortgage crisis, the markets for trading in these securities abruptly halted.

Consequently, sales of RMBS during the subprime mortgage crisis were far and few between and were limited to distressed sales. Banks and other holders of RMBS argued strenuously that being forced to value RMBS based upon these distressed fire sales would unfairly impair their regulatory capital and only accelerate and deepen the credit crisis. Banks lobbied lawmakers hard to amend the mark-to-market rules to soften their impact.

While many lawmakers on both sides of the aisle agreed with the banks and criticized then–SEC Chairman Christopher Cox for not suspending the market-to-market rules altogether, others, including then–Treasury Secretary Paulson and Fed Chairman Ben Bernanke, insisted that while some modification of the rule might be in order, a complete suspension of the rule would bring about the return of the shady accounting practices that precipitated the earlier Savings and Loan Crisis.

The problem caused by the subprime mortgage crisis and the consequent (presumably temporary) disappearance of the RMBS markets in the context of the mark-to-market accounting rules was exacerbated by the leverage used by many lenders. In an effort to bolster returns, many lenders used leverage—often through repurchase agreements or so-called "repo lines"—when purchasing RMBS. In these credit arrangements, RMBS were pledged, much like equity securities are pledged on margin loans, in order to enable RMBS investors to leverage their positions. Under the repo line facilities, a mark down of the RMBS would have triggered massive margin calls across a wide spectrum of lenders at a time when there was little liquidity in the system.

In September 2008, in response to the then–crisis conditions in the credit markets, Congress enacted and on October 3, 2008, President Bush signed into law the Emergency Economic Stabilization Act of 2008 (EESA). This act of Congress passed the $700 billion Troubled Asset Relief Program (TARP). In addition, and in response to the mark-to-market debate, EESA included a section empowering the chair of the SEC to suspend mark-to-market accounting rules and as well a section directing that a study of the mark-to-market accounting rules be conducted by the SEC in consultation with the Federal Reserve Board and the Department of Treasury.

On April 2, 2009, the FASB, in response to growing concern and following a public comment period in which leading accounting firms and experts offered their comments, promulgated FAS 157-4. A *Forbes* article described the rule change this way: "With the changes to rule 157, companies can now value the assets on their books as if they were unloaded in an 'orderly' sale rather than dumped in a forced or 'distressed' sale."[7]

The softening of the mark-to-market accounting rules may have occurred in response to legitimate concerns that the previous rule, when applied to the extraordinary market conditions that emerged in August 2008, compelled inappropriate and dangerous capital impairments. But there is an old adage among lawyers that "tough cases make bad law."

Now that the liquidity crisis has subsided, a strong case can be made that banks and other lenders are using the softened rule to carry CMBS (and RMBS) at fictional values. This in turn is contributing (by enabling) the loss-deferral strategies being employed by CMBS lenders. By making determinations that the CMBS securities are being sold in "distressed sales," banks are able to avoid booking current impairments in line with the market value of the underlying CRE collateral (less any prior senior debt).

Many banks employ aggressive cash flow models, which discount back the modeled cash flows and a hypothetical terminal sale many years out, to a present value. In this way, these banks are able to carry CMBS at far higher values than would be achieved on their debt instruments were the underlying collateral—the mortgaged CRE assets—sold at market values. Many banks are now marking to fiction, not market.

LONG-TERM HOLD BY CMBS TRUSTEE—SPECIAL SERVICER CONFLICTS

For CRE assets refinanced in the frothy debt market in place during the period 2005 through early 2008, the balance owed on the first mortgage alone is likely substantially in excess of current value. For such properties, the CMBS bondholders will generally best be served by taking back the property (whether by consensual deed in lieu of foreclosure or by a foreclosure deed) and remarketing the property on a nondistressed basis (or by selling the loan itself). Holding for an extended period of years, however, in the hopes of selling into a better market, for the reasons set forth above, will rarely yield a return superior to other new deployments of the recoupable capital.

In the case of whole loans, existing management have incentives to order the extended-period hold. Aside from their own embarrassment, these executives often hold stock in their lender-employer and taking the write-downs may cause temporary stock price declines. But what about where a special servicer is in control and has no vested interest in the prior underwriting?

It turns out this category of decision maker often has a distinct but equally compelling reason to resist a prompt sale. The special servicer makes fees from its continued servicing of the distressed loan. Thus a prompt sale, though the servicer may receive some sale-related fees, nevertheless ends its income stream. For these reasons, few underwater CMBS mortgage loans are resulting in current sales. This is clogging the clearing process and delaying CRE's eventual recovery, not to mention choking off the making of loans (and the deployment of capital) to worthier borrowers (which in turn retards GDP growth and a recovery in the jobs market).

IRRATIONAL RESISTANCE TO BORROWER DPOs

Often the borrower—or the principals holding the equity interests in the borrower—are uniquely qualified to be the buyer of the CRE collateral securing a matured and defaulted CRE loan. The property securing a defaulted CRE loan has idiosyncratic value to the existing equity holders, which no one else in the marketplace shares.

For one thing, a foreclosure event will often trigger cancellation of debt income or recapture taxes to existing equity holders, particularly if the debt arose from a cash-out refinancing, or even if it did not, if substantial accumulated depreciation deductions were taken. Thus existing equity holders sometimes can save millions of dollars in taxes by avoiding a foreclosure event. In addition, existing equity holders can spare themselves reputational damage by averting foreclosure. For these reasons, lenders often can optimize their recovery by selling the collateral back to existing equity holders in the form of discounted payoff of the loan (DPO).

Lenders, though, have shown resistance to borrower DPOs even where those DPOs yield a higher recovery than a sale to a third party. Where the loan is not securitized, the lender's management often has a vested interest in not "appearing soft" on the defaulting borrower. So too, in the case of securitized loans, the CMBS special servicer has the same incentive. Special servicers are competing in the marketplace for new special servicing assignments. Their marketing strategy includes developing a reputation for being "tough on borrowers," so DPOs don't bode well for future servicing assignments.

PROTECTION EFFORTS BY MARGINALLY OUT-OF-THE-MONEY MEZZANINE LENDERS

In some instances, out-of-the-money mezzanine lenders—that is, a mezzanine loan that would get wiped out upon a current sale of the property—will step up and "protect" by buying at par (or close to par) the foreclosing lender senior to them, provided that loan is not much larger than theirs.

This often happens where the first mortgage is "money-good," but the senior mezzanine loan forecloses (a quick nonjudicial UCC foreclosure sale).

Say, for example, that an office building presently worth $250 million has a $200 million first mortgage and four mezzanine loans of $50 million each. The building is encumbered by a total of $400 million in debt, $150 million more than it's worth. The mortgage lender may be enticed with a modest paydown from the borrower of perhaps $10 million to extend at maturity subject to an increase in its "spread" over LIBOR (its interest rate), purchasing rate caps on LIBOR to mitigate interest rate risks (assuming a floating-rate LIBOR-based loan), and a host of other terms. In such a case, the senior mezzanine lender, who is in the money, may be tempted to foreclose, wipe out the borrower, and put up the $10 million so it can own the property, recover its debt at the end of the extended term, and hopefully make a profit over and above that.

In such a UCC (Uniform Commercial Code) mezzanine foreclosure, the second, third, and fourth mezzanine loans are wiped out together with the borrower. While the third and fourth loans are hopelessly underwater, the second mezzanine loan is "just out of the money." Such a mezzanine lender may step up and buy out the first mezzanine loan just prior to the UCC foreclosure date (mezzanine lenders universally have such "protection rights" under intercreditor agreements), so that it can conduct its own foreclosure sale, wipe out the third and fourth mezzanine lenders and equity, make the $10 million investment, and hopefully recover its $50 million loan out of appreciation between the date of the foreclosure and the extended maturity date. Thus, the longer the extension the first mortgage is willing to offer, the greater the likelihood is of a marginally out-of-the-money mezzanine lender "protecting" by buying the senior mezzanine loan and conducting the UCC foreclosure sale itself.

THE MOTHER OF ALL LOSS-DEFERRAL STRATEGIES— THE BARCLAYS-PRADIUM TRANSACTION

British bank Barclays Plc sold $12.3 billion of toxic loans to a Cayman Islands fund called Protium, controlled by ex-Barclays' employees. The sale was financed by a $12.6 billion purchase money loan made by Barclays to Protium. Protium only invested $450 million.

Why would Barclays' executives agree to trade $12.3 billion of Barclays' multiple toxic loans for a single toxic loan of roughly the same aggregate size made to Protium, which is secured by a pledge back of Barclays' toxic loans? What's the point of the transaction? It seems to be entirely lacking in economic substance.

As reported in a Bloomberg News release, "It's being presented as providing a more stable, certain outcome, but you could argue they are giving away the upside but not really being sheltered from much of the downside," said Ian Gordon, analyst at Exane BNP Paribas, citing a limited capital cushion at Protium.

The toxic loans sold by Barclays to Protium included $8.2 billion of structured credit assets insured by monoline insurers, $2.3 billion of assets backed by U.S. residential mortgage-backed securities, and $1.8 billion of mortgage assets.

I would argue that this seemingly pointless transaction was done for one and only one reason: The individual toxic loans sold by Barclays have varying maturity dates all coming up before the final maturity date on the overarching $12.6 billion purchase money loan made by Barclays to Protium. By replacing the individual short-term toxic loans with a single long-term toxic loan to Protium, Barclays was insulating itself from possible mandatory impairment events as the maturities of the individual toxic loans hit.

Said differently, Barclays' executives were worried that under prevailing accounting rules, whether U.S. GAAP or International Financial Accounting Standards (IFRS, applicable throughout Europe), Barclays might have to book its losses on these toxic loans as they matured. But by trading them to Protium in exchange for a single note (secured by a pledge of those very same toxic loans), Protium, not Barclays, would be able to work out and modify the individual toxic loans as they became due or possibly foreclose and sell the underlying collateral, without Barclays necessarily having to note an impairment on its books.

The Protium loan might still be paid off in full—only time would tell. This tortured effort by management to conceal write-offs will only hurt Barclays' shareholders, as Protium got whatever upside there may be in seizing the collateral and holding it into a new market (Protium owes a fixed amount to Barclays), while Barclays' shareholders got no credit enhancement worth mentioning. The shareholders traded away upside but got no real downside protection. The transaction was a noneconomic one, driven, in my view, by management's desire to avoid reporting losses.

PUTTING OFF JUDGMENT DAY

For different reasons, the persons controlling enforcement decisions on defaulted CRE debt are motivated to put off the day of reckoning. But as Mark Twain quipped a century and half ago, "denial ain't just a river in Egypt."

This disturbing trend will have deleterious consequences, as Henry Hazlitt admonished policy makers to consider. Lenders' stakeholders are not benefited, as most often they would be better off redeploying the recoupable capital in other, more profitable loans. Banks, which put off the day of reckoning, are shorted whatever cash they could recover in the short term and thus are not able to make other, more profitable loans.

This trend results in an inefficient allocation of capital, thus retarding the overall growth of business and the recovery of the job market. And it is only exacerbated by the Obama administration's existing policies, as TARP-funded banks try desperately to pay back their TARP loans so they can get out from under the thumb of pay czar Kenneth Feinberg. That, in turn, requires that the banks pass Treasury Secretary Geithner's stress tests, which in turn requires the banks to avoid or at least defer the booking of losses. Thus the populist policy of curbing the compensation of "fat cat bankers" ends up chilling the making of new loans and job growth.

CHAPTER 6

Tranche Warfare

We shall not flag or fail. We shall go on to the end. We shall fight in France, we shall fight on the seas and oceans, we shall fight with growing strength in the air, we shall defend our island, whatever the cost may be, we shall fight on the beaches, we shall fight on the landing grounds, we shall fight in the fields and in the streets, we shall fight in the hills; we shall never surrender.
—Winston Churchill

A s CRE debt maturities and payment defaults hit individual properties or portfolios encumbered by CMBS or whole mortgage loans coupled with hierarchical mezzanine debt stacks, tranche warfare has erupted between subordinate and senior lenders, and as well between lenders and borrowers. Unusual alliances are formed, often between equity owners and some lender classes.

EXTENDED STAY—A CASE STUDY

No better example of the "tranche warfare" phenomenon is presented than by what happened on David Lichtenstein's massive 2007 Extended Stay Hotels acquisition. Another major tranche warfare battleground recently erupted at Peter Cooper Village and Stuyvesant Town, the over 11,000-unit apartment complex bought by Tishman Speyer and Blackrock Realty in 2006 for $5.4 billion from Metropolitan Life.

In June 2007, developer David Lichtenstein purchased for $8 billion the over 75,000-unit Extended Stay Hotel (ESH) portfolio—an enormous portfolio of some 683 extended stay hotel properties located in 44 states and Canada—from Blackstone (not to be confused with Blackrock, the co-investor in Peter Cooper Village/Stuyvesant Town). Blackstone had purchased the ESH portfolio (then 475 hotel properties) for less than $2 billion in March 2004, three years before it sold the expanded 683-hotel chain to Lichtenstein. In 2004, the ESH portfolio traded for $4.2 million per hotel property while just three years later it traded for $11.7 million per hotel property—a nearly threefold price increase in just three years.

Despite this frighteningly rapid rate of appreciation, investors flocked to the massive financing, desperate to hand over nearly $8 billion to Lichtenstein. Lichtenstein's $8 billion acquisition was financed by a $7.4 billion debt stack consisting of a securitized (CMBS) $4.1 billion first mortgage and 10 tranched mezzanine loans aggregating $3.3 billion.

The securitized first mortgage was itself cut up into 18 different certificate classes representing sequentially prioritized tranches. That means, putting aside senior-subordinate participation arrangements within individual tranches, the ESH debt stack was cut up into 28 prioritized tranches. Included among the ESH's mezzanine lenders were Starwood Hotels and Fortress Investment Group.

The entire $7.4 billion debt stack was originated by Wachovia, Bank of America, Merrill Lynch, and Bear Stearns. The original lenders sold out of or securitized most of the debt stack before the credit markets collapsed, but still were left holding the bag on a good chunk of the mezzanine loans (the B through E tranches). Beyond the debt financing, Lichtenstein tapped into the preferred equity market as well by selling preferred equity interests to a group led by Ivan Kaufman's Arbor Capital.

In a June 2009 suit I brought on behalf of a group of private investors who owned a $214 million participation interest in one of the junior mezzanine loans (mezzanine tranche G), my clients alleged that Lichtenstein had conspired with the original lenders—Bank of America (which had subsequently acquired Merrill), Wachovia, and U.S National Bank Association, the Fed as successor to Bear Stearns, all of whom continued to hold substantial positions in mezzanine loan tranches B–E—to manufacture a contrived event of default under the loan documents by intentionally not paying a trivial amount of the borrowers' operating expenses.

As a result of the ESH borrowers not paying these trivial operating expenses—for the most part, some cellular telephone bills—the ESH borrowers ceased being qualified as bankruptcy remote "special purpose entities" ("SPEs") as required under the terms of the loan documents. Based on the default arising by virtue of the nonpayment of the cell phone bills, the original lenders, in May 2009, the month before the entire debt stack came due, announced that they had agreed with Lichtenstein that he would turn over the entire ESH portfolio to them as a "transfer in lieu" transaction—similar to a deed in lieu of foreclosure—whereby Lichtenstein would convey the equity interests in the borrowers to the original lenders in lieu of a (threatened) UCC foreclosure by the original lenders.

Under the original lenders' plan, spearheaded by the Bank of America, it was critical that the transfer in lieu transaction whereby Lichtenstein handed the original lenders the keys to the ESH portfolio occur by midnight of June 12, 2009. The original lenders turned into pumpkins at midnight on June 12 because that day was the initial maturity date under all of the loans, and while the loan documents provided for three successive one-year extension options (the first of which had been exercised by Lichtenstein), the loan documents also called for the application of a "debt yield test" on June 12.

The debt yield test required the net operating income of the hotel properties (for the 12-month period ended the day before maturity—June 11) to be compared to the aggregate principal amount of all of the loans ($7.4 billion) on the June 12 maturity date. If the net operating income, which had been battered by the weakened economy, amounted to more than the specified percentage (about 8 percent) of the aggregate principal balances of the loans on June 12, then the debt yield test would be passed; otherwise, it would be failed.

And, if the debt yield test were failed, while the loan extensions would nonetheless remain in effect, mandatory amortization payments would then be required with respect to all of the loans. These amortization payments would cascade through the debt stack in order of priority—the $4.1 billion CMBS first mortgage would receive their interest payments and then their amortization payment, the class A mezzanine loan would then receive its interest and then its amortization payments, and so on.

It was critical to the original lenders that the amortization payments—payable with respect to the loans senior to them, the CMBS first mortgage and the class A mezzanine loan, held by Starwood—be averted. The Bank of America and the other original lenders knew that eventually the amortization payments due to the first mortgage bondholders and Starwood would dry up the cash flow and stop any payments from being made to the remaining nine tranches of mezzanine loans, the first four of which (classes B–E) the original lenders themselves still owned.

My lawsuit alleged that it was critical to the original lenders that Lichtenstein turn over the keys to them by no later than midnight on June 12 because, upon consummating the transfer in lieu transaction, all mezzanine loans junior to the mezzanine B level—the mezzanine class owned by the original lenders to whom Lichtenstein was transferring ownership—would be structurally wiped out that day. By consummating the transfer in lieu of the UCC foreclosure transaction by midnight on June 12, the aggregate principal amount of the wiped-out junior mezzanine loans (approximately $2.6 billion worth) would cease to exist as debts of the borrowers on June 12, not count for purposes of the debt yield test, and the debt yield test would be passed.

For example, if the net operating income were $500 million, while that sum would cause a failure of the debt yield test because 8 percent of 7.4 billion is $592 million, that same net operating income would result in the debt yield test being passed—and the dreaded amortization payments being averted—if on June 12 the debt stack consisted of only $4.8 billion of loans.

When the group of investors owning a majority participation interest in the class G mezzanine loan received notice from the original lenders of the operating expense-based event of default in mid-May 2009, they promptly hired me, seeking my opinion as to why the original lenders would declare a default even though all loans were then current, just one month before the common maturity date.

After reviewing the loan documents and seeing the debt yield test, I explained to them that I saw a transfer in lieu transaction in their future. Sure enough, a few days later, the original lenders sent a notice that they had miraculously come to terms with Lichtenstein, who, it seemed, had come to his senses and selflessly agreed to hand back the keys to the original lenders.

A LONG STANDOFF

I brought suit on behalf of the mezzanine G participants in the New York State Supreme Court (New York County) against the original lenders, alleging they had put Lichtenstein up to not paying a trivial amount of operating expenses—mostly cell phone bills for ESH employees—by promising him some backdoor equity participation. The suit alleged that the original lenders had colluded with Lichtenstein regarding the delayed payment of the cell phone bills in order to create a default. As I mentioned earlier, not paying operating expenses on time, because it creates exposure to an involuntary bankruptcy filing by the unpaid trade creditors, is made a violation of the "special purpose entity" covenants of the loan documents.

The suit alleged that original lenders were desperate to create a default in order to fashion a legal peg on which the original lenders could hang their hats—by affording them a basis on which to take the borrowers' interests from Lichtenstein. The suit alleged that absent the original lenders taking over the ESH portfolio by June 12, the debt yield test would have been failed and the mandatory amortization payments would have kicked in.

The original lenders, who were behind senior mezzanine lender Starwood, knew, the suit alleged, that the amortization payments due on the $4.1 CMBS first mortgage and Starwood's mezzanine loan would eventually eat up ESH's cash flow and force a payment default to the original lenders. By wiping out all the junior mezzanine lenders before midnight on June 12, however, the debt yield test would be applied to an aggregate loan principal balance, which excluded the wiped-out junior mezzanine debt—some $2.6 billion worth.

By accomplishing this junior mezzanine debt annihilation in time, ESH's net operating income would be compared to total debt of $4.8 billion (instead of $7.4 billion), the debt yield test would be passed, and thereby the dreaded amortization payments due to the senior lenders would be averted.

As an aside, it is worth noting that the transfer in lieu transaction planned by the original lenders would not have worked but for the invention of the mezzanine debt structure. Had the ESH financing been structured as 11 prioritized mortgage loans—rather than one mortgage loan and 10 tranched mezzanine loans—the original lenders would not have bothered taking a deed in lieu of foreclosure from Lichtenstein. That's because a deed in lieu of foreclosure—unlike a transfer (of equity interests) in lieu of a UCC foreclosure—does not result in wiping out junior lienholders.

On June 3, my litigation team and I appeared before New York Supreme Court Justice Richard B. Lowe III at 110 Centre Street, which houses his chambers. Nearly 50 of New York City's highest paid commercial trial lawyers, representing most of New York City's major law firms, showed up in opposition to my application for a temporary restraining order. The sheer number of lawyers presented a problem—they could not fit in the conference room Justice Lowe intended to use to hear my application. As a result, half the group had to remain in the lobby while only principal attorneys took up residence in a conference room to hear my application and present their opposition to it.

I took a seat at the conference table along with my principal associate, Stacey Ashby, and presented the case to Justice Lowe. Peter Haveles of Kaye Scholer, counsel to the Bank of America, led the opposition for the original lenders, asserting that my claims of collusion between the original lenders and Lichtenstein were sheer fabrications. After hearing the arguments for and against the restraining order, Justice Lowe granted my application,[1] issuing a temporary restraining order effectively barring the transfer by Lichtenstein to the original lenders of his interests and tolling the time within which the junior mezzanine lenders could cure the alleged operating expense default.

When the June 3 restraining order was issued by Justice Lowe, at approximately 2:00 p.m. EST on June 3, there then remained one business day and approximately 10 hours of cure period in the 10-business-day cure period prescribed by the Intercreditor Agreement among the ESH lenders. Consequently, the June 3 restraining order effectively precluded the original lenders from being able to consummate their proposed transfer in lieu transaction with Lichtenstein until one business day and 10 hours after the June 3 restraining order was dissolved.

At the request of the original lenders, Justice Lowe conditioned his granting of the restraining order upon my clients posting a bond for the amount of the unpaid operating expenses—roughly $3 million—forming the basis of the alleged default (which in turn served as the predicate for Lichtenstein's giving over the hotels to the original lenders).

Due to time constraints, my clients elected to post this undertaking by wiring the roughly $3 million requirement in cash to my attorney's escrow account. Though I offered to commit to hold these funds in that escrow account unless and until directed by Justice Lowe to disburse them, the original lenders attempted to dissolve the June 3 restraining order on the ground that the undertaking did not take the technical form of a bond. This issue was argued through a series of letters and a conference call with Justice Lowe. Justice Lowe refused to dissolve the restraining order and instead ordered that I retain and disburse the cash funds per his further direction.

On June 8, a follow-up hearing was held before Justice Lowe on the preliminary injunction my clients sought (which if granted would remain in effect for the balance of the time the case was litigated). After a lengthy hearing, this time in Justice Lowe's 60 Centre Street courtroom, Justice Lowe reserved decision but continued the June 3 restraining order pending his decision on the preliminary injunction request. This meant that if Justice Lowe did not issue his decision within four days (which was unlikely, given the complexity of the matter and the volume of the briefing), then the June 3 temporary restraining order would still be in effect on June 12.

Since the June 3 temporary restraining order specifically continued the junior mezzanine lenders' cure rights, this in turn meant that (absent a decision from Judge Lowe denying my preliminary injunction and dissolving the temporary restraining order by June 12) the original lenders would not be able to wipe out the $2.6 billion of junior mezzanine debt by the June 12 date for application of the debt yield test. In such event, the recession-strained net operating income of the ESH hotel chain would be applied to the full $7.4 billion debt stack, the debt yield test would be failed, and the amortization payments would kick in, eventually wiping out the original lenders. The heat was on.

Settlement negotiations between my clients and the original lenders ensued and at first appeared successful. A deal was struck in principle between the principals whereby my clients would be paid a cash settlement and would agree to file by midnight on June 12, on the court's electronic Web site, a discontinuance of their lawsuit. The thinking was that upon that electronic filing discontinuing the suit, the restraining order would be dissolved and Lichtenstein would be able to convey the hotel interests to the original lenders before midnight on June 12, thus enabling the annihilation of $2.6 billion in junior mezzanine debt, the satisfaction of the debt yield test, and the aversion of the dreaded amortization payments.

Unfortunately, the settlement dialogue broke down just minutes before midnight on Friday, June 12. Once the clock struck 12, the debt yield test was failed and the amortization payments were locked in. By 3:00 a.m. Saturday morning, June 13, Lichtenstein's bankruptcy counsel, Weil, Gotshal and Manges (also the bankruptcy lawyers for Lehman), had electronically filed bankruptcy petitions for the ESH borrowers in the Bankruptcy Court for the Southern District of New York located on Bowling Green at the foot of Manhattan.

This stunned me. Why had Lichtenstein authorized the ESH bankruptcy petitions? While Weil Gotshal stood to make millions in legal fees, Lichtenstein stood to lose millions (of fresh dollars) due to his having signed a nonrecourse carve-out guaranty, one of the staples of securitized lending.

As explained in Chapter 3, commercial real estate loans are almost universally structured as nonrecourse loans—the lender agrees to look solely to the pledged real estate for collection of its loan. To prevent the delays and risks attendant to the bankruptcy process, CRE lenders have taken to impregnating their loan documents with various clauses and legal mechanisms designed to minimize the chances of a bankruptcy petition being filed.

Bankruptcy-remoteness, as it called, is achieved in large part through a nonrecourse carve-out guaranty. Under this guaranty, a designated nonrecourse carveout guarantor, often the principal developer, agrees that, while he is not responsible for the repayment of the loan as a general proposition, he will become liable for the loan, or the lender's resulting losses, usually subject to some overarching cap, if any one of a number of designated "nonrecourse carve-out events" or as they are often called, "bad boy acts," occur.

The most basic nonrecourse carve-out event or bad boy act is the filing of a bankruptcy petition by the borrower. Since the principal developer signing the nonrecourse carve-out guaranty is, at least as a threshold matter, in control of authorizing a bankruptcy petition on behalf of the borrower, such developers typically agreed to sign the nonrecourse carve-out guaranty, knowing that absent their signature to that document, the loan would never have been advanced in the first place.[2]

In the case of ESH, Lichtenstein had signed separate nonrecourse carve-out guarantees in favor of the CMBS trustee and each of the 10 different mezzanine lenders. Under the terms of those guarantees, Lichtenstein's liability (where the liability was based on a bankruptcy filing) was limited to $100 million in the aggregate among all the lenders.

The ESH lenders in turn signed a lengthy (148-page) intercreditor agreement in which the $100 million nonrecourse carve-out cap was allocated among the mezzanine lenders (to the exclusion of the CMBS first mortgage) in proportion to their respective loan amounts.

In the tense hours approaching midnight on Friday, June 12—the deadline for the application of the debt yield test—Lichtenstein's bankruptcy counsel and counsel for the original lenders repeatedly threatened that Lichtenstein would throw ESH into bankruptcy. Never, I thought to myself. Why would Lichtenstein take on $100 million of additional liability beyond whatever money he had already lost?

The tense standoff persisted. I refused to succumb to the demands of the original lenders, and eventually the clock struck 12 with no deal having been reached. When I awoke Saturday morning, June 13, my e-mail inbox revealed that Lichtenstein had indeed pulled the trigger on the ESH bankruptcy filing—Weil Gotshal had electronically filed the ESH bankruptcy petitions at 3:00 a.m. on Saturday, June 13, just three hours after the debt yield test had been failed. Why the kamikaze act, I wondered?

The answer lay in a term sheet filed by Lichtenstein along with the ESH bankruptcy petition. According to this term sheet, which proposed a plan of reorganization for ESH, designated owners of senior bonds in the CMBS first mortgage—Cerberus Capital Management, the behemoth hedge fund chaired by former Treasury Secretary John Snow, and Centerbridge Capital Partners, another massive hedge fund—offered to commit $100 million of ESH's cash (otherwise presumably available to them as senior ESH creditors) to an indemnity fund dedicated to holding Lichtenstein harmless from the claims of any ESH mezzanine lenders who pursued Lichtenstein under his nonrecourse carve-out guaranty (for having authorized the ESH bankruptcy petition), $5 million more of ESH's cash to fund a litigation war chest to be made available to Lichtenstein to fund his defense (of claims by the ESH mezzanine lenders under the nonrecourse carve-out guaranty), and a potential equity participation through a new management agreement with Lichtenstein's management company.

Said differently, the proposed term sheet filed by Lichtenstein told a story of months of negotiations between Lichtenstein and these CMBS bondholders in which the bondholders agreed to provide Lichtenstein with protections against the massive liability he faced if he pulled the trigger on an ESH bankruptcy. Presumably, these senior creditors wished to use the bankruptcy process to wipe out the ESH mezzanine lenders (and perhaps some of the junior CMBS tranches as well) and take control of ESH.

Hindsight being 20/20, we now know that that strategy ultimately proved successful. A coalition of investors including Centerbridge, Paulson and Company, original ESH owner Blackstone, JP Morgan Chase, and Deutsche Bank won an 18-hour marathon bankruptcy court–sanctioned auction of the ESH portfolio with a bid of $3.93 billion, beating out Starwood's $3.88 billion bid. The winning $3.93 billion bid remains subject to bankruptcy court approval.

Once the ESH bankruptcy petitions were filed, the suit my clients had filed earlier became the subject of the automatic stay in bankruptcy because various bankruptcy debtors were listed as defendants in that suit. As a result, I voluntarily discontinued that first suit and began work on a second state court lawsuit, which removed any of the ESH debtors and added claims against Cerberus and Centerbridge.

In the second suit, my mezzanine lender clients alleged that Cerberus and Centerbridge conspired with Lichtenstein to hatch a Machiavellian scheme, whereby Cerberus and Centerbridge promised to provide Lichtenstein with a $100,000,000 indemnity (funded out of ESH's cash) with respect to Lichtenstein's liability under the nonrecourse carve-out guaranty if he caused ESH to file for bankruptcy protection, along with a $5 million litigation defense war chest (also funded out of ESH's cash) to resist the claims asserted by other lenders (such as my clients) against Lichtenstein, as well as a back-door equity participation to Lichtenstein through a new management agreement.

The second lawsuit alleged that Cerberus and Centerbridge offered these inducements to Lichtenstein as part of a comprehensive scheme designed to induce Lichtenstein to do that which ESH's lenders promised one another, under the express terms of the Intercreditor Agreement, they would never do—cause the borrowers to file for bankruptcy protection—despite the numerous other "bankruptcy remoteness" provisions built into the relevant loan documents, thereby enabling Cerberus and Centerbridge to avoid application of the cash waterfall provisions to which the other lenders had agreed.

The new suit alleged that this Machiavellian scheme had worked, and as a direct result of the protections and promises offered by Cerberus and Centerbridge, Lichtenstein caused the ESH borrowers and various affiliated enterprises to file Chapter 11 bankruptcy cases on June 13, 2009.

This new state court action made out various claims against Cerberus and Centerbridge, against Lichtenstein and his company, Lightstone Holdings, for breach of the nonrecourse carve-out guaranty, based on filing the Chapter 11 petitions and for violating the SPE covenants, and against the original lenders for their alleged conspiracy with Lichtenstein in bringing about the earlier operating expense default.

Lichtenstein, through new counsel, the Kasowitz firm (Weil Gotshal now had a conflict of interest in that it represented ESH in the bankruptcy), filed a notice of removal placing my suit before the bankruptcy judge, Judge Peck, apparently in the hopes that a bankruptcy court would be more inclined to strike down the nonrecourse guaranty on the theory that it violated public policy by closing the doors of the bankruptcy court to ESH by chilling Lichtenstein's authorizing ESH's filing of a bankruptcy petition.

I responded by moving (before Judge Peck) to remand the case back to the New York State Court. After a four-hour hearing on September 10, 2009, Judge Peck granted my motion to remand, returning the case back to Justice Lowe. Though my suit was then sent back to Justice Lowe in the New York Supreme Court, Lichtenstein, Cerberus and Centerbridge, and ESH all filed appeals of Judge Peck's decision to send the case back to State Court. Those appeals proved unsuccessful and my clients' action will be decided by Justice Lowe.

The ESH story places in stark relief the intense battles among various stakeholders in an imploding CRE debt stack. Financial institutions and private investors holding mortgage loan, mezzanine loan, and equity positions engage in fierce battles for control of the collateral, often threatening annihilation of one another's investments. Unusual alliances form, sometimes between senior lenders and equity, opposite ends of the spectrum, in order to wipe out those stakeholders in the middle—frequently the mezzanine lenders—a sort of "cram sandwich." More often than not these battles play out in our courts—business is war and litigation is its bloodiest battlefield.

OTHER CASES

The ESH story is by no means unique. Tranche warfare is breaking out in thousands of troubled CRE debt stacks across our country. Where tranche warfare erupts, some debt holder somewhere in the debt stack often ends up taking "equity back in around the horn"—meaning that in exchange for transferring ownership to a foreclosing lender, the principals of the borrower are invited back into the deal in order to participate in some reduced fashion, often through an equity kicker or percentage of the profits built into a management contract entered into between the foreclosing lender and the borrower's principals, subordinate to the return of the foreclosing lender's rescue and original capital and some specified return on that capital.

In those cases, the foreclosed lenders and the borrower would be well advised to consult experienced counsel with regard to the terms of any nonrecourse carve-out guaranty. Many characterize any deed in lieu of foreclosure or transfer of membership interests in lieu of a UCC mezzanine foreclosure as a carve-out event, and virtually all nonrecourse carve-out guarantees name fraud as a carve-out event.

In another case in which I was involved, the owner of a deeply underwater property—its value was approximately $100 million below the balance owed on the first mortgage—wanted simply to give the CMBS trustee holding the first mortgage a deed in lieu of foreclosure. Behind the first mortgage was a $25 million mezzanine loan, which had no economic value. Although the nonrecourse carve-out guaranty in favor of the mezzanine lender was not particularly well drawn in that it did not specify that the borrower giving a deed in lieu of foreclosure was a carve-out event, it did say that any fraud committed against the mezzanine lender triggered the guaranty.

While the borrower giving a deed in lieu of foreclosure to the CMBS trustee did not work a fraud against the mezzanine lender, because the property was worth far less than the balance due on the first mortgage, that valuation was subjective, and I saw no profit in the borrower taking the exposure to the mezzanine lender inherent in his giving a deed in lieu of foreclosure to the CMBS trustee.

I offered to transfer the equity interests in lieu of a mezzanine foreclosure to the mezzanine lender, but the mezzanine lender rejected the proposed turnover of its collateral to it, because a multimillion transfer tax would have been owed by the mezzanine lender. By that rejection, the mezzanine lender signified its agreement that its loan was worthless.

Despite rejecting a tender of the mezzanine collateral, the mezzanine lender continued to refuse to consent to a deed in lieu of foreclosure being given to the CMBS trustee. I brought a suit on behalf of my borrower client against the mezzanine lender (as part of a mortgage foreclosure proceeding brought by the CMBS trustee) seeking a declaratory judgment from the court that the borrower giving the property back to the foreclosing first mortgage lender would not work a fraud on the mezzanine lender, given its refusal to accept a tender of its own (mezzanine) collateral, and that in consequence the borrower's tender of a deed in lieu of foreclosure would not trigger liability under the nonrecourse carve-out guaranty in favor of the mezzanine lender.

Eventually, I was successful on that suit, but by that time, the foreclosure sale was days away. The CMBS lender opted simply to go forward with that sale rather than accept a tender of the deed on a voluntary basis by the borrower.

This story presents another aspect to tranche warfare—"hold up value." Out-of-the-money mezzanine lenders quickly realize that, while their loans have no true economic value, their ability to "gum up the works" and to cost foreclosing lenders transfer taxes can result in a small recovery for them. They can be paid to get out of the way.

In yet another case in which I was involved, the owner of the Bank of America building in Atlanta, Georgia, found himself in the unenviable position of negotiating a renewal of the Bank of America's lease during the downturn. Naturally the Bank of America pressed for reduced rents. Ultimately the renewal lease negotiated between the owner and the Bank of America was consented to by the senior CMBS trustee but not the mezzanine lender, Petra Capital.

The owner nevertheless entered into the lease, fearful that the Bank of America would leave the building absent the lease being signed. Petra, through its servicer, sued the principal of the owner, based on a nonrecourse carve-out event, arguing that the execution of the lease constituted an impermissible "transfer" of the property. In some nonrecourse carve-out guarantees, such as the one at issue here, not only deeds and transfers of equity interests but leases as well are characterized as transfers, which, if made without the lender's consent, arguably trigger liability under the nonrecourse carve-out guaranty.

While the merits of this case have yet to be decided, an interesting procedural issue was raised by the Petra suit. Petra's mezzanine loan was owned by an offshore (Cayman Islands) CDO. Rather than submit to the jurisdiction of the court—given the likelihood of lender-liability claims being asserted against Petra based on Petra's refusal to consent to the Bank of America renewal lease—Petra's servicer, Situsserve, brought suit on behalf of the offshore CDO, alleging that under its servicing agreement it had authority to bring suit.

I brought a motion to dismiss the suit, arguing that my client's guaranty ran to Petra's offshore CDO, not Situsserve, with whom my client had contractual privity. As a result, I said, Situsserve lacked legal standing to sue.

Situsserve's lawyers pointed to a clause in the servicing agreement pursuant to which Situsserve was purportedly granted a power of attorney to sue on behalf of Petra's offshore CDO. While that was true enough, I pointed out to the court that New York's power of attorney statute, authorizes only an individual—a live, flesh and blood human being—to grant a power of attorney. Situsserve's lawyers protested that the power of attorney granted to Situsserve mirrored the powers of attorney granted in hundreds of billions of dollars of securitized and mezzanine loans across the county, and that the Situsserve's power of attorney should be judged under Cayman Islands' law.

The securitized lending bar is not exempted from reading and knowing the law. If this motion proves successful, many servicers will find themselves unable to enforce lender remedies without adding the lender to the suit. Doubtless if my client does prevail, the case will go up on appeal.

Tranche warfare recently broke out at the beleaguered 56-building, over 11,000-unit apartment complex, Peter Cooper Village/Stuyvesant Town, purchased by Tishman Speyer and Blackrock at the height of the market for $5.4 billion in 2006. Claims are now being made that that complex is worth $2 billion, far less than the $4.4 billion debt stack.

TRANCHE WARFARE HITS PUBLIC PENSIONS

Often, tranche warfare pits CMBS senior bondholders or major money center or regional banks holding whole senior mortgage loans against mezzanine lenders. In such cases, the mezzanine lenders, under threat of annihilation by CMBS investors or money center or regional banks in the senior mortgage positions, are real estate private equity firms that invest money for public pension funds like CALPERS and NY Common Fund.

Thus the federal government's efforts to bail out these financial institutions—thought to be too big to fail—as the Congressional Oversight Panel's February 2010 report on CRE intimates—will have the effect of accelerating the insolvency of the states (states can't file for bankruptcy, but they certainly can become insolvent), which foolishly committed to unsustainably lavish lifelong pensions for their teachers, firefighters, and police. As we assist the major money center and regional banks in wiping out the mezzanine investments made by our public state pensions, we only assure more expensive future state pension bailouts. Once again, our policy makers must look at the long-term repercussions of their policies.

CHAPTER 7

Loans to Own and Chilling the Bid

As the CRE crisis has deepened, a host of hedge funds, real estate private equity investors, publicly traded and private real estate investment trusts (REITs), and foreign investors have sought to buy distressed commercial real estate. Unfortunately, the distressed CRE owner is rarely in a position, alone, to convey title at an attractive price. Given the 40 to 60 percent decline in CRE prices since the height of the market, and the far greater leverage levels offered in the frothy refinancing markets CRE investors tapped into during the 2003–2008 period, it is a rare CRE asset that is not leveraged beyond its current value. As a result, CRE investors must resort to indirect methods of acquiring commercial real properties—buying a "loan to own" or a short-sale by the deed holder with the consent of the lenders.

LOANS TO OWN

CRE investors anxious to acquire overleveraged properties have taken to purchasing either at or below par, depending on the situation, one or more mortgages or mezzanine loans encumbering the target property and thereafter foreclosing against the collateral. In states where mortgage foreclosures take the form of court proceedings, strategic buyers of "loans to own" often purchase both the first mortgage and senior mezzanine loan, so they can avail themselves of the streamlined (nonjudicial) UCC foreclosure proceeding available to the foreclosing mezzanine lender.

This happened when an embattled Kent Swig, grandson of a well-known San Francisco developer and owner of real estate brokerage and consulting companies, Helmsley Spear, Halstead Properties, and Brown Harris Stevens, decided to cooperate with Fortress Investment Group on its purchase of the senior mortgage loan from Wells Fargo as CMBS trustee and the senior mezzanine loan from Guggenheim Structured Finance with respect to Swig's condominium conversion on Manhattan's Westside, the Sheffield.

Swig, along with two investors, had purchased the Sheffield, an 845-unit apartment building on West 57th Street in Manhattan, for $418 million in April 2005. As a result of two 2006 refinancings of the Sheffield with Column Financial, a Credit Suisse subsidiary, the project was encumbered by a series of mezzanine loans subordinate to the CMBS first mortgage acquisition and construction financing. Guggenheim held the senior mezzanine loan with a $70 million face. JP Morgan Chase, NYLIM (NY Life), Petra Capital, Gramercy Capital, and MONY (MMA Realty Capital) held a series of mezzanine loans behind Guggenheim.

Long before Fortress bought the Wells Fargo building loan mortgage, which at the time had been paid down to a balance of just over $30 million, and the Guggenheim $70 million senior mezzanine for close to par, in June 2009, Swig had converted the Sheffield to a condominium, combined and renovated some of the apartments, and sold all but 210 apartments.

The net proceeds of the condo sales had gone to pay down the CMBS mortgage and into construction costs. Even at dramatically reduced prices, the unsold condominium units were worth a multiple of the $100 million dollar face amount the two senior loans Fortress had purchased, though such units may not have been worth as much as the entire debt stack.

I brought suit on behalf of two Sheffield investors asserting a variety of claims against Swig and some of the lenders relating to alleged improper loan advances. Almost immediately after Fortress bought the two loans, it set a UCC foreclosure sale of the Guggenheim mezzanine collateral—100 percent of the limited liability company interests in the mortgage borrower.

Fortress did not bother bringing a judicial foreclosure action even though it owned the first mortgage, as Wells Fargo would have to have done had the first mortgage matured or otherwise gone into default. Why would it? Fortress had purchased the first mortgage and senior mezzanine loan, both well in the money, knowing that the UCC nonjudicial foreclosure sale available to the Guggeneheim mezzanine lender was a much faster, much quicker, less painful, and less risky enforcement mechanism.

At the August 6, 2009, UCC auction Fortress set at its lawyers' New York City offices, bidders would be buying the equity interests in the mortgage borrower—effectively buying a company that owned the unsold condominium units subject to the first mortgage (since that company owned the units encumbered by the lien of the first mortgage). In essence, a one dollar bid at the foreclosure sale amounted to a bid of $30,000,001 for the unsold units (assuming the first mortgage balance was exactly $30 million).

The unsold condominium units, even allowing for $50 million in further renovation costs, and costs of carry and sale, were worth far more than what Fortress had paid for the $100 million face amount loans it had purchased.

At the foreclosure auction, Fortress put up an opening "credit bid" of $20 million. This meant that Fortress was not bidding with cash, but rather was bidding $20 million worth of the Guggenheim senior mezzanine debt. If successful, Fortress's $20 million bid would only go back to Fortress anyway—since it owned the first $70 million of debt (the Guggenheim senior mezzanine loan) above the CMBS first mortgage. *Vis a vis* third party bidders, however, Fortress's $20 million credit bid amounted to a $50 million bid for the unsold condominium units since anyone trying to outbid Fortress would be forced, promptly after the foreclosure sale, to pay off the $30 million first mortgage.

There was a lot of ground between Fortress's $50 million all-in bid and the sell-out value of the unsold units—likely worth well over $200 million. Several cash bidders had qualified and were at the auction table, yet not one of them bid one dollar above Fortress's $20 million credit bid, and Fortress walked away with the unsold units. Why did bidders bother to prequalify, put up the requisite cash deposit, come to the auction, only to pass on a bid when the assets being auctioned were sold for millions of dollars less than their market value?

Clearly Fortress did not buy the two senior Sheffield loans at a minor discount to par in order to make a trivial profit on getting the notes paid off. When an investor buys a mezzanine loan at a discount and conducts a UCC foreclosure sale of the mezzanine collateral, if the investor is outbid and a cash bidder wins the auction, the proceeds, after the expenses of the sale (the auctioneer's or broker's fee, for example), go to the holder of the mezzanine loan, up to the total amount due under the mezzanine loan (including default rate interest). Here, though Fortress's purchase of the CMBS mortgage and Guggenheim's senior mezzanine loan was a private transaction, word on the street was that Fortress had paid close to par for both the first mortgage and Guggenheim's mezzanine loan—after all, they were both deeply in the money. Everyone knew Fortress did not get involved in the Sheffield to make a couple of million dollars.

The cash bidders therefore knew that Fortress could and would "credit bid" the full $70 million sum owed on the Guggenheim mezzanine loan (thereby amounting to a $100 million overall bid when adding in the $30 million first mortgage balance). Indeed, Fortress was not obligated to stop there—it was perfectly free to continue bidding, with any overbid being a cash, not a credit bid—beyond the $70 million balance owed to it under the Guggenheim mezzanine loan. In such event, the overbid amount would go to the next mezzanine lender, JP Morgan Chase (up to the balance owed under its second mezzanine loan). Said differently, everyone at the table knew Fortress had bought the two senior Sheffield loans as "loans to own"—they were in it to win it, and winning meant getting the unsold condo units.

Since all the qualifying cash bidders knew Fortress would bid to an overall bid value of $100 million and likely more (on a cash basis), and since the terms of sale were quite onerous, no one bid and Fortress walked away with the unsold units.

Unlike a judicially supervised mortgage foreclosure sale (or even a nonjudicial mortgage foreclosure sale where statutory requirements are specific), a mezzanine lender setting a UCC foreclosure sale of mezzanine collateral is free to set the terms of the sale, subject to a court ruling that they are commercially unreasonable should a party with standing such as the borrower or junior mezzanine lender bring a suit challenging the sale.

Thus Fortress was able to set the terms of its own sale. It chose to say that qualifying bidders had to put up $3 million by bank check or wire transfer three business days prior to the sale, that bidding had to be in $100,000 minimum increments, that a bidder had to close in cash on its bid within five business days (or face losing its deposit), and that Fortress could designate a "back-up bidder" whose deposit would remain unreturned pending the high bidder's consummation of the sale. And, if the high bidder failed to close, then the back-up bidder would be designated as the winning bidder and be obligated to close, failing which he or she would lose the deposit.

Bidders had to represent and warrant that they were qualified investors, that they were not intending to resell the securities they were bidding on—the limited liability company interests being purchased—and were required to indemnify Fortress against losses sustained by reason of any misrepresentations by the bidder. Bidders were cautioned that Fortress had confidential information concerning the auctioned property that it was under no obligation to disclose and was not in fact disclosing. Fortress also retained the right to reject all bids and terminate or adjourn the sale, as Fortress in its discretion adjudged appropriate, by announcement prior to or at the sale.

It is easy to see how the bidding was chilled. Not that anything Fortress did violated the New York Uniform Commercial Code. The UCC was never designed by its draftsmen to handle the sale of mezzanine collateral. The UCC was drafted long before the advent of mezzanine loans. In fact, the UCC as a general proposition handles tangible goods—personal property—but not real estate. Thus the UCC draftsmen would have assumed that real estate foreclosures would be governed by the several states' judicial or nonjudicial foreclosure laws. These mortgage foreclosure laws build in protections to defaulted borrowers and junior lien holders. The UCC, conversely, must deal with a panoply of goods including perishable goods such as crops. Imagine trying to draft a single foreclosure statute that must set a single set of timeframes for selling collateral ranging from tomatoes to condominium units.

It makes no sense for acquisitive mezzanine loan buyers to be able to set the terms of their sale, subject only to a vague and amorphous "commercial reasonableness" standard, as the UCC draftsmen envisioned would apply in the broad spectrum of "goods" covered by the UCC.

Given that the UCC will now be governing hundreds of billions of dollars worth of CRE foreclosures via mezzanine loan collateral sales, the UCC draftsmen would be well advised to call out a separate category for CRE mezzanine collateral sales and set forth objective criteria for these foreclosure sales. These criteria could include 30 to 45 days advance notice and bidding qualification and minimum bidding increments tied to a fractional percentage of the foreclosed loan. Qualified investor representations could be standardized as would bidder indemnification exposure.

Reasonable, objective bidding standards take on added importance because the injured parties, where bidding is effectively chilled, as in the case of the Sheffield, are the next most senior lenders. In the case of the Sheffield, this lender was JP Morgan Chase. Had the overall bidding been driven up over $100 million, JP Morgan Chase would have walked away with cash even if it were not a bidder.

And in a society where the taxpayers bail out those financial institutions adjudged too big to fail, a UCC that fails to ensure competitive bidding can and does hurt taxpayers.

The 182-page February 2010 Congressional Oversight Panel report (COP Report) on CRE discusses at length the systemic risks to our banking sector presented by the impending tidal wave of CRE foreclosures, suggesting that more bank failures are imminent and that absent more taxpayer bailouts of some of those failed banks, particularly smaller regional banks, we risk another seizure of our credit markets. But a simple amendment to UCC foreclosure mechanisms could mitigate bank losses at no cost to the taxpayers (but only to some opportunistic CRE buyers who might have to pay closer to market value).

This suggestion takes on added significance when one considers that in many instances the junior mezzanine lenders being short-changed by chilled bid auctions are real estate private equity firms, which invest public pension money. By now it should be no surprise to anyone that our states are being rendered insolvent by their public employee pension funds, where public employee unions negotiated against "management"—state executives— who had no real interest in holding down pension costs. (Worse, "management" often took the form of elected officials, who took bribes in the form of massive campaign contributions from public sector unions—like the $80 million the Service Employees International Union contributed to

Democrats' campaign coffers in the 2008 election cycle.) Most state employees retire with astronomical defined benefits—sometimes as much as 90
percent of their full salaries—for life.

Insolvent states like California reflexively look to the federal
government—meaning the U.S. taxpayers (or, more accurately, the half of
them that pay any taxes)—for bailouts. Some simple changes to the UCC
as adopted by each state could mitigate losses to public pensions indirectly
invested in mezzanine loans being wiped out in mezzanine foreclosures.
Why are our politicians so focused on the risks to banks engaging in
proprietary trading, yet have no interest in regulating the investment of
teachers,' firemen's and policemen's retirement funds in risky junior mezzanine loans? (The answer is that state pension plans need to make unreasonable assumptions about investment performance in order to conceal
their true insolvency levels.)

In the COP Report, much is made of the risks CRE debt defaults present
to our banking sector, particularly smaller regional banks. Though the COP
report makes no concrete recommendations, the report strongly suggests
that many banks, particularly smaller banks, will fail as a result of their
exposure to CRE debts, and that while not every failed bank will need to
be bailed out, some will:

> *There are no easy solutions to these problems. Although it endorses
> no specific proposals, the Panel identifies a number of possible
> interventions to contain the problem until the commercial real
> estate market can return to health. The Panel is clear that govern-
> ment cannot and should not keep every bank afloat. But neither
> should it turn a blind eye to the dangers of unnecessary bank fail-
> ures and their impact on communities.*[1]

Maybe the Panel is "clear," but I'm not. Putting aside the utter lack of
practical utility in the COP Report's conclusion (can you imagine either body
of Congress agreeing on which bank failures are "unnecessary bank failures"
and which are necessary?), there are a host of government "interventions"
that do not involve the ubiquitous liberal solution—a taxpayer bailout.

As suggested above, why not mitigate the losses of the banks that
have made CRE mezzanine loans (along with state pension funds that have
invested in mezzanine loans via real estate private equity firms) by redrafting
the UCC to provide basic minimal protections to junior lienholders in the
UCC foreclosure process, similar to those that already exist in nonjudicial
foreclosure statutes? Notice and advertisement requirements could be standardized, as could bidding increments, down payment requirements, and
closing timeframes.

TURBO-CHARGING THE LOAN TO OWN STRATEGY— BUYING THE REPO LINE

Some CRE mezzanine loan investors leveraged their investments by borrowing back a portion of the capital they had loaned out. Typically this leverage would take the form of a "repurchase agreement," commonly called a "repo line."

This credit facility works in a manner similar to stock or bond margin loans. The CRE mezzanine lender, immediately after advancing a mezzanine loan, would pledge the mezzanine loan note and collateral (typically membership or equity interests in the fee title–owning enterprise, or a borrower parent enterprise in the case of a multitiered mezzanine debt structure) to the repo lender (by delivering the original note and membership interest certificates, for example). The repo lender would then advance to the mezzanine lender (who was a borrower *vis a vis* the repo lender) a stipulated percentage of the pledged mezzanine loan, often 50 percent. These facilities were sometimes structured as "repurchase agreements" rather than pledges. The repo lender would buy the pledged mezzanine loans subject to the right of the repo borrower to repurchase them (by paying off the repo line).

Repo lines on mezzanine loans were used, for example, by Lehman Brothers, who had an ongoing repo facility with State Street Bank, whereby Lehman was continually delivering its "mezz paper" to State Street, whereupon Lehman would get readvanced 50 percent of the face amount of the pledged "mezz paper," so that Lehman could redeploy that capital.

As CRE debt stacks have matured or otherwise gone into default, mezzanine loan repo borrowers have been defaulting on their repo lines in droves. When that happens, the repo lender simply sends a notice to the mezzanine borrowers (under the pledged mezzanine loans) advising the mezzanine borrower that the repo lender is the new owner of the mezzanine loan and demanding that the borrower remit its future payments to the repo lender.

If the mezzanine borrower fails to pay, the repo lender has the same UCC foreclosure rights as the mezzanine lender had, and it can auction the mezzanine collateral (assuming it has any value—i.e., that the underlying CRE asset has a market value greater than all the debt ahead of the mezzanine loan in question).

Some repo lenders have made a critical error when their repo borrower defaults. Rather than reviewing the various mezzanine loans pledged to them before sending out notices demanding that future payments be made to them as successor mezzanine lender, some repo lenders have indiscriminately sent notices to all borrowers under the pledged mezzanine loans.

This is a dangerous practice. Some mezzanine loans have continuing construction funding obligations, as when the costs to pay for contemplated improvements were to be advanced in stipulated percentages pursuant to an approved budget by all stakeholders (i.e., all lenders and equity). In such a case, if the mezzanine loan has no economic value because the underlying CRE asset is worth less than the senior debt, the pledged mezzanine loan is a pure liability.

By reflexively sending a notice to the mezzanine borrower to remit its future payments to the repo lender, the repo lender steps into the shoes of the mezzanine lender and takes on lender liability exposure if it then refuses to fund future construction draws. In a case in which I was involved concerning a Manhattan office building, exactly that happened with respect to a Lehman mezzanine loan pledged under a repo line to State Street.

Although the pledged mezzanine loan was underwater, State Street sent a notice to the mezzanine borrower (my client) and to the master servicer, advising the mezzanine borrower to send future mezzanine loan payments to State Street. I responded to State Street by advising them in turn to send their future construction advances to my client. This notice was sent by State Street itself and not a single-purpose subsidiary, and thus my lender liability claim for State Street's future failure to fund required construction draws accrued against State Street itself.

Although State Street's litigators, after realizing State Street's blunder, attempted to argue that State Street had only succeeded to the right to receive payments and did not undertake any of Lehman's funding obligations, the common law provides that an express assumption is not required under those circumstances—once State Street took payments on the Lehman mezzanine loan from the master servicer, it signed on to make the funding obligations contained in the same loan.

Sometimes the repo lender elects to sell the entire portfolio of pledged mezzanine loans instead of dealing with them singly as State Street did in the case of the Lehman repo line. This happened when Credit Suisse (Column Financial) made a repo facility available to failed Australian mezzanine lender Rubicon. Rubicon had pledged 17 different mezzanine loans made on U.S. commercial real estate assets to Credit Suisse.

Many of Rubicon's mezzanine loans went into default, and Rubicon consequently went into default on its repo facility with Credit Suisse. Though Rubicon and Credit Suisse were negotiating with various individual mezzanine borrowers, including one of my clients, a New York developer, ultimately Credit Suisse sold a repo line secured by a pledge of the entire Rubicon mezzanine loan portfolio to a joint venture formed by FBE and Lane Capital for $15 million, even though the aggregate balance owed under the 17 mezzanine loans was over $123 million. That transaction offers a glimpse of the extent of the losses CRE mezzanine lenders (and repo lenders) face in the current environment.

I do not believe the FBE/Lane joint venture was playing to become the owner of all 17 underlying properties, as Fortress was in the case of the Sheffield. Rather, the FBE/Lane joint venture was playing for a payoff—either from equity or more junior mezzanine lenders. Rubicon's parent had previously filed the Australian equivalent of a bankruptcy petition, and shortly after the FBE/Lane-Credit Suisse transaction was concluded, Rubicon's U.S. subsidiaries—the owners of the 17 U.S. mezzanine loans pledged to Credit Suisse—filed for a Chapter 7 liquidating bankruptcy.

FBE and Lane promptly moved for relief from the automatic bankruptcy stay, which was granted on consent of Rubicon's bankruptcy trustee because, apparently, Rubicon had no equity in its mezzanine loan portfolio beyond the amount owed under the Credit Suisse repo line. This sum was vastly in excess of what FBE and Lane had paid Credit Suisse.

After obtaining a lift of the bankruptcy stay, the FBE/Lane joint venture was able to conduct a single UCC foreclosure against Rubicon. Prior to that foreclosure sale, FBE and Lane published terms of sale (given the lack of specific requirements set forth in the UCC) under which any bidder would have to make a holistic bid for all 17 different mezzanine loans.

Thus none of the 17 different Rubicon mezzanine borrowers had the ability to bid on buying (i.e., paying off) their individual mezzanine loans except in connection with a bid to buy 16 other mezzanine loans such borrower had nothing to do with.

Not surprisingly, the only bidder for all 17 Rubicon mezzanine loans was the FBE/Lane joint venture on a credit bidding basis. As a result, the FBE/Lane joint venture became the successor mezzanine lender under each of the 17 Rubicon mezzanine loans. FBE and Lane became the owner of the 17 Rubicon mezzanine loans and were thereafter free to set separate (nonjudicial) foreclosure sales on each of the 17 Rubicon mezzanine loans. On their mezzanine collateral foreclosure sales, FBE/ Lane joint venture will be looking to get paid on each by either the mezzanine borrowers or some junior mezzanine lender under threat of annihilation.

The strategy of buying a mezzanine loan portfolio from a repo lender is made more potent because of the lack of objective standards governing UCC foreclosures and the freedom such statutory void gives to opportunistic buyers of mezzanine loan repo lines.

Once again, simple objective guidance in the UCC foreclosure process as it pertains to mezzanine collateral, a function the UCC draftsmen never contemplated the UCC governing, would have the effect of mitigating losses to borrowers and junior mezzanine lenders, often banks and public pensions, beyond the true economic losses inherent in the underlying CRE collateral value.

THE FORGOTTEN DEFENSE FROM THE MIDDLE AGES—CHAMPERTY

Before leaving a discussion of "loans to own," a word on the ancient English common law doctrine of champerty is in order. The crime of champerty arose to combat abuses in medieval England. Some unscrupulous nobles took to the habit of lending their good names to writs or other complaints to enhance the credibility of false claims in return for a share of the recovery. As judicial independence grew, judicial fear of the nobleman's sword diminished, the effect of the nobleman's backing of the writ became less significant, and champerty took on less importance. Nevertheless, in many states, champerty exists as part of the common (decisional) law inherited from England (this is the case, for example, in Delaware). In other states, champerty has been codified as statutory law, as is the case in New York.[2]

Thus, where an investor acquires a note or loan with the advance intention of bringing a foreclosure proceeding, including, arguably, a nonjudicial UCC foreclosure proceeding, the tort (and in New York, the crime) of champerty has been committed. While there is little to no practical chance of champerty being criminally prosecuted, it may, in limited circumstances, serve as a useful defense to a borrower.

Where codified, as is the case in New York, champerty statutes often provide statutory exemptions so as not to present an impediment to modern commerce. Thus, in New York, a statutory safe harbor is created where a note is purchased for $500,000 or more. In New York, if the price paid for the note is $500,000 or more, the purchase is not considered champertous even if the loan were purchased by the investor with the express and sole purpose of commencing a foreclosure action.

This statutory exemption provides an interesting twist in the case of a portfolio purchase of mezzanine loans, as occurred in the case of the FBE/Lane joint venture purchase of the Rubicon repo facility from Credit Suisse. Although the sum paid by FBE and Lane for the entire portfolio was far in excess of the $500,000 statutory exemption threshold, it is likely that there is no allocation of the overall price to individual mezzanine loans. Since some are performing and others are not, and since there are 17 different loans, it may be that many of the individual loans have fairly allocable prices below the $500,000 champerty exemption threshold, when considering varying principal balances and performing versus nonperforming status of the pledged mezzanine loans.

CHAPTER 8

Funding Cessations and Extension Fights

Once a lender, whether the whole loan owner itself or the servicer for a CMBS loan, determines that the loan is underwater—that the CRE asset has a market value less than the balance due on the loan—a series of obvious economic motivations become set in stone.

For one thing, the lender does not want to get in any deeper—it does not want to advance any more money. Second, if the property is income-producing, the lender is loathe to allow net cash flow (even after debt service) to leak to junior stakeholders (whether junior mezzanine lenders or equity participants in the borrower). Such excess net cash flow, from the perspective of the senior lender, ought to be applied toward reduction of the principal balance of the senior loan—thereby reducing the senior lender's eventual loss—instead of going to any subordinate stakeholder. However, typical loan documents do not permit the senior lender to trap all net cash flow available after servicing the senior debt interest, provided the borrower is not in default.

These economic motivations have spawned two recurring themes in lender-borrower conflicts: funding cessations and extension fights.

FUNDING CESSATIONS

Construction loans are the riskiest of CRE loans and by percentage of loss will undoubtedly be among the worst performing CRE loans in the current down cycle. CRE construction loans on (eventual) income-producing assets like office buildings, multifamily rental housing, retail projects, and hotel properties are typically financed against a "permanent take-out" commitment.

A "permanent lender" issues an advance commitment that upon completion and lease-up, the permanent lender will take out the construction lender with a permanent loan. The term "permanent loan," in this context, is something of a misnomer, as the permanent loan in modern CRE financings is usually a relatively short-term loan—often three to five years—with little or no amortization, and thus the "permanent" loan must itself be refinanced by another permanent loan when the first permanent loan matures.

In the case of apartment buildings or other multifamily projects designed and built as condominiums, the permanent loan phase is skipped, and the construction lender looks to condominium unit sales for its "take-out," requiring release prices usually equal to 115 to 120 percent of the *pro-rata* loan amount payable as and when the condominium units are closed.

In recessionary times, particularly the current severe downturn, permanent lenders are quick to renege upon their take-out commitments, often by "finding" that one or more conditions to their commitment have not been satisfied. Realizing that the take-out lender will likely renege, or in the case of condominium projects, that the sales simply will not be there—at least at the per square foot prices needed to pay off the construction loan—many construction lenders simply stop funding midstream.

This causes a host of serious problems. Short-funded construction projects experience a cessation of construction activity, become dormant, are vandalized, and have mechanics' liens filed against them. Often, such disruptions result in a stigma. Customers (tenants or condominium buyers) either lose interest in bidding on space at the troubled project (or drop their bids), and contractors likewise become leery of continuing to perform work or supply materials. This results in a vicious negative feedback loop, whereby contractors' liens scare away jittery tenants or buyer prospects, and the resultant lack of leasing or sale activity causes the lender to dig its heels in further, steeling itself against future advances.

As one might expect, construction lenders do not readily admit to their defaults. Loan documents are for the most part adhesion contracts—even for larger CRE loans—and it is a rare construction lender who cannot find a legal peg on which it can justify its refusal to fund.

This destructive process—and the negative feedback loop it entails—is regrettably not limited to pure construction loans. In modern CRE financing, acquisitions of existing income-producing properties, whether office buildings, multifamily rental properties, retail projects, or hotels, are almost always acquired with a view toward upgrading, modernizing and "repositioning" the property. Older class B office buildings are slated for modern glass curtain walls and upgrading to Class A status, while multifamily rental properties get set to receive new amenity packages and modernized kitchens and baths in apartment interiors. Often building-wide systems like electrical, plumbing, HVAC, roofs, elevators, and smart building systems are planned by prospective new owners.

Typically CRE lenders to these to-be-refurbished properties underwrite the greater rents or hotel rates and occupancy levels expected from the modernized project and consequently insist on "reserving" for the planned capital expenditures. Said differently, many "permanent loans" to existing income-producing CRE properties have substantial construction loan components in the form of loan holdbacks (or funded reserves) to cover the capital outlays associated with the contemplated improvements. In consequence, funding cessations and the associated negative feedback loops are not limited to pure "ground-up" construction loans.

My own caseload abounds with examples of construction funding–cessation cases: a consortium of lenders to a New York City office building undergoing a massive modernization project including an entirely new curtain wall stop funding midstream; a multifamily rental property whose owner vacated the buildings as part of plan to renovate and upgrade them finds himself receiving notices from his lender that it will not approve the main contractor and fund draw requests.

These lenders inevitably find some legal peg to hang their hat on—some nit in the loan documents—but often the e-mail traffic and appraisals make clear what is really driving the lenders' refusals to fund: the property is underwater. It is worth less than the debt, so the lender would rather take the *legal* risk of a borrower's lender liability lawsuit than the *market* risk of increasing its principal balance. In some instances, lenders stop funding, put the borrower under pressure, and then offer a discounted payoff (DPO), essentially trying to pressure the borrower into paying off the loan at a discount prior to maturity.

THE DESTINY CARD

This dynamic implicates an interesting, but largely unresolved, legal question: Can construction loans be specifically enforced? As a general proposition, the law of contracts awards only money damages to a contracting party claiming the other party's breach of the contract. If I hire a painter to paint my house and he fails to show up to do the job, and I sue him, I cannot get a judgment ordering the painter to paint my house. Rather, I will get a judgment awarding me the monetary equivalent of his performance. I must go into the market and cover—hire another painter to perform the same scope of work. If that painter charges me $10,000 more to perform the same scope of work, the court will award me that $10,000 (plus reimbursement of any deposit I paid my original defaulting painter).

The policy underlying this theory of monetary substitutes for actual contractual performance is a threefold one: One, commerce is promoted by awarding a monetary substitute, rather than being clogged by court-ordered performances unwanted by the breaching party (and likely by the non-breaching party in many cases); two, costs of enforcement are reduced—the courts would become mired in endless follow-on disputes were specific performance the general rule; and three, on some level, monetary substitute damages promotes the libertarian ideal (which Washington seems to have forgotten) of minimizing the sovereign's control—in this case through the courts—over its citizens' behaviors.

But the law does recognize exceptions to the general rule of substitute monetary damages for breaches of contracts. One notable exception—arguably the quintessential exception—is a contract to purchase real estate. Due to the inherent uniqueness of real estate—no two parcels are identical—the law, out of a fear, I suppose, that monetary damages would never fully redress the harm caused by a defaulting seller of real estate, often awards the complaining buyer an order of specific performance.

Such a judgment orders the defaulting seller to convey title to the complaining buyer upon payment, of course, of the balance of the price due. In theory, a recalcitrant seller who fails to perform such an order is accountable under the court's contempt powers for failure to comply (including fines and theoretically incarceration).

Loan agreements are nothing more than contracts to rent money. The lender gives its dollars to the borrower for the term of the loan and the borrower pays the lender "rent" for the right to use the lender's dollars for the term in the form of interest—and at the end of the term, the borrower must return the rented funds. As a general rule, loan agreements are enforceable by affording the borrower money damages for the lender's breach. This only makes sense since money is the ultimate fungible commodity—one dollar (of a given currency) is exactly the same as another, the antithesis of a unique asset (such as real estate).

But what about a loan agreement where the loaned funds are to be used to improve a designated parcel of real property—a construction loan? While the funds to be loaned are fungible, the resultant improvements—a building, for example—are not. Can borrowers argue that while loans as a general rule should not be specifically enforced, a limited category of loans—construction loans—should be specifically enforceable (like contracts to acquire real property), because the ultimate object of the construction loan—a building to be built—is itself unique real property?

On this issue the courts are split, though in my view the majority of courts favor not specifically enforcing real estate construction loans. Given this split of authority and the irreplaceability of construction loans in the credit market, it is likely lenders' and borrowers' lawyers will find themselves frequently slugging out this interesting question of law.

In one recent high-profile decision, New York's intermediate appellate court, the Appellate Division (Fourth Department), decided this issue in favor of the borrower, ordering Citibank to fund a massive construction loan.

In *Destiny USA Holdings, LLC v. Citigroup Global Markets Realty Corp.*,[1] Destiny USA's development and construction of a regional mall project (designed as a "green mall") in Syracuse, New York was funded, in part, by a $155 million loan from Citigroup. After honoring the first 26 draw requests made by its borrower, Destiny USA Holdings, Citigroup refused to honor the next three draw requests on the ground that the loan was out of balance and therefore in default (thus excusing Citigroup from honoring further draw requests).

Citigroup claimed that the reasonable estimated cost of the planned improvements exceeded the undisbursed balance under the loan and that the out-of-balance condition constituted a default under the loan agreement. Destiny Holdings USA disagreed, asserting that Citigroup had erroneously included the estimated costs of tenant improvements—finishes to the interiors of tenant spaces—in determining that an out-of balance-loan condition existed when, according to the developer, such improvements were not to be financed under the loan and therefore should not have been taken into account in Citigroup's calculations.

When Destiny failed to cure the purported out-of-balance condition (by refusing to invest additional equity in the project), Citigroup declared the loan to be in default and ceased funding further construction draws. In consequence, construction at the project abruptly halted. Destiny filed suit seeking an emergency preliminary injunction compelling Citigroup to fund the pending loan advances.

Shortly after filing suit, the New York State Supreme Court in Onondaga County granted Destiny's motion for emergency relief, ordering not only that Citigroup fund the three then outstanding draw requests (totaling over $68 million), but that it fund future draw requests in accordance with the terms of the loan documents.

On appeal, New York's intermediate appellate court, the Appellate Division, Fourth Department, by a 3 to 2 split decision, modified, and as modified, affirmed, the lower court's ruling, holding that Citigroup's failure to fund the pending draw requests would cause irreparable injury to Destiny, reasoning that construction loans (to improve real property) are exceptions to the general rule that monetary damages are an adequate remedy, that Destiny's damages could not be calculated with any reasonable precision, and that there was potential for harm to Destiny's reputation and the reputation of the project.

Significantly, the court noted that, given the economic climate, it was unlikely that Destiny could secure replacement financing and, in turn,

Destiny would be unable to complete the project without an emergency order compelling Citigroup to fund the outstanding draw requests. Citigroup was ordered to fund the three draw requests then outstanding, totaling over $68 million, but the portion of the lower court order compelling Citigroup to fund future draw requests in accordance with the loan documents was stricken by the appellate court.

In addition, the Appellate Division ordered Destiny to post a bond (to secure Citigroup against damages should it ultimately be found that there was indeed a loan default) in the sum of $15 million, the amount of the out-of-balance condition Citigroup had claimed to begin with. Thus, if, after a full trial, it were determined that Citigroup had correctly declared a default based on the out-of-balance loan condition, Citigroup would be made whole by drawing down on the bond—since Citigroup had admitted that had Destiny invested an additional $15 million into the project the alleged out-of-balance default would have been cured.

In a dissenting opinion written by Justice Fahey and joined by Justice Green, Judge Fahey, quoting from an older decision, said: "New York courts will not order specific performance of a contract to lend money to a plaintiff, on the ground that money is fungible, and an injured party can borrow funds elsewhere and recover damages based on the higher costs it was forced to pay to the replacement lender."

Even though the *Destiny* decision was decided by a 3 to 2 split court, Citigroup does not have a present right to appeal to New York's highest court, the New York Court of Appeals, because an order granting a preliminary injunction is not a final one. However, once the case is over, assuming it does not settle, the Appellate Division's decision affirming the specific performance preliminary injunction can be brought up for review before the Court of Appeals.

It thus remains to be seen whether New York's highest court will affirm or reverse the Appellate Division's decision in *Destiny*. An affirmance would be helpful to borrowers nationwide while a reversal would be helpful to lenders nationwide since the New York Court of Appeals' decisions on unresolved questions of common law are carefully watched and well respected.

Doubtless many borrowers will rely on *Destiny*, or at least make the argument advanced by the borrower therein—that construction loans result in unique improvements to real property and as such are specifically enforceable; or said differently, that a construction lender may not willfully breach a construction loan and tell the borrower it is relegated to a money damages judgment against the lender for its breach. A right without an effective remedy is no right at all.

Once a construction project is stopped by a lender's refusal to honor its obligation to make construction cost advances, a money judgment will never make the borrower whole. The dissent's view in Destiny will only have the effect of placing a punishing amount of negotiating leverage in the hands of lenders who, in reality, have simply stopped funding due to their own view that the value of the completed project will not exceed the loan balance that will then be owed to them.

Lenders were free to insert in their loan documents not only loan balancing requirements, but a prematurity loan-to-value test (judged by a third-party appraisal). Lenders who either never asked for such loan-to-value tests to be inserted in their loan documents—or worse, who did ask but were turned down by their borrowers—should not be permitted to make up for what their loan documents do not say, by gaming the system through the intricacies of the law of damages.

In many of the cases now on my desk, where construction lenders have ceased funding draws, e-mail traffic plainly shows that the lenders have stopped funding not because of borrower defaults but because of dropping CRE values. In some cases, the lender defaults are so brazen that following the refusal to fund, the lender has demanded that the borrower prepay the loan—at a discount to par suggested by the lender.

In essence, such lenders are saying to borrowers—you better pay me off, we are never going to honor our commitment to fund construction. Such wanton breaches of contract should not be countenanced by our courts under the theory that loan agreements are not specifically enforceable and that an eventual money judgment will suffice. It takes years for any complex commercial case to wind its way through our courts, and no construction project can survive such a delay. As the old legal adage goes, justice delayed is justice denied.

EXTENSION FIGHTS

A related area of lender-borrower conflict frequently arises in connection with loan extensions. Many CRE loans, particularly those of more recent vintages (2003–2008), were underwritten with short initial terms ranging anywhere from two to five years, but contained explicit loan extension options. Often modern CRE loans were underwritten with an initial term of three years and coupled with either a single two-year extension option or two successive one-year extension options, in order to afford the borrower a five-year term (or at least the illusion of one). Sometimes, they were underwritten with an initial two-year term and three successive one-year extension terms.

CRE lenders opted to break up the bargained-for five-year term into multiple pieces for at least two distinct reasons. First, CRE lenders often charge a loan origination fee payable in consideration of the extension of loan term. Thus each extension option affords the CRE lender a separate "billable event," where extending a single five-year term (even with prepayment penalties being imposed for early payment) does not. In the case of a two-year initial term followed by three successive one-year renewal options, the lender can charge and collect four different origination fees, while it would only charge one in the case of a single five-year term (even if the origination fees payable upon the exercise of the one-year renewal terms are appropriately downsized to reflect the brief period of the extension—frequently an eighth of 1 percent for a one-year extension).

Second, breaking a five-year term up into an original term and multiple extension terms affords the lender the opportunity to apply conditions as a prerequisite to each loan extension. I have yet to see a loan agreement that does not specify a variety of such preconditions to each extension—that the borrower is not in default, coupled with the satisfaction of a debt yield or debt service coverage ratio test, and sometimes (usually found in construction loans) a loan-to-value test.

These tests have taken on enormously heightened importance in the current downturn, because of the confluence of two factors—historically not coincident with one another—both of which are undeniably present in today's CRE market. These two factors are near zero-base interest rates and dramatically reduced CRE values.

The confluence of these two factors makes for an anomalous condition in many CRE loans. The borrowers are underwater, frequently vastly underwater (i.e., the loan balance greatly exceeds the reduced market value of the underlying CRE collateral), yet the borrower is easily able to make the required debt service payments, despite faltering fundamentals—reduced rents and increased vacancies—because the loan is structured as an interest only, no-floor LIBOR-based loan.

In the majority of securitized (and many whole loan) CRE debt stacks, all loans in the stack require payments of interest only, which floats at fixed spreads above 30- or 90-day LIBOR rates. Since the beginning of 2009, when the unprecedented injections of liquidity at near zero rates were introduced by the Fed (and other central banks worldwide) in response to the then alarming seizure of global credit markets, LIBOR has floated at around one quarter of one point—25 basis points (see Figure 4.2, Chapter 4), increasing only slightly in the spring of 2010 as the Greek contagion hit.

While spreads—the margins lenders charge above LIBOR—vary inversely with loan priorities, that is, senior loans take smaller spreads and junior loans take larger spreads in order to make for sensible risk-adjusted returns, the blended spreads on most complex CRE debt stacks work out to less than 3 percent (300 basis points).

Senior mortgage loans were frequently written with margins barely above 1 percent (100 basis points) while junior mezzanine lenders were able to charge increasing margins, sometimes approaching or even exceeding 5 percent (500 basis points). However, generally the senior loan made up a bit more or less than half of the overall debt stack (in terms of principal amount), and thus blended weighted spreads were typically around 3 percent or less.

Since LIBOR has floated around 25 basis points for all of 2009, this put many CRE owners in the fortunate position of having interest-only loans bearing interest at a blended rate of around 3.25 percent, sometimes even less.

In contrast, when many of these CRE loans were underwritten, LIBOR was over 5 percent. Because most of these floating-rate CRE loans were underwritten as no-floor loans (in contradistinction to floating rate residential loans, which almost universally have both a floor and a ceiling), CRE owners have been the fortunate beneficiaries of a vast reduction in interest costs on the order of $5 million per $100 million of principal amount. This cost savings makes up for a lot of rent reductions and vacancy increases.

In fact, in many cases, CRE properties throw off significant cash flow above current debt service requirements, despite faltering fundamentals and despite the fact that such owners are vastly underwater—they owe more than their properties are worth.

In one case I recently handled, a New York City commercial property generated nearly $20 million in distributable cash flow after paying all required interest, yet arguably had a market value substantially less than what was owed to all lenders in the debt stack. The series of loans encumbering this particular property matured (i.e., the initial maturity date fell) in mid-2009. The borrower exercised its first extension option.

While the first mortgage lender agreed that the borrower had properly exercised its extension option, one of the junior mezzanine lenders disagreed, insisting that the borrower did not qualify for the extension. Threatened litigation and negotiations ensued, and ultimately the matter was resolved in the borrower's favor.

From the lenders' perspective, it is anathema to allow excess cash flow to leak to equity when the lenders are undersecured. For that matter, it is anathema to a senior lender to allow cash flow to leak to a junior mezzanine lender when the senior lender is undersecured. In such a circumstance, the senior stakeholders want the excess cash flow to be used to pay down (amortize) their principal balances instead of being leaked to equity or junior mezzanine lenders. Senior secured stakeholders do not want to find themselves in a position where they allowed cash flow to leak to junior stakeholders during an extension term, only to find themselves suffering a principal loss at the extended maturity date.

These battles can be ferocious and often turn on technical provisions of loan documents. We have already discussed the debt yield test in place in the Extended Stay Hotel debt stack (see Chapter 6). Another version of that same concept is the debt service coverage ratio (or DSCR) test. In a DSCR test, "underwrite-able" net cash flow (rents less real estate taxes and operating expenses determined pursuant to a conservative formula approved by the lender) is compared to the debt service due.

Almost universally, just as the net cash flow is determined pursuant to a lender-approved formula, which stresses actual cash flows by imputing mandatory minimum expense assumptions and vacancy rates, so too, the lenders have imposed artificial minimum debt service assumptions. Thus, while a CRE owner who has an actual blended cost of capital on the debt stack of, say, 2.75 percent when LIBOR is at 25 basis points (i.e., the weighted spread is 2.5 percent), and thus such borrower has a current actual interest cost of $2.75 million on each $100 million of principal amount, DSCR tests almost always require the borrower to perform the DSCR calculation based on a stipulated minimum rate. Frequently this stipulated rate is between 7 and 8 percent.

If the stipulated rate (including the spread above LIBOR) is 7.5 percent and the debt stack aggregates $200 million, the borrower will be required to demonstrate $15 million of "underwrite-able" net cash flow in order to be entitled to exercise its explicit renewal option, even though its actual cost of capital at the time of renewal (assuming LIBOR is then 25 basis points and a weighted average spread of 2.5 percent) is only $5.5 million (2.75 percent times $200 million).

In such a circumstance, a borrower whose property is generating $10.5 million (or $5 million per year in excess of all actual debt service) will be unable to meet the DSCR test because such test requires the property to be adjudged solvent based on an assumed interest rate of 7.5 percent, or in our example, a rate requiring $15 million per year in net cash flow.

Such a CRE owner is likely to meet enormous resistance to exercising an explicit renewal option, even though under the express terms of that option, the owner is also required to purchase contracts hedging against the risk of LIBOR increases, known as rate cap agreements. In a rate cap agreement, a solvent counterparty (both Lehman Brothers and AIG were big rate cap issuers) agrees, in consideration of a cash fee, to bear the risk of LIBOR rising above a specified price (called the strike price) during the term of the cap agreement. Where, as is most often the case, and as is the case in our hypothetical example, the extension term is only for one year, the borrower is required, under the express terms of the extension option, to obtain a rate cap agreement for the one-year extension term.

The required rate cap agreement will likely include a strike price below the difference obtained by subtracting the stipulated rate (in our example 7.5 percent) from the blended spread (in our example 2.5 percent). Thus, in our example, the borrower will likely be required, under the express terms of renewal option, to purchase, in advance of renewal, a rate cap agreement, running for the entire one-year renewal term and covering a notional amount equal to the outstanding principal balance, at a strike price at or below 5 percent, so that if LIBOR somehow did rise above 5 percent during the renewal term (and therefore the borrower's blended cost of capital rose above the stipulated all-in rate of 7.5 percent), the rate cap counterparty and not the borrower would pay that excess interest cost. Thus the sanctity of the renewal underwriting would be preserved regardless of how high LIBOR rises during the renewal term (assuming the continued solvency of the rate cap counterparty).

In our hypothetical example, the borrower could offer to buy a rate cap at a strike price far below the 5 percent strike price set forth in the loan document and thereby insure the lender that the actual underwrite-able net cash flow is sufficient, given the low strike price rate cap agreement, to protect the lender during the extension period.

For example, given a cash flow of $10.5 million and a debt stack having a principal balance of $200 million, an all-in rate of 5 percent would be covered. Given that the spread in our hypothetical example is 2.5 percent, our borrower could propose buying a rate cap at 2.5 percent or even 2 percent, thus insuring the lender against the risk of LIBOR rising above the level currently supportable by the collateral. Such a rate cap, being at a strike price many times the current 25 to 50 basis point LIBOR rate, is likely to be very affordable, especially for a short-term extension.

While logic would dictate that a borrower should be given the option to purchase a rate cap agreement at a lower strike price, thus justifying a lower stipulated interest rate, I have never seen such foresighted optionality (from the borrower's perspective) built into any loan agreements. Though a borrower confronted with the situation presented by our hypothetical example might implore its lenders to allow the extension based on the $10.5 million of actual net cash flow by offering to buy a rate cap agreement at a strike price of 2 percent instead of 5 percent, thereby assuring that the borrower never pays an all-in rate exceeding 4.75 percent during the renewal term (2 percent strike price plus 2.75 percent margin, which assures the sufficiency of the $10.5 million actual net cash flow), such a borrower is not likely to find a sympathetic ear among its lenders.

In such a circumstance, the lenders are far more likely to deny the borrower the extension and call the loan due. Now an interesting dynamic arises. Assuming the lenders (and borrower for that matter) agree that the property is worth less than the outstanding debt (let us assume the property is worth $131 million—$10.5 million of net cash flow at an 8 cap), the last thing the lenders in such circumstance want is a foreclosure sale. Upon such a sale, they will lose $69 million, if not more (cap rates tend to go up, and prices down, in fire sales).

What the lenders really want is to grant the borrower its extension, but with a modification requiring that all the free net cash flow (available after payment of debt service), in our example, $5 million annually, be applied toward amortizing the principal balance due (the senior lender). Said differently, the lenders do not want the borrower to pocket cash during the renewal term given that the borrower is underwater.

Often in such circumstances litigation ensues over the borrower's entitlement to exercise the renewal option, and often the conflict is resolved by a negotiated compromise whereby some of the excess cash flow is paid to the lenders (to reduce the senior loan principal balance) and some is leaked to junior mezzanine lenders or equity members, and in addition the loans are repriced at higher spreads, given how low LIBOR now is.

Things get even trickier where the debt stacks are complex and tranched. Suppose in our example that our $200 million debt stack consists of a $150 million senior CMBS loan and two $25 million mezzanine loans. In that circumstance, the CMBS servicer is faced with the prospect of a loss of $19 million ($150 million loan less a collateral value of $131).

In that situation, the CMBS servicer is duty bound to resist allowing interest to be paid even to the two mezzanine loans (during the extension term), until the CMBS loan principal balance is reduced below $131 million.

I had a debt stack exhibiting these unfortunate characteristics implode in mid-2009. The senior lender understandably wanted to condition the loan extension upon a modification to the loan agreements requiring all net cash flow above interest on its mortgage loan being paid (but before interest on any of the debts owed to the junior mezzanine lenders was paid), to be trapped by and paid to the CMBS trustee, until the senior debt was amortized to a balance equaling the then-appraised value of the property.

This left all the junior mezzanine lenders with no interest payments whatsoever. The most senior mezzanine lender agreed to this proposal, realizing that pretty soon the first mortgage would be reduced to safe levels and that it would then start to receive interest payments. But that senior mezzanine lender then wanted to mirror the deal proposed by the first mortgage lender—that is, it wanted to apply excess cash flow toward the amortization of its senior mezzanine debt until its debt was fully secure (based on a current appraisal) before releasing any excess cash flow to the next junior mezzanine lender in line.

It did not take long for the junior mezzanine lenders to realize that with mandatory amortization cascading through the debt stack in order of priority, the junior mezzanine lenders were likely to receive no money whatsoever during the term of the extension. Making the matter even more complex, some of these junior mezzanine lenders were themselves leveraged, having pledged their mezzanine loans under "repo lines."

In such a circumstance, the borrower must not only secure the consent of every lender in the debt stack, but in essence its lender's lenders as well. Such a broad-based consent is elusive, to say the least. In the case I handled, unanimous lender consent proved elusive and a foreclosure eventuated whereby the equity interests and junior mezzanine lenders were wiped out.

In many CRE loan agreements containing extension options, the borrower is afforded safe harbor (from the stipulated interest rate) via an interest reserve, which the borrower is allowed to prefund at the time the extension option is exercised.

To go back to our example, were such an interest reserve clause attached to the extension option, our borrower could fund into the reserve the hypothetical shortfall created by the excess of the stipulated interest charges ($15 million at the stipulated rate of 7.5 percent) over the net cash flow (in our example $10.5 million), or a prefunding requirement of $4.5 million ($15 million minus $10.5 million). In many situations, the borrower will find the interest reserve already containing cash at the time of renewal, since one was likely established at the opening of the loan and funded based on then prevailing (much higher) LIBOR rates.

Nevertheless, even where such safe harbors are explicitly provided, lenders and borrowers still find ambiguities in loan documents and much to fight about, given what is at stake. I had one mezzanine lender take the position that while the loan agreement expressly provided for an interest reserve, the amount on deposit in such reserve could not be taken into account in determining compliance with the DSCR test.

On other occasions, lenders have taken the position that the prefunding requirement must be satisfied from scratch—that the entire shortfall (in our example $4.5 million) must be funded by a fresh cash infusion from the borrower, without taking into account the existing cash balance in the interest reserve. Each of these positions, in my opinion, is spurious.

In some loans, DSCR tests measured by stipulated interest rates can only be satisfied by the borrower posting additional collateral—usually a letter of credit. In such cases, the loan balance is considered reduced by the letter of credit face amount for purposes of calculating the DSCR test. For loan agreements bearing these features, outlier mezzanine lenders may find that it behooves them to make a deal with the borrower and convert their mezzanine loan to preferred equity in order to satisfy the DSCR test and claim entitlement to an extension of the loan. Intercredit agreements in such cases need to be consulted carefully by experienced counsel.

In the end, borrowers and lenders find themselves playing a game of high-stakes "chicken" when a CRE debt stack with an extension option matures: Neither really wants a foreclosure, but the lender nevertheless threatens and often proceeds with one. Stressful brinksmanship often results with deals getting cut on the courthouse steps at the last minute. In one such case I handled, not once but twice I was on the courthouse steps about to file a suit to protect a borrower's right to extend, when my cell phone rang and I was advised that meaningful negotiations were in process. Realizing that delays in my asking for emergency relief (I was seeking an emergency restraint on foreclosure) would not sit well with any judge, I gave all concerned (including my own client) a limited mini-reprieve, and walked around Manhattan's South Street Seaport (which is near the courthouse) for an hour. Sure enough, I received an e-mail on my BlackBerry that the parties had reached consensus before the hour was up, despite the fact that the same parties had been negotiating for months prior thereto without success. Often the uncertainty of litigation serves as a great driver in making deals happen.

Sometimes, extension battles erupt between a borrower and a loan-to-own buyer of a CRE loan, rather than the borrower's original lender. This situation—the intersection of loan-to-own disputes and extension battles—happened in a case in which I represented an office building developer.

Over a period of many years, the developer had put together an assemblage of several small parcels forming a contiguous building footprint. After designing and constructing a state-of-the art office building, a terrible fire broke out, resulting in many millions of dollars in damage.

The developer pressed his insurance claim and with the cooperation of his lenders—there were three loans, a senior mortgage and two mezzanine loans—rebuilt the severely damaged building.

All three loans had a common initial maturity date and all three offered two six-month extensions. The mortgage loan and senior mezzanine loan each imposed a loan-to-value test as precondition to extension.

Oddly, the senior mezzanine loan stipulated that the mortgage and senior mezzanine loan could not in the aggregate exceed 65 percent of the as-is value of the building on the extension date, while the mortgage loan said that it alone could not exceed 75 percent of the as-is value of the building. Obviously, if the mortgage lender had advanced to 75 percent of value, then the senior mezzanine lender, being subordinate to the mortgage loan, would have advanced to a much higher percentage of value, perhaps 85 to 90 percent.

The extension option set forth in the senior mezzanine loan was illusory. The junior mezzanine loan had no loan-to-value test and simply required that both the mortgage loan and senior mezzanine loan be extended.

A few months prior to the maturity day, an owner-operator of office buildings purchased the mortgage loan for a major discount off its face value. After purchasing the mortgage loan, the owner-operator retained an appraiser to perform an appraisal of the as-is value of the then nearly complete (reconstructed) building.

The appraisal showed an as-is value that was several million dollars less than the owner-operator had paid for the mortgage. Despite being underwater on its investment, at least according to the appraisal, the owner-operator, after getting the appraisal and seeing its valuation, purchased the senior mezzanine loan at a steep discount to par (but nonetheless paying millions of dollars for it).

I prepared appropriate extension notices, which were sent, along with the requisite extension fee payments, with respect to all three loans. Not surprisingly, the owner-operator rejected the extension exercises, complaining that the loan-to-value tests in both the mortgage and senior mezzanine loan had been violated, and demanding massive paydowns of both loans as a precondition to their extension.

On the maturity date, I appeared in court seeking a preliminary injunction restraining a UCC mezzanine foreclosure by the owner-operator. My position was simple—why would the owner-operator have purchased the senior mezzanine loan after it learned that the amount it had paid for the first mortgage loan alone exceeded the value of the building, as determined by its own appraiser?

When the owner-operator purchased the mortgage loan, it stepped into a preexisting contractual relationship with the developer—it became the developer's first mortgage lender. Under the contract governing that relationship—the first mortgage loan agreement—the developer had a right to the first loan extension if it met the 75 percent loan-to-value test contained in that loan agreement. By buying the senior mezzanine loan after its own appraisal indicated the property was worth less than the first mortgage loan balance, the owner-operator had, I argued, violated the implied covenant of good faith and fair dealing inherent in all contracts.

The owner-operator had bought the senior mezzanine loan, I argued, strictly for the purpose of depriving the developer of the fruits of his first mortgage loan contract, which included a loan extension. The owner-operator, I said, had bought the senior mezzanine loan precisely in order to obtain the far tougher extension test it contained—under the senior mezzanine loan the loan-to-value test yielded a value requirement many millions of dollars greater than the value required under the first mortgage loan value test. The matter was settled, with the extension being granted.

CHAPTER 9

Bankruptcy Considerations

Bankruptcy filings are infrequent, relatively speaking, for commercial real estate. For one thing, the vast majority of CRE assets, as noted earlier (see Chapter 3), are held by single-purpose enterprises (SPEs). These SPEs generally do not directly employ on-site personnel, who, more often, are employed by a separate management company, even if that management company is controlled by the same principals who own the SPE. In consequence, the majority of CRE-owning SPEs are not operating companies in the true sense of that term, but rather are dedicated legal vehicles for maintaining CRE ownership in an isolated format, offering protection (via liability immunization) to the SPE's equity holders and their other assets (including other CRE assets).

As a result, commercial real estate–owning SPEs are not well suited to classic bankruptcy reorganization, which contemplates a leaner going concern exiting the bankruptcy process, though bankruptcy reorganization can be used to force the deleveraging of an overleveraged CRE asset.

There are, of course, exceptions to this generalization—CRE assets held by public and private real estate investment trusts and hotel chains, for example, do present true operating companies capable of benefiting from the bankruptcy reorganization process. Recent examples of CRE-based going concerns that have entered the bankruptcy process include Extended Stay Hotels (discussed in Chapter 6) and shopping mall giant General Growth Properties, a New York Stock Exchange–listed company.

GENERAL GROWTH PROPERTIES—A RECENT TEST CASE FOR THE BAD FAITH FILING STANDARD

Although admittedly not insolvent when General Growth's senior management filed bankruptcy petitions for some 388 different enterprises in April 2009, these executives were painfully aware that the CMBS and whole-loan

CRE refinancing markets had deteriorated so dramatically since the onset of the subprime mortgage crisis, that there was no practical chance of General Growth refinancing the substantial part of its over $18 billion in project level debt coming due in the two to three years following these bankruptcy filings.

General Growth's project level debt encumbered some 200 shopping centers in 44 states across the country. Faced with billions of dollars worth of maturing and irreplaceable mortgage and mezzanine debt, General Growth's management experienced insurmountable problems in trying to reach a consensus on restructuring conversations with its large body of creditors. According to the General Growth Web site:

> The decision to pursue reorganization under chapter 11 came after extensive efforts to refinance or extend maturing debt outside of chapter 11. Over many months, the Company has endeavored to negotiate with its unsecured and secured creditors to obtain the time needed to develop a long-term solution to the credit crisis facing the Company. Unable to reach an out-of-court consensus, the Company reluctantly concluded that restructuring under the protection of the bankruptcy court was necessary. During the chapter 11 cases, the Company will continue to explore strategic alternatives and search the markets for available sources of capital. The Company intends to pursue a plan of reorganization that extends mortgage maturities and reduces its corporate debt and overall leverage. This will establish a sustainable, long-term capital structure for the Company.[1]

Several of General Growth's secured creditors, including Metropolitan Life and Clarion Capital, brought motions to dismiss the General Growth bankruptcy case, asserting that the case was a "bad faith filing" given that General Growth had reported consolidated revenues of $3.4 billion in 2008 and, though there were technical defaults, General Growth was still current on its debts. The case was assigned to the United States Bankruptcy Judge for the Southern District of New York, Allan L. Gropper, who in a 47-page decision issued on August 11, 2009,[2] sustained General Growth's bankruptcy filings.

A number of significant and interesting legal issues were presented by the General Growth bankruptcy case. First, the secured lenders seeking dismissal of General Growth's bankruptcy case argued that the corporate (SPE) structure at General Growth—each of the malls is held by a separate special-purpose entity or SPE—precluded the upstreaming of operating cash surplus (i.e., net operating cash after payment of current nondefault rate interest on project-level debt). This upstreaming of project-level cash surplus was vital to General Growth's general and administrative operations, including payment of the salaries of many of its approximately 3,700 employees (exclusive of those employed at the various project sites).

The effort by General Growth's secured lenders to halt the upstreaming of project-level cash surplus is a recurring theme in the current ultra-low interest rate environment. It is the same battle that raged in the Extended Stay Hotel matter (Chapter 6), and as well the same battle that underlies the refusal by CRE lenders to honor explicit loan extension options (Chapter 8).

In the current 25–50 basis point LIBOR environment, operating cash surpluses often exist—there is money left over after paying interest based on near zero base rates; yet, in many instances, the senior lender is nevertheless not fully secured because, despite the operating surplus, the principal balance of the senior debt exceeds the current value of the CRE collateral. Hence, the senior lender wants to trap all such cash surplus and apply it toward amortization of the senior loan. Judge Gropper ruled that the "SPE structure did not require that the project-level Debtors be precluded from upstreaming their cash surplus at a time it was needed by the Group."[3]

Another issue presented by the General Growth bankruptcy was the alleged "prematurity" of the filing—the secured lenders argued that there was no imminent threat to the financial solvency and stability of General Growth—and that, as a result, the bankruptcy petitions were premature and should be dismissed. Here again, Judge Gropper ruled that the secured lenders' arguments were unavailing, finding that the collapse of the credit markets had made a future financial catastrophe at General Growth inevitable. Judge Gropper thus declined to dismiss management's bankruptcy filings on this basis.

The secured lenders also argued that General Growth's filings were submitted in bad faith, because General Growth could not confirm a plan of reorganization without the consent of the secured lenders, and they had no intention of consenting. Here again, Judge Gropper declined to dismiss, ruling that the likelihood of a plan of reorganization being confirmed was not a prerequisite to a bankruptcy filing.

Similarly the secured lenders urged Judge Gropper to dismiss General Growth's bankruptcy filing because management had failed, the lenders said, to try to negotiate with the lenders before the filing. This argument highlights one of the catch 22s present in the current CRE environment.

CMBS loans are handled by master servicers. Earnest restructuring dialogues cannot occur with the master servicer; rather, they can only occur with the "special servicer." But a loan is not "put into special" until there is a default or imminent default. In essence, CMBS borrowers cannot get to meaningful discussions until they are in real trouble, and thus, where cash flow is swept and trapped by the lender and a strategic default is prevented, a bankruptcy filing may be the only way of initiating a meaningful dialogue in advance of a payment default—it is one sure-fire way of grabbing the lenders' attention.

Here again, Judge Gropper was not persuaded by the secured lenders' argument and held that there is no prenegotiation requirement to the filing of a bankruptcy petition.

Another interesting issue—and one likely to see much more litigation—was General Growth's handling of the so-called "independent director" issue. As explained in Chapter 3, the loan documentation used for nearly all CMBS-financed CRE includes various "bankruptcy remote" provisions. The two leading bankruptcy-remoteness devices are the springing nonrecourse carve-out guaranty (which makes a lead principal, parent enterprise, or fund liable for all or part of the loan in the event of a bankruptcy filing) and the independent director clauses, which require the borrower-SPE to engage special independent directors, who, most lenders believe, are there reflexively to vote no to any bankruptcy filing.

In other words, secured lenders insist that their borrowers' organizational documents call for the engagement of special (professional) independent directors, who only vote on one issue—whether to file a bankruptcy petition. While many lenders believe these independent directors are there to vote no to a bankruptcy filing, in fact many of them are (correctly) worried about properly discharging their fiduciary duty and their own liability (to the SPE and its stakeholders) if they act unreasonably in voting against a proposed bankruptcy filing.

This is a sensible concern since, in most states, the fiduciary duty owed by directors to a corporation's shareholders shifts to the creditors of the corporation when the corporation becomes insolvent (or in some cases when the corporation enters the "so-called" zone of insolvency)[4] because, when insolvency strikes, the equity of the shareholders has been wiped out. In essence, the creditors then own the equity.

Although General Growth's senior management has never admitted as much, in the case of the General Growth bankruptcy filing, it appears that senior management and General Growth's lawyers were worried that the existing independent directors would do the secured lenders' bidding and vote no to a bankruptcy filing. As a result, General Growth fired its independent directors (without notifying them) and replaced them with new independent directors. Loan documents typically do not specify independent directors by name, but rather simply require that the borrower have two independent directors on its board and set out objective qualifications for determining independence.

General Growth and its lawyers were careful to replace the original independent directors with persons who met the objective criteria for independence set forth in the loan documents, and then convened a board meeting with the new (but not the old) independent directors, at which presumably management made out a detailed case demonstrating the need for a bankruptcy filing. The new independent directors agreed and cast their votes in favor of General Growth's bankruptcy filing.

In their motion to dismiss General Growth's bankruptcy filing, the lenders attacked General Growth's firing of the original independent directors and their replacement with new ones. It was not disputed that the original independent directors were not even made aware of the fact that they had been fired until after General Growth had filed for bankruptcy.

Although General Growth's management said that the surreptitious firing of the original independent directors was done in order to avoid subjecting General Growth to "publicity about potential restructuring strategies,"[5] it is clear to me that General Growth and its lawyers felt an urgent need to get the bankruptcy petitions filed in advance of anyone having knowledge that they were firing and replacing the independent directors, lest some creditor attempt a state court action aimed at restraining the firing of the independent directors before the filing could be made.

Despite the eyebrow-raising tactics of a surreptitious firing of its independent directors, Judge Gropper sustained General Growth's bankruptcy filing, reasoning that the corporate documents did not prohibit the firing and replacement of the independent directors, and noting that such directors had a fiduciary duty to the corporation and its shareholders.

It remains to be seen whether CMBS and whole-loan CRE lenders endeavor to close this gap in loan documents by requiring the secured lender's advance consent to the replacement of independent directors (or at least the existing independent directors' advance knowledge of their being fired). I would be surprised if they do not do so soon, though lenders would be well advised to act cautiously in this regard as they too may find themselves taking on liability to creditors if they block the appointment of independent directors in order to prevent a bankruptcy filing. Indeed, even providing for such consent in loan documentation may prove to be detrimental to lenders as a measure of "control" that exposes them to potential liability.

While General Growth managed to clear all the hurdles to its bankruptcy filing, the same cannot be so easily accomplished for commercial real estate–owning SPEs that are not part of a larger publicly traded REIT or other going concern (such as the Extended Stay Hotel chain, which, though private, employed over 10,000 people).

As Judge Gropper noted in his decision upholding the GGP bankruptcy filing, the factors bankruptcy courts look at in determining whether a bankruptcy filing should be dismissed as a bad faith filing include the following:

- Whether the debtor has only one asset (for example, a single building)
- Whether the debtor has few unsecured creditors whose claims are small in relation to the claims held by the secured creditors
- Whether the debtor's single asset is already the subject of a state law foreclosure proceeding when the debtor files for bankruptcy
- Whether the bankruptcy is really a two-party dispute between the debtor and its secured creditor or creditors, which can be resolved by a pending state court (or nonjudicial) foreclosure proceeding
- Whether the timing of the bankruptcy filing by the debtor evidences an intent to frustrate the legitimate efforts of the debtor's secured creditors to enforce (typically via foreclosure) their rights
- Whether the debtor has little or no cash flow
- Whether the debtor cannot meet current expenses including payment of personal and real property taxes
- Whether the debtor has no employees

Unlike General Growth and Extended Stay, many CRE assets are held by stand-alone SPEs with no or very few employees and with few trade or other creditors. In such cases, it may prove difficult for such SPEs to resist similar motions to dismiss their bankruptcy filings as bad faith filings, particularly if they are commenced on the eve of a foreclosure sale. Of course, the bad faith determination is fact-specific, and there are undoubtedly many situations in which a bankruptcy filing is appropriate for even private stand-alone SPEs.

NONRECOURSE CARVE-OUT GUARANTIES

Owners of stand-alone SPEs often find themselves facing an even more difficult burden than the bad faith filing standard at issue in the General Growth bankruptcy case. As detailed in Chapter 3, nearly all SPEs financed by CMBS (and some financed by whole-loan lenders) are burdened with a springing nonrecourse carve-out guaranty (an "NRCOG"). The NRCOGs are typically signed by a lead principal (the developer) or parent enterprise, or in the case of CRE owned by real estate private equity firms, the underlying fund enterprise (which normally is a net worth enterprise with hundreds of millions of dollars worth of assets separate and apart from the specific CRE owned by the SPE borrower).

These NRCOGs provide for springing liability to the guarantor (often limited to a capped sum) in the event the SPE files for bankruptcy, or if the SPE commits any one of a number of specified "bad boy" acts including a failure to follow the independent director rules set forth in the organizational documents (though in the case of the latter, the lender is generally entitled to recover only its actual damages arising from the bad boy act, while in the case of a bankruptcy filing, no such proof of damages is required).

Thus, for stand-alone SPEs, it frequently does not pay for the developer or real estate private equity fund to expose its other assets to the risk of liability for the loan to the lender under the NRCOG, in order to gain whatever potential advantages can be had from a bankruptcy reorganization.

An interesting twist on this issue took place in the Extended Stay bankruptcy case, where developer David Lichtenstein (the signer of the NRCOG) obtained the agreement of certain senior secured creditors to use $100 million worth of Extended Stay's cash assets to provide an indemnity fund to protect Lichtenstein from a suit on his NRCOG as a result of Extended Stay's bankruptcy filing, as well as a $5 million litigation war chest to fund the defense of suits against Lichtenstein (by other lenders) under his NRCOG. (See Chapter 6.)

I brought such a suit on behalf of two mezzanine lenders in the New York State Court (New York County) against Lichtenstein after he authorized the Extended Stay bankruptcy filings. Lichtenstein's counsel removed my case to the Bankruptcy Court (Southern District of New York), and I moved to have Bankruptcy Judge Peck remand the case back to the New York State Court.

In arguing that remand motion, Lichtenstein's counsel asserted that the NRCOG Lichtenstein signed should not be enforced because all NRCOGs close the doors of the bankruptcy courts to debtors in need of the benefits of bankruptcy reorganization and thus are void for violating the public policy underlying our federal bankruptcy laws. Lichtenstein said that the NRCOG he signed should be voided as a matter of public policy because it tends to chill a director's exercise of the fiduciary duty to file a bankruptcy proceeding as the companies whose debts are guaranteed entered the zone of insolvency. Therefore, Lichtenstein's counsel argued, any suits seeking to enforce such guarantees must be heard in the Bankruptcy Court because federal law preempts the area. The Extended Stay bankruptcy judge, James M. Peck, rejected these arguments and remanded the cases back to the New York State Court (that decision was subsequently affirmed on appeal).

On a practical level, hundreds of billions of dollars of commercial real estate loans were made in the last decade and a half based, in large part, on the bankruptcy remoteness offered by NRCOGs, which render the otherwise nonresponsible guarantor liable for a loan in the event of a bankruptcy filing. Most major law firms throughout the United States, as a routine part of their practice over the past many years, have drafted—and signed opinion letters confirming the enforceability of—these so called nonrecourse carve-out guaranties for hundreds of billions of dollars worth of commercial real estate loans. As several analysts[6] and commentators have recently noted, a staggering volume of commercial real estate loans are coming due in the next few years—at least $1.4 trillion between 2010 and 2014.[7]

For all practical purposes, there is neither a fully functioning commercial real estate refinancing market in existence today capable of dealing with the impending tsunami of commercial mortgage foreclosures, nor in consequence a fully functioning resale market, though both have been improving since the beginning of 2010. One shudders to think how much worse the systemic risks to our banking system would be (given that banks hold most of the maturing loans) were a court to invalidate the nonrecourse carve-out guaranty—a staple of commercial real estate loan documentation in the United States.

It is quite clear that the nonrecourse carve-out guaranty at issue in Extended Stay did not have a chilling effect—the petitions were in fact filed. Finally, unlike so-called "ipso facto" clauses where, for example, a lease terminates or goes into default upon the filing by the tenant of a bankruptcy petition, in the case of a nonrecourse carve-out guaranty, there is no such ipso-facto forfeiture of a bankruptcy *debtor's* property.

The fact that a nondebtor's assets—such as Lichtenstein's assets in the Extended Stay case—are exposed to liability takes nothing away from the (bankruptcy) debtors. Ipso facto or bankruptcy clauses automatically terminate a contract or lease to which a debtor is a party or permit the other contracting party to terminate the contract or lease *with a petitioning debtor* in the event of bankruptcy.

In the case of Extended Stay, Lichtenstein's NRCOG did not involve an executory contract or unexpired lease (or other property) of Extended Stay, and thus did not implicate an ipso facto clause. All that happened was that a nondebtor party (Lichtenstein) took on liability by virtue of the bankruptcy filings.

At best, because the Bankruptcy Code fails to regulate, much less invalidate, nonrecourse carve-out guaranties, there has been no federal preemption in this area. At worst, by invalidating a limited class of ipso facto clauses in such a tailored way as to specifically not include nonrecourse carve-out guaranties, when clearly, given their proliferation, they were undoubtedly on the congressional radar, Congress preempted the area in a manner validating (by nonobjection) such nonrecourse carve-out guaranties.

Despite Lichtenstein's argument that his guaranty is void as against public policy, so-called "springing guarantees" have routinely been upheld and enforced by bankruptcy, federal district, and state courts.[8]

In an important New York case, *First Nationwide Bank v. Brookhaven Realty Associates*, 223 A.D.2d 618, 637 N.Y.S.2d 418 (2d Dep't 1996), the plaintiff bank agreed that the borrower, under a nonrecourse mortgage agreement—and therefore its principals since the borrower was a general partnership—would only be personally liable in the event of certain "bad boy" acts, including the borrower filing a bankruptcy proceeding that was not dismissed or resolved within 90 days after filing.

The borrower defaulted on the mortgage and the bank brought a foreclosure proceeding. Following the commencement of the foreclosure action, the borrower filed for bankruptcy, and while the proceeding was eventually dismissed, the dismissal did not take place until after the 90-day deadline (i.e., the dismissal took place more than 90 days after its filing).

Based on this bankruptcy default trigger, the bank sought a deficiency judgment against the borrower and its general partners in the foreclosure action. Upholding the enforceability of the bankruptcy-based termination of the affirmative exculpation clause of the loan agreement (thereby creating pass-through liability to the borrower's general partner), the New York Appellate Division, Second Department held that:

> As a bankruptcy default clause is enforceable under the laws of this State, the one at issue here should be enforced. The [borrowers] are bound by the terms of the contract and enforcement of the bankruptcy default clause is neither inequitable, oppressive, or unconscionable. Moreover, the recovery of a deficiency judgment is specifically contemplated by statute.[9]

The lenders to Extended Stay all insisted in their respective loan documents that New York law would govern, knowing in advance New York's case law (which holds that springing guarantees are enforceable). For all these reasons, New York, which is the financial capital of the world, has a keen if not overwhelming interest in ensuring that its already stated policy of enforcing springing bankruptcy–based (nondebtor) liabilities be scrupulously enforced.

If the federal courts were to invalidate NRCOGs, the results would be problematic given our already anemic refinancing market, the precipitous drop in commercial real property values in 2008 and 2009, and the mind-numbing dollar volume of commercial real estate loans maturing in the next several years.

In another recent decision, *111 Debt Acquisition LLC v. Six Ventures, Ltd.*, No. C2-08-768, 2009 WL 414181 (S.D. Ohio Feb. 18, 2009), the bankruptcy court considered the nondebtor guarantors' objections to the enforcement of springing recourse guarantees. Those guarantors, much like Lichtenstein, argued that springing recourse guarantees encumbered access to the bankruptcy courts. The Ohio bankruptcy court, rejecting this argument, held:

> *Obtaining a judgment against the guarantors of a corporation's debt is not void as contrary to public policy. Rather, the inverse is true. Individuals are permitted to contractually obligate themselves to pay the debts of another and, if those debts are not paid, obtaining a judgment is the only manner by which a plaintiff can obtain a judicial declaration that the guarantors are indebted to the lender.*[10]

The Ohio bankruptcy court held that the springing recourse clause did not place the defendants in the untenable situation of choosing between filing for bankruptcy and triggering the recourse guarantees, or not filing for bankruptcy to protect themselves to the detriment of creditors. According to the court:

> *Guarantors' argument that the bankruptcy filing/Springing Recourse Event clause places them in an "untenable situation" lacks merit. This Springing Recourse Event created liability for the individual guarantors—it did not prevent Six Ventures from seeking protection afforded by the Bankruptcy Code.*[11]

Lichtenstein also argued that "contracts that encumber the free exercise of fiduciary duties are void as a matter of public policy." In the end, Bankruptcy Judge Peck ruled against Lichtenstein, granting my motion to remand the case back to the New York State Supreme Court (though that decision remains under appeal).

In so doing, Judge Peck found that Lichtenstein benefited directly from the springing guaranty at the outset—that is, but for the springing guaranty, he might not have received $7.4 billion in loans. Lichtenstein made the business decision to execute the NRCOG. It was his fiduciary duty, once the Extended Stay companies entered the zone of insolvency, to act in the best interests of creditors regardless of how such actions would impact him personally. As Judge Peck held:

The Court reiterates its previous findings, set forth earlier in this Memorandum Decision, regarding the public policy argument. Disincentives to the filing of bankruptcy cases and so called non-recourse carve-out guarantees are within the domain of bankruptcy-remote structuring. Guarantees of the sort executed by Lichtenstein and Lightstone are intended to make bankruptcy cases less likely, to the point that they are remote risk factors for lenders. But here, the structure failed to achieve that objective.... The fact that [Lichtenstein's] liability may be tied to bankruptcy filing does not lead to the conclusion that federal bankruptcy policy is implicated in any way.[12]

Since the mid-1990s' advent of CMBS, borrowers have showed that they were not afraid to file for bankruptcy in an effort to stave off foreclosures—and to take other actions adversely affecting the value of collateral when a foreclosure became imminent. Necessity being the mother of invention, CMBS (and whole loan) lenders discovered the potency of springing nonrecourse carve-out guaranties as bankruptcy remoteness devices.

By virtue of this necessity, commercial real estate lenders developed these so-called "bad boy" guaranties, affording lenders recourse for what were otherwise nonrecourse liabilities—that is, while the loan was generally not recourse to the borrower, certain "bad boy" acts will result in recourse liability for the borrower, its principals, or guarantors. The occurrence of a voluntary bankruptcy is the quintessential nonrecourse carve-out event. It exists in hundreds of billions of dollars worth of commercial real estate loans. The nonrecourse carve-out at issue in Extended Stay was clearly written and negotiated by sophisticated businesspeople, and Lichtenstein agreed to the nonrecourse carve-out guaranty knowing full well that it was a material term in obtaining $7.4 billion of financing for the Extended Stay acquisition.

In short, stand-alone SPE owners are likely to find the execution of an NRCOG a substantial impediment to a bankruptcy filing and they are likely to find invalidation of such guarantees an uphill legal battle. Further, given the possibility of such a filing being dismissed as a bad faith filing, there would seem to be little incentive to NRCOG signers taking the chance of liability associated with a bankruptcy filing, although they need to balance this with their fiduciary duty which, in some circumstances, such as in the case of General Growth, may justify a bankruptcy filing.

Said differently, a bankruptcy filing may trigger liability for the NRCOG signer despite that same bankruptcy petition later being dismissed at the behest of the lender as a bad faith filing—leaving the guarantor with personal liability for the loan but no bankruptcy reorganization to look forward to.

One possible exception to the NRCOG having its intended effect arises where the NRCOG obligates the guarantor to pay "actual losses" suffered by the lender which "arise from" the bankruptcy filing (instead of simply making the guarantor liable for the loan). Where NCRCOGs are drafted to cover only actual losses arising from the bankruptcy filing, it remains to be seen how effective a bankruptcy-remoteness device they turn out to be. Some intrepid developers will doubtless test the efficacy of this strain of NRCOG soon enough.

For all these reasons, I think we are likely to see relatively few CRE bankruptcy filings, especially in the case of CRE assets encumbered by CMBS loans (which are almost universally supported by NRCOGs), except in rare cases like Extended Stay Hotel and General Growth Properties, which truly involve operating businesses and going concerns, and not stand-alone SPEs.

TRANSFER TAX EXEMPTIONS

One potential exception to this general rule comes from Bankruptcy Code Section 1146(a). This section provides for the exemption of transfer taxes when real property is transferred pursuant to a confirmed bankruptcy plan of reorganization. This is not an inconsiderable benefit.

In many jurisdictions, transfer taxes are quite high. For example, in New York City, combined state and city transfer taxes approach 3 percent of the consideration payable, which, in the case of a deed in lieu of fore-closure, is based on the amount of debt being forgiven. Thus where the CRE is encumbered by a $200 million mortgage, the combined New York State and City transfer taxes will be on the order of $6 million.

While in some instances such transfer taxes are covered by the NRCOG, in most cases they are not. Thus, the foreclosing lender in such a circum-stance is placed in the unenviable position of having to increase its losses by the amount of the transfer taxes (even if the borrower is willing to give up and tender a deed), in my example, $6 million.

However, by doing a "bankruptcy prepack" with the borrower—a prebankruptcy agreement in which the lender and borrower agree in advance to the terms of the plan of reorganization—the lender may be able to escape the $6 million transfer tax liability by having a preagreed plan of reorganization pursuant to which the property is conveyed by the borrower to the lender for no additional consideration beyond the forgiveness of the lender's mortgage.

In such a situation, the Bankruptcy Code trumps the state and local transfer tax laws and exempts the transaction from transfer tax. In such a case, the lender is likely to agree to waive the NRCOG and perhaps even pay the borrower a portion of, in my example, the $6 million transfer tax savings in order to gain the borrower's cooperation, without which the lender must pay the full $6 million transfer tax. It remains to be seen, however, whether bankruptcy prepacks whose sole object is transfer tax exemption will be challenged by the states and municipalities whose transfer taxes are being avoided, or by proactive bankruptcy judges who dismiss such filings as bad faith filings whose sole or principal purpose is tax avoidance in violation of section 1129(a).

COMPLEX DEBT STRUCTURES

A final instance in which bankruptcy filings may prove valuable comes in the case of CRE encumbered by complex debt stacks including several layers of mezzanine loans junior to the first mortgage. In such cases, when the debt stack matures (they always mature in unison), each lender is likely to refuse to extend except upon terms requiring that such lender trap all surplus cash until its debt is paid down to the point where such lender is fully secured.

This understandable requirement often means that the more junior mezzanine lenders will receive nothing throughout the term of the contemplated extension (because senior lenders will be trapping cash flow to amortize their loans until they are paid down to such a level that such lender becomes fully secured). In such cases, these junior mezzanine lenders are not likely to go quietly into that good night.

This leaves the senior lenders and borrower with two options—a UCC mezzanine foreclosure sale (which would wipe out the junior lenders) or a so-called Bankruptcy Code section 363 sale. Under a section 363 sale, the borrower, having filed a bankruptcy petition, enters into what is commonly called a "stalking horse" contract with a senior lender whereby that senior lender offers to buy the encumbered CRE (typically for the amount of such bidding lender's loan and any loans senior to the bidder). Such a contract is called a stalking horse contract because the deal is subject to higher and better bids at an auction conducted with the approval and under the supervision of the bankruptcy court.

If a higher bidder emerges at the bankruptcy court–supervised auction, the property is sold to that higher bidder, and the stalking horse bidder usually receives a "break-up fee," often a few percentage points on the sale price. This is intended to compensate the stalking horse bidder for the considerable costs and expenses incurred in pursuing the sale. Given our anemic CRE debt markets, it is often difficult for stalking horse bidders to be outbid.

If the stalking horse bid is successful, the arrangement can include allowing the borrower's principals coming back into the equity of the enterprise purchasing the CRE. In this way, the junior lenders are wiped out, yet equity owners can preserve some of their equity.

However, it should be noted that in order to accomplish a successful stalking horse bid, the first step is the borrower's bankruptcy filing, an event that will likely trigger liability under an NRCOG if there is one. In such event, the borrower is likely better off trying to work out a "transfer in lieu" transaction or a cooperation agreement in connection with a UCC mezzanine foreclosure to accomplish the same purpose. That is, if the senior mezzanine lender can declare a default and accelerate its loan, such lender is then free to enter into a transaction (called a transfer in lieu transaction) whereby the borrower conveys the equity interests securing such senior mezzanine lender's loan to a new company established by such lender, in exchange for the borrower's principals being readmitted to such new company. This transfer in lieu structure will wipe out any junior mezzanine lenders while allowing the borrower to preserve some of its equity. This must be done, however, without arranging a trivial and complicit default with the borrower's complicity, as my clients alleged occurred in the Extended Stay case.

CHAPTER 10

Multifamily Market

In many cases rent control appears to be the most efficient technique presently known to destroy a city—except for bombing.

—Assar Lindbeck, Swedish socialist and economist

The multifamily sector presents unique considerations not affecting other CRE asset classes. First, multifamily lending is the only category of CRE asset lending supported by government-subsidized loans—loans on multifamily properties are made by Fannie Mae and Freddie Mac. Second, the multifamily sector is the only CRE asset class subject to price controls, the most severe restriction on the free market possible, short of a government takeover. For these two reasons, the multifamily sector presents both risks and benefits not found in other CRE asset classes.

GSE SUPPORT OF THE MULTIFAMILY SECTOR

According to its Web site, "Fannie Mae provides multifamily financing for affordable and market-rate rental housing. We operate nationally, in all multifamily markets and under all economic conditions. Every day, Fannie Mae delivers economical, flexible and tailored financing for investors. In 2008 Fannie Mae invested over $35.5 billion in the multifamily affordable housing market. Eighty-nine percent of the homes and rental housing financed by Fannie Mae lenders are affordable to families at or below the median income of their communities." Likewise, Freddie Mac boasts that its "multifamily division supports the acquisition, refinance, rehabilitation and construction of apartment communities across America."

Unlike other CRE asset classes, such as retail, office, and hospitality, the multifamily rental market, much like the housing market, continues to enjoy the support of government-subsidized lending. Indeed, Fannie and Freddie dominated the multifamily lending market in 2009. According to the Co-Star Group, a commercial real estate information company, Fannie Mae and Freddie Mac overwhelmed private-sector multifamily financing in 2009: "The two federal government sponsored enterprises financed 81 percent of multifamily activity based on Freddie Mac's accounting. Their combined activity totaled $36.4 billion. Fannie Mae, through its lender and housing partners, provided $19.8 billion in debt financing for the multifamily rental housing market in 2009."[1]

In contrast, the CMBS market for other CRE asset classes remained moribund. Due to government support of the multifamily sector, existing private multifamily lenders can expect less pain than lenders to other CRE asset classes as private sector loans mature. On the other hand, multifamily fundamentals (rental and vacancy rates) remain under stress and will likely continue to experience downward pressure so long as unemployment remains high (home foreclosures may or may not provide a net increase in renters); and underwriting criteria, even at Fannie and Freddie, have substantially tightened. Thus, while private lenders to multifamily assets can look forward to a Fannie or Freddie refinancing, it is doubtful the proceeds will be sufficient to avoid a loss.

Though private-sector mezzanine lending business today is virtually extinct, Freddie Mac recently launched a program under which it will partner with a few mezzanine lenders to expand its multifamily mortgage loan program.[2] These mezzanine lenders will make mezzanine loans behind mortgages originated by Freddie Mac that are earmarked for securitization and will also acquire junior participations in Freddie's CMBS mortgages called B-pieces. The federal government is thus subsidizing the multifamily sector (up to 85 percent financing, based on optimistic appraisals), in an effort to soften the blow of maturing multifamily loans. Nothing like this exists outside of the multifamily sector, where owners and their lenders are left to their own devices in dealing with maturing CRE loans.

It remains to be seen whether a new generation of highly leveraged Fannie Mae and Freddie Mac multifamily loans will go into default as 17 percent effective unemployment rates continue to ravage multifamily fundamentals. It also remains unclear whether there exists the political will to have taxpayers continue to write checks to multifamily rental property (as opposed to home) owners. As of this writing, the taxpayer bailout of Fannie and Freddie stands at $148 billion. There are, in my view, another $300 to $500 billion more of baked-in losses in their residential portfolios. As the profligate spending of the Obama administration continues to operate as an anchor around the neck of private enterprise, I question the political will to commit taxpayers to support both residential mortgages—ostensibly trying to help individual homeowners—and as well the investors who own multifamily rental properties.

RENT CONTROL

While the vast majority of the approximately 17 million rental apartments in the United States are priced by the free market, some major U.S. cities (like New York, the District of Columbia, and San Francisco), as well as some smaller towns in New York, California, New Jersey, and Maryland, have chosen to fix rents through rent control laws.[3] Few legislative efforts in our history have proven as misguided or resulted in more damage than our rent control laws, though it remains to be seen whether Obamacare gives rent control a run for its money on the worst-legislative-idea-ever list.

Oddly enough, universal condemnation of rent control has been advanced by economists on both the right (Nobel Prize winners Milton Friedman and Friedrich Hayek, for example) and on the left (Nobel laureate Gunmar Myrdal, an architect of the Swedish Labor Party's welfare state). In fact, Myrdal said that "rent control has in certain Western countries constituted, maybe, the worst example of poor planning by governments lacking courage and vision."[4] Another Swedish socialist and economist, Assar Lindbeck, bluntly put it that "in many cases rent control appears to be the most efficient technique presently known to destroy a city—except for bombing."[5]

As with any price control, rent control—by mandating prices below the level dictated by a free market—inevitably creates a shortage of the price-controlled commodity—here housing. Said differently, in a price-coordinated or free market economy, suppliers furnish more of a given commodity as the price goes up while buyers do the reverse—buy more as prices go down. The market price, in a constant state of fluctuation, tentatively settles where buyers' and sellers' desires are optimized, resulting in the most efficient allocation of scarce resources (with alternative uses) possible.

Since the core function of any economic system is the allocation of scarce resources with alternative competing uses, housing (a commodity like any other) must be allocated—only with price control, the market can no longer perform that function. In a rent-controlled housing market, cronyism, succession rights, gamesmanship, and luck replace price as the resource allocator. In the end, no serious economist quarrels with the notion that rent control results in a reduction in both the quality and quantity of housing, and to boot creates crushing inequities to market newcomers.

No place is more notorious than New York City for the cronyism infecting the allocation of below-market rent-controlled apartments. Stories about the wealthy elite occupying vastly below-market rent-regulated apartments abound. Actors Mia Farrow and Dick Cavett, for example, held rent-regulated apartments in New York City.

As for cronysim, nothing can match Congressman Charles Rangel's four rent-stabilized apartments in Harlem's Lenox Terrace. Imagine a public servant hoarding four different below-market rent-regulated apartments in a city with the lowest vacancy rates and greatest housing shortage of any major U.S. city.[6] That's what rent control enables.

In 2007, Rangel paid about $4,000 per month for all four apartments, easily half the market rate. One of them was located on a different floor than the others and used solely as an office, even though rent-stabilized apartments in New York City must be used solely as primary residences. Worse, Rangel took a homestead tax break on his Washington, D.C. house during the same years he occupied his four Manhattan rent-stabilized apartments, thus simultaneously claiming a primary residence in two different cities.[7]

Rangel's brazen abuse of his position of privilege and power (though that hardly makes him stand out among New York politicians)—would not have yielded him four apartments absent rent control. Said differently, rent control (the absence of a free market) enables unscrupulous politicians like Rangel to game the system and cheat other people out of apartments they need. That could never happen, even at the hand of the powerful (former) chairman of the House Ways and Means Committee, if a free market prevailed.

Despite these manifest failures, confused tenants, courts, and legislators continue to press the rent control agenda. Indeed, I would make the case that the moral hazard created by the confluence of the greatest recession and unemployment rates since the Great Depression coupled with the frenzy of government giveaways and bailouts (particularly in the housing sector) have led to increased rent controls. That is one possible explanation for a blatantly wrong recent decision by New York's highest court.

In *Roberts v. Tishman Speyer Properties*,[8] New York's highest court—the Court of Appeals—overturned the deregulation (or removal from rent controls) of nearly 4,000 apartments at Peter Cooper Village—Stuyvesant Town, a sprawling 91-building complex containing more than 11,000 apartments on over 80 acres running along the East River on Manhattan's lower East Side, even though the complex's owners decontrolled the apartments over a nearly 15-year period pursuant to the express rules of the New York State agency in charge of administering New York City's rent control laws.

This massive complex, known in New York as Stuy Town, was constructed in the early 1940s by the Metropolitan Life Insurance Company as part of the postwar effort to accommodate returning G.I.s. In those days—the complex was built before the end of segregation—MetLife chose forced to build two separate projects, one for whites and the other for blacks. A similar project was built by MetLife in Harlem called Riverton. Both Riverton and Stuy Town have already been bankrupted by the current Great Recession.

After the complex was opened, blacks were barred from living in the complex, with MetLife's then president, Frederick H. Ecker, stating that "Negroes and whites do not mix."[9] Lawsuits were filed asserting that, because the project was built pursuant to a public-private joint venture between MetLife and New York City, the city's then antidiscrimination laws for public housing had been violated.

In a vivid demonstration of just how far society has changed in the last six decades, in July 1947, the New York Supreme Court determined that the development was private and that, in the absence of laws to the contrary, the company could discriminate as it saw fit. The court wrote, "[i]t is well settled that the landlord of a private apartment or dwelling house may, without violating any provision of the Federal or State Constitutions, select tenants of its own choice because of race, color, creed or religion. . . . Clearly, housing accommodation is not a recognized civil right."[10]

Near the height of the market, in October 2006, MetLife agreed to sell Stuy Town to a joint venture consisting of Tishman Speyer Properties and real estate private equity firm BlackRock for the record-breaking price of $5.4 billion. The sale to the Tishman-BlackRock joint venture took place only after the venture outbid the complex's tenants, who, having been organized by New York City Council member Daniel Garodnick, submitted a bid within $100 million of Speyer's $5.4 billion offer.

New York's senior senator, Charles Schumer, is reputed to have urged C. Robert Henrickson, MetLife's chief executive, to accept the tenant-sponsored offer for the complex. Clearly, Senator Schumer in his long and illustrious career never did more for more tenants than he did by failing to persuade Henrickson to accept the Stuy Town tenant bid. Sometimes the deals a man does not make are his greatest achievement.

Witnessing the inevitable deterioration of New York City's rent-controlled housing stock (because owners were unable to afford continuing repairs and improvements), the New York State Legislature, hoping to encourage owners of rent-regulated properties to invest in crucial building upgrades, in 1955 enacted the "J-51" real estate tax exemption program, which grants benefits and tax relief to owners making such building repairs.

Pursuant to New York's Rent Stabilization Law, hundreds of thousands of apartments in New York City buildings completed prior to 1974 are rent regulated, including Stuy Town. By granting owners of preexisting rent-stabilized buildings tax breaks when they invested in crucial improvements, the J-51 tax program endeavored to encourage such investments, similar to the credits energy utilities might give for updated "green" building improvements.

As a general proposition, New York City's Rent Stabilization Law does not apply to buildings completed on or after January 1, 1974.[11] In order to make the J-51 program available to all building owners, even those who owned unregulated (free-market) buildings, in 1975 the New York Legislature amended the Rent Stabilization Law to add a section[12] that permits building owners, including owners of free-market buildings with high market rents already in place, to qualify for J-51 tax benefits upon making qualifying improvements, but only if the owner opted into the Rent Stabilization system for the period of the J-51 abatement, generally 12 years—with initial rent-stabilized rents set at then-prevailing market rents.

Once that 12-year J-51 abatement period ends, the building returns to free-market rents. Free-market building owners who elected to avail themselves of J-51 tax benefits were not required to roll back rents to the levels of similar long-term "rent stabilized" apartments in the area, which have been rent stabilized since the 1974 enactment of the Emergency Tenants Protection Act (or the earlier 1969 Rent Stabilization Law), but rather to subject the building to the rent stabilization laws at then-prevailing market rents on a going-forward basis for the 12-year J-51 tax abatement period.

Nearly four decades later, deterioration of New York City's rent con-trolled housing stock had once again reached alarming proportions. For that reason, in 1993, the New York Legislature amended the Rent Stabilization Law once again, this time by enacting the Luxury Decontrol Law, which permitted landlords of rent-controlled buildings to decontrol (or remove apartments from the rent regulation) where (a) the legal regulated rents reached $2,000 per month, and (b) such apartments were vacant, or were occupied by tenants whose household income for each of the two preceding calendar years exceeded $250,000 per year.[13] The Luxury Decontrol Law, however, contained the following narrow exclusion:

> *Provided, however, that this exclusion shall not apply to housing accommodations which* became or become *subject to this law (a)* by virtue of *receiving tax benefits pursuant to [the J-51 law].* . . .

RSL §§ 26-504.1 AND 26-504.2(A)

The New York Legislature thus created a narrow exception to the Luxury Decontrol Law by prohibiting the decontrolling of apartments only at buildings that "became or become" subject to the Rent Stabilization Law—that is, first entered Rent Stabilization—as a result of receiving J-51 benefits. This only makes sense, since the already high fair-market rents forming the basis of initial regulated rents in the fair-market J-51 buildings were often above the $2,000 monthly threshold set forth in the Luxury Decontrol Law. Therefore, absent this limited exclusion, the owners of such fair-market buildings would have been able to commit to being subject to the Rent Stabilization Law (for their respective J-51 abatement periods), and then immediately decontrol their apartments (before the abatement period expired).

Concerned about a potential conflict between the J-51 tax abatement law and the Luxury Decontrol Law, New York City's building owners sought clarification from the New York State agency in charge of administering New York City's Rent Stabilization Law, the New York State Division of Housing and Community Renewal (the "DHCR").

The DHCR responded in the mid-1990s with a letter ruling and later official policy statements clearly stating that the decontrolling of apartments in buildings built before January 1, 1974, pursuant to the Luxury Decontrol Law was lawful and would be permitted. According to the DHCR, such older buildings, having been rent regulated long before first receiving J-51 benefits, did *not* "become" rent stabilized "by virtue of" their owners having opted to apply for J-51 tax benefits.

The New York City agency in charge of administering the J-51 tax abatement program, the New York City Department of Housing Preservation and Development ("HPD"), likewise responded by adopting regulations prorating down the J-51 tax benefits available to owners of older J-51 benefited buildings, as the percentage of apartments in those J-51 benefited buildings were decontrolled, so that the only the portion of the J-51 benefits attributable to rent-stabilized apartments remained available to building owners, thus preserving the sanctity of the policy underlying the J-51 program—promoting capital investment in rent-regulated apartments.

Having obtained the necessary guidance from the two governmental agencies in charge of administering the Rent Stabilization Law and the J-51 tax abatement program, respectively, the DHCR and HPD, owners of pre-1974 buildings, including originally MetLife and thereafter the Tishman Speyer/BlackRock joint venture, followed a path of applying for both J-51 tax abatements (when they made qualifying improvements) and decontrolling apartments (for the most part when apartments with legal regulated rents in excess of $2,000 per month became vacant).

As apartments in Stuy Town and other pre-1974 J-51 benefited buildings were decontrolled, future J-51 tax benefits were prorated down by HPD so that only the J-51 tax benefits attributable to remaining rent-stabilized apartments were allowed.

As a result, since being enacted, both the Luxury Decontrol Law and the J-51 program worked in tandem to revitalize New York City's housing stock. In essence by giving incentives for capital improvements and certain building repairs, and permitting high-rent units to go to fair market, the wealthier free-market tenants have effectively subsidized the long-term rent-stabilized tenants, exactly as the New York Legislature intended.

Because of the higher rents paid by the nearly 4,000 decontrolled apartments at Stuy Town, massive capital expenditures and improvements were justified, and long-term rent-stabilized tenants benefited. Absent those decontrolled units, the quality of life for long-term rent-stabilized tenants at Stuyvesant Town—Peter Cooper Village would be a far cry from what it is now. This was precisely the object of the Luxury Decontrol Law and the J-51 program.

Ever since the enactment of the Luxury Decontrol Law, tens of thousands of high-rent New York City apartments have left Rent Stabilization as they were vacated (or if their occupants earned more than $175,000 per year), and formerly regulated rents were brought above $2,000 per month under the Rent Stabilization rules, exactly as envisioned by the New York Legislature. Owners and lenders long relied on the explicit rules and policies articulated by the DHCR—which allowed the decontrolling of apartments in pre-1974 J-51 benefited buildings—and underwrote and valued buildings based on the total rent roll resulting from the mix of decontrolled and regulated apartments in every building.

THE *ROBERTS* CASE

In early 2007, a group of fair market tenants at Stuy Town (who knowingly and willingly signed fair-market leases for renovated, decontrolled apartments) brought a class action suit[14] seeking hundreds of millions of dollars of alleged rent overcharges, asserting that by virtue of the J-51 benefits applied for and received first by MetLife and later by the Tishman Speyer/BlackRock joint venture, their apartments had been illegally decontrolled (before they had rented them).

In essence, these tenants, all of whom had voluntarily and knowingly signed fair-market leases in which they agreed to pay fair-market rents, sought to break the contracts they had signed by arguing that the (by then) 15-year-old DHCR rules and policies expressly allowing such decontrol were invalid and contrary to statute. The complaining fair-market tenants' lawyers stood to make a fortune as they took the case on a contingency fee basis.

The case was assigned to Justice Richard B. Lowe, III, a judge in New York County's Commercial Division, who dismissed the case, in my opinion correctly, ruling that Stuy Town, having been rent stabilized for about 18 years prior to receiving its first dollar of J-51 benefits, could not possibly be said to have "become" rent stabilized "by virtue of" receiving those benefits.

Stuyvesant Town—Peter Cooper Village was originally constructed in the 1940s as a Redevelopment Companies Law[15] project, but entered the Rent Stabilization program in 1974. Nearly two decades later, in 1992, MetLife, the owner at the time, for the first time applied for and began receiving J-51 tax benefits. Justice Lowe declined to cast aside as irrational the rules and policies of the DHCR (upon which owners and lenders had reasonably relied for 15 years) and dismissed the fair-market tenants' class action suit.

However, the fair-market tenants appealed. New York's intermediate appellate court (the Appellate Division, First Department) reversed Justice Lowe's decision and thereafter New York's highest court, the Court of Appeals, affirmed that reversal of Justice Lowe's decision, in what I contend is a tortured reading of the plain language of the Luxury Decontrol Law—one which I submit might be explained by the moral hazard now infecting all branches of government, including our judicial system.

Both the Appellate Division and New York's high court misconstrued the words "become or became" and held that any building that merely receives J-51 benefits—as opposed to one that *became* rent regulated by virtue of receiving such benefits—was ineligible for luxury decontrol. Such a result was not and could not have been the intention of the New York Legislature in enacting the Luxury Decontrol Law, which was specifically designed to remove from Rent Stabilization apartments for which there was no housing emergency, while enabling owners to increase their capital investments in New York's aging rent-stabilized housing stock by having higher priced apartments and higher income tenants subsidize the others.

Nor is the result of the appellate courts' decisions consistent with the purpose of the J-51 program, which was intended to incentivize capital improvements and renovations to the existing rent-stabilized housing stock—investments that many of the owners of such housing stock were unable to afford absent the program—and not as a backhanded method of increasing the inventory of rent-stabilized housing stock (which was the province of the Rent Stabilization Law, not the J-51 law).

In my view, both appellate courts held that if the New York Legislature had meant to limit the decontrol exclusion to apartments that became subject to Rent Stabilization "solely" by virtue of the receipt of J-51 benefits, then the word "solely," which did not appear in the Luxury Decontrol Law, would have been inserted by the legislature. Accordingly, the appellate courts reversed Justice Lowe's decision dismissing the case, and in so doing, declined to give deference to, and ultimately overturned, the DHCR's rules and policies, upon which Justice Lowe and building owners and lenders had relied (in the case of the latter for many years), which permitted luxury decontrol to take place notwithstanding an owner's receipt of J-51 benefits provided the building was rent stabilized before first receiving J-51 benefits.

Both the New York Appellate Division and Court of Appeals got it wrong. Justice Lowe's interpretation of the language of the Luxury Decontrol exclusion was correct, and the DHCR's rules and policies should have been upheld. New York's appellate courts, in reversing Justice Lowe's decision, focused on the wrong three words of the exclusion appearing in the Luxury Decontrol Law—"by virtue of"—holding that, because Stuy Town was rent stabilized by virtue of having entered the Rent Stabilization program in 1974 and was "redundantly stabilized" by virtue of later receiving J-51 benefits in 1992, the decontrolled units were, at least in part, rent stabilized "by virtue of" receiving J-51 benefits and as such were not eligible for luxury decontrol.

According to these appellate courts, since the New York Legislature did not say "solely by virtue of" when writing the Luxury Decontrol exclusion, both the DHCR regulations and Justice Lowe impermissibly read into the exclusion a missing word—"solely."

However, the word "solely" need not be read into the statutory exclusion to support Justice Lowe's (and the DHCR's) interpretation of the Luxury Decontrol Law. The Luxury Decontrol Law provides that apartments cannot be decontrolled if they "became or become" subject to Rent Stabilization "by virtue of" receiving J-51 benefits. Since all of the apartments at Stuy Town "became" rent stabilized in 1974, and since MetLife first applied for J-51 benefits nearly two decades later in 1992, native speakers of the English language would not say that any of these apartments "became" rent stabilized in 1992 or any later year.

By using the word "became," the New York Legislature made perfectly clear that, if an apartment was subject to the Rent Stabilization Law before ever receiving J-51 benefits, then that apartment remained eligible for luxury decontrol. The word "became" makes the use of the word "solely" unnecessary and redundant.

In order to achieve the twisted interpretation of the plain statutory language necessary to overturn 15 years of DHCR rules and policies and thereby recapture into the rent-controlled housing stock the apartments previously decontrolled by owners who relied on those explicit DHCR policies, Court of Appeals Judge Robert Smith remarked at oral argument that he had "become" a grandfather for the third time recently and thus he saw no reason why a project that was rent stabilized in 1974 could not likewise "become" rent stabilized in 1992 when it first received J-51 benefits.

The colloquialism that Judge Smith cited, however, twists the plain meaning of the word "become," which every English-speaking person on the planet knows like the back of his hand. I would have asked Judge Smith, "Judge, you 'became' a teenager on your 13th birthday. Did you also 'become' a teenager on your 14th, 15th, 16th, 17th, 18th, and 19th birthdays?"[16]

The Merriam-Webster dictionary of the English language defines the verb "become" to mean "to undergo change." Like any human being who became a teenager upon reaching the age of 13 and not at any later time, Stuy Town became rent stabilized only on the particular day in 1974 when it first entered Rent Stabilization and not on any subsequent day.

The reference to becoming a grandfather for the third time is a colloquial deviation from proper English—a deviation no doubt spawned by the joyfulness of that occasion. Human beings are understandably so thrilled at "becoming" a parent or grandparent that they have taken (in common parlance) to saying that they became a parent or grandparent for the second or third time each time an additional child is born. It is a harmless way of celebrating that moment and a way of elevating the birth of subsequent children and grandchildren to a level coequal with that of first child or grandchild. Well, it was a harmless colloquial deviation from proper English until Justice Smith got hold of it.

Permitting buildings that were already subject to the Rent Stabilization Law, having been built before 1974, to be deregulated notwithstanding the mere receipt of J-51 benefits subsequent to such buildings first entering the Rent Stabilization system makes perfect sense. The architects of the J-51 program laid out a coherent plan—encourage owners of rent stabilized buildings to invest in capital improvements and renovations by giving them tax incentives based on those investments, and also, to be fair, permit owners of free-market buildings to avail themselves of J-51 benefits provided they opt into Rent Stabilization for the 12-year abatement period without the benefit of luxury decontrol, in order to make sure that *quid pro quo* is honored—that all of the apartments in such otherwise free-market buildings remain subject to the Rent Stabilization Law for the full

12-year J-51 abatement period. It is therefore perfectly logical to provide, as the New York Legislature did, that only those free-market owners be prohibited from availing themselves of the Luxury Deregulation Law during the pendency of the 12-year J-51 abatement period.

Absent the narrow exclusion to the Luxury Decontrol Law enacted by the New York State Legislature, first-time entrants to the Rent Stabilization system, such as newer buildings that truly "became" rent regulated by virtue of receiving J-51 benefits, by reason of their higher initial regulated rents and higher income tenants, would be able to avoid rent stabilization by entering the Rent Stabilization system and then immediately luxury decontrolling high-income tenants paying regulated rents exceeding $2,000 per month.

Had the New York Legislature not enacted the narrow exclusion to Luxury Decontrol, newer buildings first becoming rent stabilized by virtue of J-51 benefits would have entered a revolving door rather than the Rent Stabilization system, as they would have entered and then been able to use their higher initial regulated rents and tenant incomes to luxury decontrol many or all of their units long before their respective J-51 tax abatement periods ended.

Thus, absent the limited exclusion wisely drawn by the New York Legislature, J-51 tax-benefited *first-time entrants* to Rent Stabilization would have been able to exit the system before the 12-year tax abatement period ended. None of these concerns apply to older buildings rent stabilized since 1974, like Stuy Town, which, by virtue of having become rent stabilized long before ever receiving any J-51 benefits, did not present the case of an owner breaching the commitment to enter the Rent Stabilization system for the duration of the owner's tax abatements as a condition of receiving such tax benefits.

The narrow Luxury Decontrol Law exclusion therefore was an artful attempt by the New York Legislature to prevent first-time Rent Stabilization entrants from immediately returning to deregulated status, and it was decidedly not intended to recapture into the Rent Stabilization system apartments and tenants that the New York Legislature in its wisdom, by the Luxury Decontrol Law, sought to remove from the Rent Stabilization system.

Aside from the obvious inequity of changing the rules after everyone relied on them for 15 years, the *Roberts* decision will likely throw many New York City apartment buildings into foreclosure, which otherwise would be successfully carried by their owners through the current tough economic times. Rather than face forward-looking rent reductions and backward-looking rent overcharge claims, owners will likely leave the already beleaguered lenders to deal with the problem.

The *Roberts* decision is bad for owners, bad for our already distressed banks, and bad for New York City—both because the city's housing stock will deteriorate as owners are unable to afford upkeep and because the city will potentially be required to refund enormous amounts of J-51 benefits and devalue the tax assessments of J-51 benefited buildings.

Justice Lowe, the DHCR, and HPD therefore got it right when they permitted apartments in older buildings subject to the Rent Stabilization Law to be luxury decontrolled notwithstanding their later receipt of J-51 benefits, and the HPD prorated down the J-51 benefits appurtenant to such buildings as apartments therein were deregulated. This is not an "incongruous" result as the Appellate Division held, but rather an eminently—really the only—logical approach, given the architecture of the J-51 program and the Luxury Decontrol Law.

The Court of Appeals' strained reading of the phrase "become or became" in the *Roberts* decision—one of the most highly respected courts in the country—I submit, is a casualty of the times. The *Roberts* decision stands as stark evidence of the fact that judges are human beings and as such are subject to the pressures of the times. The current severe recession and joblessness must have weighed heavily on the minds and hearts of New York's senior jurists, who ultimately fell prey to twisting the plain language of the statute in order to achieve what they considered a just result.

The moral hazard created by Obama's bailout mania is thus not limited to underwater homeowners' defaulting on their mortgages. Ironically, however, the *Roberts* decision is the worst thing that could have happened to New York City's poorer rent-stabilized tenants, as they always remained protected (and would have remained protected had the *Roberts* decision gone the other way), and now they will lose the subsidies formerly coming from fair-market tenants.

In January 2010, Speyer and BlackRock stated their intention to hand back the keys to the project to its lenders, who must now wade through the aftermath of this tragic decision, which will doubtless spawn at least another decade of further litigation and uncertainty.

CHAPTER **11**

Governmental Actions Caused the Affordable Housing Crisis

To kill an error is as good a service as, and sometimes even better than, the establishing of a new truth or fact.
—Charles Darwin

Government inflicts us with disease and then rushes to our aid with a cure. In this chapter, I explain how the "affordable housing crisis" was really brought about by earlier governmental actions. Regrettably, the cures the government has offered to respond to the disease of its own making are even worse than the disease.

GOVERNMENTAL MUNCHAUSEN BY PROXY

Named after the 18th-century Baron Munchausen, the psychological disorder Munchausen syndrome describes someone who intentionally harms himself in order to gain medical attention and sympathy. In a different form of this awful syndrome called "Munchausen by proxy," the afflicted individual, a parent, secretly harms his or her child, so that the child is hospitalized and treated, thereby achieving the clandestine object of the mentally ill parent: aggrandizement for his or her excellent care-giving. In extreme cases, afflicted parents have poisoned their children in order to be lavished with praise for their ensuing dedication to the care and welfare of the poisoned child.

Munchausen by proxy offers an instructive analogy to various governmental actions. Examples abound in which government initially takes some action that causes great harm to society and then later responds with some legislative "cure" for the societal ill brought about by the original ill-advised governmental intervention. Though the examples are legion, for our purposes, a good starting place is the congressional reaction to the so-called affordable home ownership crisis—a situation which, though hardly qualifying as a crisis at all, was brought about largely by earlier misguided governmental actions.

NANTUCKET—A CASE STUDY IN THE DEATH OF COMMON SENSE

Poorly thought out local government regulation caused housing to become unaffordable in those areas of our country where it did become unafford- able. To illustrate this point, I will resort to some anecdotal evidence, since it happens to be readily available to me, in one of America's least affordable communities, Massachusetts' Nantucket Island, located off the south coast of Cape Cod.

In 2000, I formed a development company, Nantucket Residential Design LLC, with my wife, Melissa, an architect, to acquire land and design, build, and furnish high-end waterfront and waterview "spec" homes in Nantucket. Over the next 10 years we developed a handful of high-end Nantucket homes, selling for prices ranging from $5 million to over $12 million each.

Roughly half of Nantucket's nearly 48 square miles is titled in perma- nent protected trust and thus forever immune from development. Much of Nantucket's conservation efforts were accomplished by the formation of the Nantucket Islands Land Bank. According to the Nantucket Islands Land Bank Web site:

> *The first program of its kind in the United States, the Nantucket Islands Land Bank is a land conservation program created to acquire, hold, and manage important open spaces, resources and endangered landscapes for the use and enjoyment of the general public. Since 1983, the Land Bank has served as a model for several communities across the country. The success of these efforts and those of other public and private conservation groups is evident in the quality of life on Nantucket for both residents and visitors. To date, nearly half of Nantucket is forever-protected open space.*[1]

At an annual Town Meeting held on April 5, 1983, the citizens of Nantucket voted on a home rule petition:

> *To vote on Article 23: Nantucket County Land Bank stated: "To see if the Town will vote to instruct its representative in the General*

Court to file a bill in the Legislature, in the form of a home rule petition to establish a Nantucket County Land Bank ... said bill, when approved by the Legislature and signed by the Governor, to be approved in its final form by the voters at Town Meeting in order for it to be implemented." Based on a recommendation from the Planning Board, the article was later amended to include the words, "A two-percent registration fee for certain transfers of real estate." The vote was taken by a show of hands: Yes, 446; No, 1.[2]

The 2 percent Land Bank fee added on at the recommendation of Nantucket's Planning Commission applied to all nonexempt transfers of real property on Nantucket and became the funding source for the Land Bank. With transactions approaching a billion dollars annually at the height of the market, this tax raised more than $20 million per annum in the boom years including over $23 million in 2005. All of this revenue is committed to and spent on acquiring vacant land so that it can be placed into Nantucket's ever-increasing stockpile of permanent protected open spaces (and to maintaining preexisting protected land holdings).

The title to each parcel the Land Bank acquires is then restricted in perpetuity so that it can never be developed. Since the Nantucket land mass is finite (disregarding for the moment erosion and accretion), and since land parcels acquired by the Land Bank never return to unprotected status, each year the universe of parcels eligible for acquisition by the Land Bank steadily diminishes. Conversely, since houses are forever trading hands, the income stream payable to the Land Bank from the 2 percent Land Bank tax is perpetual. Thus, each year, the Land Bank is forced to stretch further and further in its efforts to buy properties worthy of protection—each year falling prey to acquiring parcels less and less worthy of permanent protection.

For the most part, all of the major undeveloped tracts on Nantucket have already been preserved. Thus in recent times, the Land Bank has taken to buying minor subdivisions from developers promptly after they have received the relevant approvals. These tracts would otherwise have been developed with houses (mostly at the lower end of the price range), but only up to the limited density levels imposed as part of Nantucket's rigorous subdivision approval process.

For example, on March 14, 2007, one of Nantucket's two daily newspapers, *The Nantucket Independent,* ran a front-page story, with the following opening paragraph:

Snatching 19.2 acres from the jaws of development, the Nantucket Islands Land Bank will buy five of six lots on Pout Pond Road in mid-April. The purchase—Land Bank Director Eric Savetsky cannot disclose the price until the deal closes—is important to the Land Bank because the land is part of the subdivision, Pout Pond Road, that could be developed at any time by its owners, Glenn Shriberg, Morton I. Kaufman, Dorothy Kaufman and Barry Zlotin into two-dwelling lots.

Despite Hollywood's efforts, it would seem it is the jaws of development and not the jaws of the great white shark that send tremors of fear through the hearts of Nantucket's wealthy summer residents.

In order to build a house on Nantucket, the exterior of the house must be approved by the Nantucket Historic District Commission, a board that endeavors to ensure that the architecture of Nantucket's homes is consistent with its rich historical heritage. It is not uncommon for this process to take many months, sometimes over a year, requiring many expensive redesigns and of course requiring the landowner to carry the land (taxes, insurance, and interest) during this extended review period.

When my wife and I first began developing "spec" houses on Nantucket, the Town of Nantucket had voted to impose an outright moratorium on building permits. In other words, even after obtaining all requisite sign-offs and approvals including the rigorous Historic District Commission review process and the building and zoning inspectors' sign-offs, the approved application for a building permit would wait in a long queue during the years when the moratorium was in effect, as the Nantucket Building Department was then limited by law to issuing a fixed number of building permits a year.

In addition, Nantucket strictly enforces both state and local conservation laws. These laws affect a great many of Nantucket's developable land parcels, as few land parcels on the island are not within the regulated 100 feet of some coastal or inland resource area. According to the Nantucket Conservation Commission Web site:

The Massachusetts Wetlands Protection Act (the Act) requires that no person shall remove, dredge, or alter any bank, freshwater or coastal wetlands, beach, dunes, flat, marsh, meadow or swamp bordering on any resource area as defined in the Act without filing written notice of the intention to perform such work with the Conservation Commission of the Town in which the land is located and receiving a permit from the Commission to perform the work. This mandated authority was reinforced by the 1963 Annual Town Meeting which authorized the establishment of a Conservation Commission for the Town.

In February 1988, the Commission passed local regulations which provide for more strict controls in and around both inland and coastal wetlands than are provided by the State's enabling legislation and ensuing regulations. The Commission's protected interests of public and private groundwater protection, prevention of pollution, erosion control and storm damage prevention provide great benefit to the Town's seasonal and year-round economy. The additional interests of protection of land containing shellfish and fisheries play an important part to the summer recreational fisherman and the local commercial scalloper.

The Commission is comprised of seven members appointed by the Board of Selectmen. The Commission function is to review, condition and permit activities within 100 feet of inland and coastal wetlands. The Town has a separate Wetlands By-law, Chapter 136, that increases protection over the State Wetlands Protection Act. The State Wetlands Protection Act and the Nantucket By-law requires that files presented to the Commission must be opened within twenty-one days.[3]

On many occasions, the approval of other government agencies besides the Nantucket Conservation Commission must be procured as a prerequisite to development. For example, a Nantucket landowner must not only seek Conservation Commission approval if he or she is contemplating work within 100 feet of a state or local resource area (such as a wetlands or coastal bank), the owner must also check data published by Mass Wildlife, the Massachusetts Division of Fisheries and Wildlife, to see if there are protected habitats for any "threatened species" or species of "special concern" on the parcel slated for development. According to the Mass Wildlife Web site:[4]

The Natural Heritage and Endangered Species Program (NHESP), part of the Massachusetts Division of Fisheries and Wildlife, is one of the programs forming the Natural Heritage network. NHESP is responsible for the conservation and protection of hundreds of species that are not hunted, fished, trapped, or commercially harvested in the state. The Program's highest priority is protecting the 176 species of vertebrate and invertebrate animals and 259 species of native plants that are officially listed as Endangered, Threatened or of Special Concern in Massachusetts.

The overall goal of the Program is the protection of the state's wide range of native biological diversity. Progress towards this goal is accomplished through the following:

- *Biological Field Surveys*
- *Research and Inventory*
- *Data Management*
- *Environmental Impact Review*
- *Rare Species Recovery*
- *Ecological Restoration of Key Habitats*
- *Land Protection*

As a result, the Nantucket Conservation Commission often requires Mass Wildlife to be informed of contemplated development activities, whether a house is being built from scratch or an existing deck is being expanded. On its Web site,[5] Mass Wildlife, speaking of the Nantucket Core Habitat, says:

> *One of the most effective ways to protect biodiversity for future generations is to protect Core Habitats from adverse human impacts through land conservation. For Living Waters Core Habitats, protection efforts should focus on the **riparian areas**, the areas of land adjacent to water bodies. A naturally vegetated buffer that extends 330 feet (100 meters) from the water's edge helps to maintain cooler water temperature and to maintain the nutrients, energy, and natural flow of water needed by freshwater species.*

Not only are some birds, large and small, protected, such as owls, harriers and plovers, but as well hundreds of species of plants, and vertebrate and invertebrate fauna are protected including various salamanders, moths, beetles, and worms. Some beach grasses are considered protected species. Imagine being told after purchasing an expensive plot of land that your planned home will destroy the home of certain earthworms, not currently threatened but of "special concern" and that you must recreate the worm habitat elsewhere in order to move forward.

Obtaining the approval of the Nantucket Conservation Commission is no small matter. Abutting landowners must be notified. Nantucketers have a nasty habit of abandoning their conservational proclivities when it comes time to developing their own properties but suddenly "getting religion" when their neighbors want to break ground. These NIMBY ("not in my backyard") folks could not care less about the environment—just their own views and privacy.

Newly minted environmentalist neighbors are not the only adversary of someone desiring to develop a lot on Nantucket. More often than not, the complex labyrinth of statutes and regulations governing Nantucket architecture and land development, including most notably its conservation laws and rules, become potent weapons in the hands of environmental extremists.

On Nantucket, private nonprofit organizations such as the Nantucket Land Council regularly review single-home projects, often hiring, out of funds from charitable contributions, botanists, zoologists, and soil geologists, who appear before the Conservation Commission public hearings to make cases for expanding resource areas or finding threatened species of flora and fauna on a homeowner's parcel. By creating a record on these issues supported by credentialed so-called experts, the Nantucket Conservation Commission is understandably hard pressed to approve the homeowner's application. While the efforts of such nonprofits are ostensibly proconservational, often their budgets are funded by wealthy local summer residents who already own homes and simply want to make sure no further development occurs.

These activities take on a decidedly antidevelopment rather than proconservation feel. It is difficult and expensive for a typical individual homeowner or even a developer to take on the resources and expertise of nonprofits like the Nantucket Land Council, and the result often is a negotiated compromise, whereby the homeowner or developer agrees to restrict the development of the parcel in a fashion desired by the wealthy residents backing the Nantucket Land Council.

Worse than the antidevelopmental efforts of a homeowner's neighbors cloaked in the respectable garb of a not-for-profit conservation foundation are the unabashed direct efforts of a neighbor whose obvious purpose is the protection of his or her own views and privacy. In the hands of such unscrupulous NIMBY neighbors, conservational rules and regulations provide a powerful club. Here's a personal example of just how much cost, delay, and injustice can be wielded by a NIMBY abutter pretending to be interested in conservation.

My wife and I owned an expensive waterfront property on Nantucket's tony Monomoy Road, with direct frontage on Nantucket Harbor. After developing a main house on a landward knoll, we sought approval of a small waterfront cottage, entirely within all applicable rules and regulations. After spending months designing and redesigning the cottage per the suggestions of the Nantucket Historic District Commission (concerning the external architectural appearance of the house), we dutifully applied to the Nantucket Conservation Commission for an order of conditions allowing the construction of the cottage where we had sited it, as that location was within 100 feet of a coastal bank (the bank being a protected resource area) but outside of the proscribed 50-foot buffer zone.

There were houses on either side of our proposed location, each sited parallel to and just as seaward as ours. In fact, the abutter to the west, a New York real estate developer, whom I considered a friend, had only months previously himself gone to the same Conservation Commission where he had sought and obtained approval for the construction of his own cottage. As part of my neighbor's application, he engaged soil geologists to ascertain the location of the landward boundary of the coastal bank not only on his property but extending eastward of his property over ours.

Though I was noticed as an abutter by my neighbor when he sought approval for his cottage, I did not appear or oppose his application. But when it came time for my application, on which I duly notified my neighbor, he not only appeared; he hired a soil geologist and attorney who testified and submitted reports stating that the coastal bank located on my map was wrong. This was the exact same coastal bank location my neighbor had himself plotted and submitted only months previously. In fact, we had used his data.

Despite this blatant hypocrisy, my neighbor and his attorney and geologist pressed forward with their "new-found" evidence on the location of the coastal bank, which it seems had migrated vastly inland over the few months since my neighbor's application. Miraculously the coastal bank's migration only took place within the lateral boundaries of my lot. Besides contradicting his own previous application (and the soil science data supporting it), my neighbor and his team were required to advance the laughably preposterous position that the coastal bank ran parallel to the harbor shoreline and roughly 50 feet inland therefrom throughout the lateral width of his lot—otherwise his brand-new cottage would itself have been illegal—but then the coastal bank made an abrupt 90-degree inland turn right at the boundary line between our two lots and moved inland another 50 feet, where it once again ran parallel to the shoreline (only 50 feet further inland on my lot than on his).

Of course the neighbor to my east was there at the hearing too, and she would have had her property adversely impacted had the "new"—50 feet more inland—coastal bank location continued onto her property. Somehow, the coastal bank miraculously migrated back to its original position—50 feet more seaward—right at the boundary line between my property and the easterly neighbor.

It is remarkable that during the last great ice age, roughly 10,000 years ago, the forces of nature had the prescience to arrange for the deposition of glacial moraine so the resulting coastal bank would precisely follow the lot boundary lines laid out by a surveyor thousands of year hence in the 1920s when the lots of Monomoy were subdivided.

Despite the absurdity of this position, the fact that it contradicted the science recently submitted by the very party advancing this idiotic position, the fact that that prior science had been approved by the same commission we were then before, and the transparent self-serving (nonconservational) motives of my wonderful neighbors, they nevertheless had no difficulty finding a lawyer and geologist to support them.

I was required not only to hire my own attorney, but also a surveyor and soil geologist. The geologist took core samplings and did soil studies of the cores to prove that the coastal bank did not make abrupt inland and seaward turns precisely overlaying my easterly and westerly lot boundary lines. After months of delays and $50,000 of needless additional expense, my cottage was approved.

During the boom years, Nantucketers, not surprisingly, became enraged at the appalling lack of affordable housing on their island. The same crowd who urged the adoption of these impossible development-thwarting rules decried the lack of affordable housing.

Land cost is a very substantial component cost of all housing—be it multifamily rental housing or individual homes. Laws and regulations reducing the yield of a single-family lot—the square footage of gross building area that may be built upon a lot (whether by bulk or zoning restrictions or overlaying conservation restrictions, which curtail building footprints)—drive the price of housing up.

With nearly half of Nantucket's land mass already in permanent protected trust, with the area of Nantucket's protected land mass continually expanding due to the efforts of the taxpayer-funded Nantucket Land Bank, and with the island's remaining land mass being subject to a complex of extremely burdensome rules and restrictions, enforced not just by the governmental agencies charged with the responsibility of doing so, but as well by well-heeled NIMBY neighbors and not-for-profit foundations funded by larger NIMBY collectives, is it any wonder that the supply of buildable lots on Nantucket was severely limited? And is it really a surprise to anyone that the immutable law of supply and demand would drive up the price of Nantucket housing as a result?

Nantucketers easily could have solved their affordable housing problem. They could have allowed mid-rise construction of garden apartment buildings in some appropriate zone, but they did not want to see those buildings. Instead, they chose to continue to their path of thwarting development and to complain about "greedy" developers who refused to develop affordable housing—never mind that vacant lots started at half a million dollars thanks to withdrawing land from development altogether and the dizzying array of land regulations.

Nantucket voters—being only the full-time residents of the Island—were happy to burden the development process beyond any commonsense boundaries because they believed—incorrectly, I might add—that the exorbitant costs of compliance would be borne solely by the wealthy (non-voting) summer residents who were buying up land lots and building homes.

But year-round Nantucketers pay for those burdensome development costs every time they go grocery shopping, dine out, or pay their school taxes. That's because the checkout clerks at the local supermarket, the waiters and waitresses, and the schoolteachers all need to be housed. Either they are housed on Nantucket at sky-high costs or they live on Cape Cod and commute from and to the Cape daily either by plane or ferry. Either way, these important workers cannot sustain themselves—and will seek employment elsewhere—unless their salaries compensate them for those increased housing (or commuting) costs. No one on Nantucket escapes these costs, whether they know it or not. Groceries on Nantucket are, as a result, prohibitively expensive.

Not surprisingly, when the costs of a governmental policy are directly borne by Nantucket's year-round residents, they suddenly turn frugal. Nantucket high school students must travel off island to engage in the competitive sporting events so important to the high school experience.

The Nantucket Whalers cannot play another Massachusetts high school football team without the entire team getting on a boat or plane. Often, the team members travel to their away games by one of the twin Cessnas operated by Cape Air, the local airline. Generally, Cape Air runs its fleet on a single pilot basis and sells a ticket for the right front seat—the place a copilot would sit if there were one.

While Cape Air has a good safety record, there is at least one instance I know of where a disaster was narrowly averted by a passenger who happened to be a student pilot. The pilot lost consciousness shortly after takeoff (as I recall, he was a diabetic who had improperly failed to disclose that medical condition) and could not be revived. After a harrowing ride, the student pilot landed the twin Cessna wheels up in Provincetown, many miles from the intended destination, Hyannis. Miraculously, no one was hurt.

Some years ago, one of the Nantucket parents sought to get Cape Air to put a copilot on board the flights transporting Nantucket High School team members. Cape Air graciously offered to do so without being compensated for lost ticket revenues, but wanted reimbursement of the copilot's compensation, about $50 per flight. With 10 or more kids on each flight, this came to $5 per child—a pretty reasonably priced insurance policy. The measure got voted down.

Are the people of Nantucket so unworried about the safety of their own children that they are unwilling to spend $5 per child per flight for extra safety, yet so worried about certain species of endangered earthworms that they are willing to cause their grocery (and all other living) expenses to be driven to sky-high levels to protect the earthworms? Hardly. A more likely explanation is that Nantucketers, like many people throughout the United States, simply do not see the true costs of their governmental policies.

This inability to see the true long-term costs of governmental policies and who bears them is one of the greatest shortcomings of our political system. Although I used Nantucket as a handy example, this story repeats itself in thousands of communities throughout the United States. In fact, I daresay wherever housing is exorbitantly priced, development-thwarting regulations may be found. While affluent communities from Puget Sound to Nantucket concern themselves with recreating endangered earthworm habitats without regard to cost, I tend to doubt these lowly creatures generated as much concern among those in charge of inner city planning in the Detroit neighborhoods about to be bulldozed.

In this way local governments throughout the United States created pockets where home ownership (and for that matter housing in general) was no longer affordable. They did this by taxing home buyers and using the proceeds to buy and place undeveloped lands in permanent protected trust and by enacting a labyrinth of common-sense-defying zoning restrictions and conservation rules, many of which became powerful weapons in the hands of NIMBY neighbors or not-for-profit groups funded by NIMBY collectives.

Our federal government then came to the rescue—governmental Munchausen by proxy—via the forced lending to low down payment buyers (the Community Reinvestment Act) and explicit quotas on Fannie and Freddie buying low down payment mortgages. Local government created the affordability crisis—the disease—and our federal government came to the rescue with the cure—subprime mortgage loans. Unfortunately, the cure turned out to be far worse than the disease.

This analysis raises a critical threshold question—should government concern itself (at all) with the form of ownership of its citizen's housing? Said differently, is not government's role ensuring the decency and quality of housing and not whether it is owned by the housed citizen or the landlord? Governments have a place making sure citizens' housing accommodations are safe, heated, perhaps air conditioned in some areas, and free of vermin and pests, but why should our government concern itself with a citizen's decision whether to own or rent housing?

IT'S NOT AS GOOD AS IT SEEMS

In the end, home ownership is not all it's cracked up to be. It often consumes the family stretching to afford home ownership, and as result forces too much of the family's resources into the cost of housing and leaves too little of the resources left to pay for other important things like educating children and saving for retirement.

If the goal is to make sure our citizens benefit from building up wealth through home equity appreciation, boy, did that policy backfire. The governmental responsibility for safe and sound housing, of course, rests squarely on the true sovereigns, the states, and not with the federal government, which had no business sticking its nose in the housing tent to begin with.

CHAPTER 12

Governmental Reactions to the Housing Crisis

The Obama administration's efforts to combat the housing crisis have been worse than miserable failures. They have only compounded the crisis, as the White House insists on printing more subprime paper. The administration's efforts at financial reform are really nothing more than a power grab and do little to mitigate the risks of a repeat crisis. In order to get reform passed without even mentioning the real culprits, Fannie and Freddie, Obama waged and won a propaganda war against business.

Obama's out-of-control spending has brought our publicly held national debt from $5.4 trillion on August 1, 2008 to $8.8 trillion on August 1, 2010. This amounts to $1 trillion of public debt accumulated every seven months—an impossibly insurmountable debt tragedy, which threatens all Americans. (Almost all the TARP funds advanced in the waning days of the Bush administration have been repaid, so this explosion of public debt is entirely on Obama.)

The Obama administration's multiple past attempts to fix housing have been frighteningly expensive failures. First, through his Home Affordable Modification Program (HAMP), Obama tried to pay both delinquent homeowners and their banks to modify defaulted loans—an attempt to stop foreclosures (and the resulting resetting of housing prices). It failed.

Next—call it HAMP 2.0—Obama tried to pay the banks holding second mortgages—the piggyback home equity lines—thinking they were getting in the way of the modifications. That failed too. He attacked the demand side of the equation as well, hoping to stimulate buying—only at the lower end, of course—in an apparent realization that his attempts to stop foreclosures would not work.

Through the First Time Home Buyer's tax credit, we ended up paying $8,000 apiece to 1.5 million people who would have bought homes anyway, borrowing sales from the future, inviting billions in taxpayer fraud, and chasing out of the market middle and upper price bracket buyers who waited in the wings astutely fearful of a double dip in housing prices once the unsustainable government supports fell away.

It all failed. We got less than 10 percent of the 4 million modifications Obama promised us; handouts to first-time homebuyers resulted in billions of dollars being paid to those who would have eventually bought houses anyway; and foreclosures, while delayed, continued to stack up in the legal pipeline. Housing prices will remain flat for years, or worse, double dip in foreclosure-rich regions, as the foreclosed homes finally hit the market.

Meanwhile, to stimulate demand for purchases and refinancings, we've pumped $1.4 trillion into the mortgage market, taking rates to the lowest level in decades. Yet neither has occurred in a meaningful way: Middle- and upper-market buyers continue to wait in the wings for the bottom that has yet to come, while overleveraged homeowners found themselves unable to refinance.

In Obama's latest effort to help housing—call it ObamaHome 5.0— instead of subsidizing delinquent homeowners, this program benefits homeowners who are underwater on their mortgages but continue to pay.

Obama will subsidize upper-income homeowners (owing mortgage balances up to $729,750) by paying their banks if they reduce the principal balance to 97.5 percent of the home's value and payments to "affordable" levels—31 percent of the homeowners' income. For homeowners who owe second-mortgage loans, the balance need only be reduced to 115 percent of the home's value. Obama will pay billions of taxpayer dollars to the principal-forgiving banks from 10 to 21 cents per dollar of principal forgiven, depending upon the overall percentage of principal forgiven.

Even so, banks would never take the principal hit, unless they were getting cashed out on the unforgiven principal balance. After all, the redefault rate on Obama's prior modifications has been abysmal. And the amounts at stake are huge: One in four homeowners is underwater— around $2.75 trillion of loans.

So the administration declared that the Federal Housing Administration (FHA) would insure refinancings of qualifying underwater loans. Where first and second mortgages are reduced to 115 percent of the home's value, Obama will use additional TARP money to insure the portion of the reduced principal balance exceeding the 97.5 percent HFA limit.

Mind you, the FHA is now insuring 30 percent of all home mortgages, up from just over 3 percent in 2005. Plus, it's running at one-quarter of the required minimum capital reserves, before taking into account the additional loans insured under this new program. Lenders will see seize the one-time chance to shed their riskiest nondelinquent mortgages by laying them off on the taxpayers. It's a bailout of lenders who've refused to do short sales or work things out with borrowers.

And it will never end up costing the taxpayer only the incentives paid up front to get those lenders to reduce principal balances. The real bill will come down the road when the HFA-insured refinancings default, and the homes are foreclosed and sold for less than the new loan balance. And it still can't stop home prices from falling.

In normal times, 15 million homes would turn over during the three-year period 2010 to 2012. But the market will also have to absorb likely another 10 million foreclosed homes over the same period—which means we need to draw in two new buyers for every three we would normally have to find. Only a price drop will attract those additional buyers.

All Obama's efforts can't stop this inevitable free-market adjustment; at best, he'll delay it—at the price of shifting the risk of hundreds of billions in losses on underwater loans from lenders to taxpayers.

Maybe he sees that as a worthwhile price for kicking the can down the road. (With elections coming up in November, 2010, maybe that's the plan.) But it's not worth it for the rest of us. The sooner we take the pain, the better off we'll be.

FEDERAL SUBSIDY OF HOUSING MARKET BENEFITS YIELD-HUNGRY INVESTORS

Mortgage rates hit new lows just before the July 4, 2010, holiday weekend as investors gobbled up residential mortgage-backed securities—the very financial instruments that triggered the subprime mortgage crisis.

Some see this as a boom for consumers—many cash-strapped home-owners will be able to refinance and lower their monthly interest payments— and as much-needed support for the beleaguered U.S. housing market, the recovery of which has stalled and may even double dip.

But what the mini-boom in mortgage refinancing really represents is a ticking time bomb—one that will soon blow up in the face of the taxpayers. Until April 1, 2010, the Fed made massive purchases of residential mortgage-backed securities (RMBS). The central bankers claimed that absent their support—they accumulated $1.25 trillion worth of RMBS—there would be no mortgage market, and without a mortgage market, housing could not recover.

But when the Fed stopped buying MBS, a funny thing happened. Investors jumped into the RMBS market with both feet. Why are investors flocking to MBS, the very investment that spawned the great recession? Are they convinced the U.S. housing market has really bottomed?

Hardly. Given the European debt crisis and worldwide investor sentiment that risk levels are too high, investors see RMBS as an opportunity to earn more than they could on Treasury bonds without taking on any additional risk given the U.S. guarantee of all mortgages. That's because, between Fannie Mae, Freddie Mac, and the mortgage insurance issued by the Federal Housing Administration, the United States presently guarantees or insures virtually every mortgage loan being made—about 97 percent of all mortgages.

Because the United States is backing all mortgages, rates have been dropping as investors compete to purchase MBS, which offer higher rates than comparable treasury bonds. Mortgage rates—on Friday, July 2, 2010, 4.58 percent for a 30-year fixed loan—were low enough to induce homeowners to refinance, but high enough to attract risk-averse investors who would otherwise buy 30-year Treasury bonds—they were yielding only 3.94 percent that day.

But what will happen if the U.S. housing market double dips? Many of the mortgage loans backed by the United States have razor-thin equity cushions. The FHA has been insuring loans with as little as 3.5 percent down. That means that if the housing market falls just another 4 percent, the homeowners of new FHA-insured loans will be "underwater"— their loan balances will exceed what they owe.

One thing the bursting of the housing bubble has taught us is that many homeowners who are underwater on their mortgage loans eventually default. This is especially so in the United States because several states have "nonrecourse" laws, which prevent a bank from pursuing the homeowner for any shortfall following a foreclosure sale.

As investors compete to purchase MBS and rates are driven lower and lower, it pays for more and more homeowners to refinance—for example, a homeowner with a rate of 5 percent might not refinance when rates are 4.75 percent but would refinance if rates drop to 4.25 percent.

Recently, all U.S. mortgages totaled $10.7 trillion, and more than half of them—$5.5 trillion worth—are presently backed by the federal government. But with rates dropping the way they are, and the United States backing virtually all mortgage loans, the $5.2 trillion segment of the mortgage market currently not backed by the United States is bound to go down, and the $5.5 trillion segment currently backed by the United States is bound to go up.

And the government backing of the mortgage market will not stop the inevitable correction to home prices commanded by market forces—it only delays the price corrections we must put behind us for the housing market to begin healing in earnest. Because so many foreclosed homes are being listed for sale, existing home sales plunged 30 percent in May 2010, while new home sales fell 33 percent that month.

Canada's housing market, on the other hand, is already well on the road to recovery. That's because Canada does not have Fannie or Freddie;

it does not protect defaulting homeowners from being sued by banks for deficiencies; its banks, for the most part, hold onto rather than securitize their mortgage loans; and its tax code does not encourage its citizens to take on excessive mortgage debt by making mortgage interest tax deductible.

As of July 2, 2010, U.S. taxpayers have bailed out Fannie and Freddie to the tune of $148 billion. The Congressional Budget Office recently increased its estimate of what the mortgage giants will cost the taxpayers to $389 billion, but I put the eventual cost at closer to $1 trillion.

The FHA will never be able to make good on all the guaranteed mortgages that eventually go into default. The FHA's reserves are at half of 1 percent of all insured mortgages, and 4.2 percent of FHA-insured mortgages are seriously delinquent within one year, while its up-front insurance premium is 2.25 percent.

But this hidden federal subsidy only helps yield-hungry investors, often foreign banks and sovereign wealth funds—they earn 15 to 20 percent more by buying MBS instead of Treasury bonds—and bails out existing mortgage lenders in advance of future mortgage defaults by paying them off with U.S.-backed refinancings.

While MBS investors and existing mortgage lenders are being helped by this unbudgeted federal largesse, the taxpayers will end up with nothing but a massive tax bill over and above the one they will get stuck with anyway, to fund the deficit spending disclosed in President Obama's budget.

THE SEC SUIT AGAINST GOLDMAN SACHS

On Friday, April 16, 2010, the Securities and Exchange Commission filed suit against Goldman Sachs based on its role in marketing a collateralized debt obligation (CDO) called ABACUS 2007-AC1, formed in early 2007. Goldman created ABACUS to buy and hold about $1 billion worth of credit default swaps relating to a specified group of residential mortgage-backed securities. Even though the swaps were synthetic—neither side would actually own the portfolio of referenced RMBS—if those RMBS remained in good standing with the rating agencies, Goldman, the issuer of the swaps, would be required to make large payments to the ABACUS equity investors.

Like a sports bookmaker who needs to match up opposing bettors on a football game, Goldman had to secure the other side to the credit default swap—an investor willing to risk a billion dollars on the ABACUS RMBS going into default quickly. Texas billionaire John Paulson's hedge fund, which had for some time been placing, up until then, losing bearish bets against the housing market, took that side of the ABACUS credit default swaps.

The SEC said that ABACUS had two equity investors—ACA Management, the "portfolio selection agent," and IKB Deutsche Industriebank, a German bank. ACA invested or insured $951 million worth of the ABACUS RMBS and IKB invested $150 million. Paulson risked about the same amount—$1 billion—taking the opposite side by betting the specified RMBS would be downgraded by the raters. All three investors were highly sophisticated players in the RMBS space.

The SEC alleged that Goldman allowed Paulson to participate in the selection of the RMBS and that ACA and IKB did not know Paulson was betting on the bear side. But synthetic securities must have both a short and long side. ACA had to know.

The SEC expressed that Paulson came to Goldman first. So what? This is no more eyebrow-raising than saying that a Las Vegas bookmaker took a million-dollar Super Bowl bet from a Saints fan before he was able to lay off the other side of that bet to a gambler willing to bet on the Colts.

The SEC said Goldman allowed Paulson to participate in the selection of the RMBS. But ACA had the final say. In any event, this is no more alarming than saying that a bookmaker discussed the "spread" with the two opposing big bettors before setting it. If either gambler thought that the spread was unfair to him, then he would not place his bet, and without his bet, the bookmaker can't take the other gambler's bet.

On the only real question—whether Goldman misled ACA and IKB about which way Paulson was betting—the SEC allegations were weak and watery.

In an e-mail sent by ACA to Goldman, ACA said: "We didn't know exactly how they [Paulson] want to participate in the space. Can you get us some feedback?" So what? Couldn't that mean that ACA did not know the precise credit default swap terms on which Paulson wanted to place its bear bet?

Goldman employee Fabrice Tourre, also an SEC defendant, sent ACA an e-mail calling Paulson a "Transaction Sponsor" and saying it was taking a "pre-committed first loss" position. Isn't it possible that these terms could describe Paulson's bear bet?

ACA sent an e-mail to Goldman saying: "I can understand Paulson's *equity perspective* but for us to put our name on something, we have to be sure it enhances our reputation" (emphasis mine). Couldn't that have been a reference to Paulson's view that ACA, by selecting only high-quality RMBS, was being too favorable to equity—to ACA's own long position? And that unless the RMBS reference portfolio included a fair sampling of more aggressively underwritten loans, Paulson would not commit to the bear side, and there would be no deal?

The SEC said Paulson drove the selection of the RMBS, but the specific allegations say that ACA selected the RMBS out of a list given to ACA by Paulson and even added some mortgage-backed securities not on Paulson's list.

ACA asked, "Did [Paulson] give a reason why they kicked out all the Wells [Fargo] deals?" Wells was regarded as a stronger underwriter with less risky mortgages backing its private-label RMBS. If, as the SEC said, Goldman told ACA and IKB that Paulson was investing on the same side as they were, wouldn't Paulson's removing all Wells Fargo's less risky mortgages have tipped off ACA and IKB that Paulson was on the bear side of the swaps?

Goldman would not go through with the ABACUS deal unless ACA not only insured against defaults in the ABACUS RMBS reference portfolio, but insisted that ACA secure a major bank to back ACA up. Major European bank ABN Amro agreed to serve in this role and ultimately paid Goldman $840 million. It is laughable to suggest, as the SEC did, that ABN Amro did not independently scrutinize the ABACUS portfolio before committing itself to an $840 billion exposure.

Goldman claimed it lost $90 million on ABACUS (even after ABN Amro's $840 million payoff on the ACA credit insurance)—$75 million more than the $15 million in fees Goldman made. This means Goldman participated as an equity investor in ABACUS alongside ACA (and ABN Amro) and IKB.

In January 2007, betting on a housing crash was a contrarian view. With Goldman having invested on the equity side of ABACUS, and a major bank like ABN Amro having issued credit insurance after scrutinizing the selected portfolio, the SEC would have had a real uphill battle proving Goldman intentionally structured ABACUS as a losing investment, had Goldman not later elected to settle with SEC for $550 million—a decision undoubtedly driven by Goldman's desire to avoid further reputational damage.

The SEC suit did not charge Goldman with criminal fraud—only civil fraud. The SEC knew its case was far too weak to support a criminal fraud charge. The evidentiary standard for making a civil fraud charge stick is much lower.

The timing of the SEC lawsuit—in the midst of the debate on financial regulatory overhaul—speaks volumes. To get Senator Dodd's proposed bill passed—long before the Financial Crisis Inquiry Commission's findings were published and without so much as mentioning Fannie and Freddie—Obama needed to wage and win a propaganda war. It was necessary that he convince Americans that Wall Street, not Washington, was to blame for the financial crisis.

Goldman formed ABACUS in early 2007, and neither AKA nor IKB complained to the SEC, so far as I know. Harry Markopolos spent 10 years trying to convince the SEC to investigate Bernie Madoff, to no avail. After cooperating with the SEC since this investigation began in 2008, Goldman was blindsided by these charges with no substantive effort to resolve the matter through settlement. That's because propaganda value, not redress for alleged securities violations, was the government's goal.

The SEC complaint read like a press release. Where both procedural rules and litigation strategy call for a civil plaintiff merely to notify the defendant of the nature of the allegations being made, specific items of evidence—in commercial litigation, frequently e-mails—are left for trial. Other e-mails may be uncovered during the discovery phase and innocent explanations may be preferred by the defendants for seemingly damaging correspondence.

No experienced lawyer ever would have committed to laying bare all his or her proof in the first salvo—unless, of course, the idea was to try the case in the press and not a court of law. Here, the SEC not only laid bare their trial proof in their complaint, they offered the legally superfluous allegation that Goldman "contributed to the recent financial crisis by magnifying losses associated with the downturn in the United States housing market," and included embarrassing quotes from then 29-year-old Goldman employee Fabrice Tourre, the self-described "Fabulous Fab"—precisely because they knew that superfluous allegation and those quotes would bury Goldman in the court of public opinion.

Democrats had a field day with the SEC suit. Vermont's socialist Senator Bernie Sanders said: "I applaud the SEC. . . . the illegal behavior of major Wall Street firms . . . helped cause the worst recession since the 1930s." Dodd, anticipating a possible SEC failure in its effort to hold Goldman liable even civilly, said: "We don't need to know the outcome of this case to know that the opaque nature of unregulated asset-backed securities fueled the financial crisis."

Obama, Dodd, Frank, and other left-wing Democrats leading the charge for regulatory overhaul of the financial sector knew it would not matter whether the SEC ultimately lost its suit against Goldman. The wheels of justice grind slowly. Long before the SEC suit's outcome could be known, regulatory reform—including the federal government's right to dismember financial institutions—became law.

To deflect criticism of the government's role in the financial crisis, Obama paid Google, so that, the day the suit was filed, when Americans searched "Goldman Sachs SEC," Obama's head shot filled their screens and a message appeared saying: "There's too little accountability on Wall Street and too little protection for Main Street. It's time for real change."

Shortly after the SEC filed its suit, we learned that the Paulson trader responsible for the ABACUS deal, Paolo Pellegrini, told the SEC point blank that he had met with ACA and told ACA that Paulson was taking the bear side. In a letter to his investors sent after the SEC filed suit, John Paulson said he did not originate or structure the ABACUS transaction, and that he did not have the final say over the portfolio composition. Just days after its filing, the SEC case began unraveling. But it nevertheless paid for Goldman to settle—when you're fighting a propaganda war, the merits are not so important.

I am not suggesting that Goldman is innocent of all wrongs. Nor am I saying there should be no financial reform—targeted reform like making derivatives trade through a clearinghouse, limiting bank leverage, opening up the government-sponsored oligarchy on rating agencies, and requiring mortgage securitizers to keep skin in the game—are indicated.

But neither Goldman nor Wall Street at large is guilty of *causing* the financial crisis. At worst, they intensified and spread a government-spawned contagion by securitizing and distributing risky subprime and Alt-A mortgages commanded by Congress and past administrations.

The SEC suit will galvanize the plaintiffs' class action bar and unleash a flood of strike suits against Goldman and other investment bankers when we can least afford it. Reputational damage alone will drag down Goldman and others in the financial sector. Goldman cannot brush off its missteps, even if they are only perceived, as easily as politicians like Frank and Dodd. Washington is far more forgiving than Wall Street. Imagine what Dodd would say if Blankfein got caught taking multiple below market rate interest loans from one of the lenders whose mortgages Goldman securitized?

Like it or not, we need the investment banking community to get capital where it needs to go in order to grow businesses and create jobs. Even Obama needs Wall Street. Running a deficit triple anything ever before seen requires Wall Street to place U.S. debt and keep us afloat. Obama is Wall Street's biggest customer—he is making them rich by lending to them at zero and borrowing back the same money at long-term Treasury rates.

For Obama, "change" requires that he wage and win a propaganda war against business, even if doing so risks our fragile economic recovery and risks the funding of his own out-of-control deficit spending. That war will have its casualties. Unfortunately those casualties will not be limited to Wall Street investment bankers—they will include millions of hard-working Americans.

Following on the heels of the SEC suit against Goldman, Senator Carl Levin, chairman of the Permanent Subcommittee on Investigations, convened his televised Goldman hearing. The senator betrayed a shocking level of financial and economic illiteracy in the Goldman hearing, and worse, made clear that Democrats are waging a war not just against Goldman Sachs or Wall Street, but against free-market capitalism.

The subcommittee senators showed that they do not understand the fundamental distinction between a market maker—someone who makes a market in a given security by selling that security to investors whose purpose is to take on risk in the hopes of being compensated for doing so—and an investment advisor—someone who advises an investor on whether or not to take on investment risk. *Customers* of market makers should not and do not care about the long or short positions of the market maker. *Clients* of investment advisors should and do care about what their advisor thinks.

Another thing Senator Levin does not understand is that markets speak. They convey information through the prices they set. The prices set by a free-market economy replace (for free) the tens of thousands of central planners otherwise needed in a socialist system and do a far better job to boot.

The equity markets spoke loudly the day of the hearing, when they proclaimed that the SEC's case against Goldman was a loser. The very day that the senator grilled Goldman executives for 10 hours was a terrible day for equities. The DOW sold off 213.65 points. Of all the financial companies included in the S&P 500, every single one traded lower that day, save one—Goldman. However, days later the Department of Justice announced it was opening a criminal investigation concerning Goldman's trading activities and Goldman stock sunk.

Markets speak too when credit default swap spreads widen. That says defaults may soon happen. CDS are the smoke detectors of our financial system. Eliminating smoke detectors is not a good strategy for stopping fires. In all likelihood, CDS dampened what would otherwise have been an even worse financial crisis.

In 1989, after Ronald Reagan got the Berlin Wall torn down, the tragic failures of the Soviet central planners were exposed to the world. Following the dissolution of the Soviet Union, Russian and Chinese privatization and capitalism put hundreds of millions to work. Regrettably, much of the savings of those newly employed workers fueled and were lost in the recent financial crisis.

The timing of the SEC lawsuit—in the midst of the debate on financial regulatory overhaul—and Senator Levin's farcical Goldman hearing mark the high water mark (to date) in the construction of a "virtual Berlin Wall" designed to conceal the failure of the European-style socialism that has crept into the United States economy.

By waging a propaganda war against free-market capitalism and seeking to blame it for the unforeseen consequences of ill-advised and radical governmental market interventions, left-wing Democrats seek to blame bit players for the crisis and obfuscate its root causes.

Senator Levin railed against Goldman executives for what he said were their conflicts of interest. Was it a conflict of interest for Senator Dodd to take six undermarket mortgage loans from Countrywide's Angelo Mozilo? Was it a conflict of interest for Rahm Emanuel to stop an investigation of his own activities while on the board of Freddie Mac? Was there a regulatory failure when for 10 years the SEC refused to investigate Bernard Madoff, the protestations about his impossibly smooth returns by Madoff-tipster Harry Markopolos notwithstanding? How about the SEC's handling of the Stanford Ponzi scheme?

Where was Levin—the regulator of regulators—when those blatant conflicts of interest and regulatory failures came to light?

Levin and his minions are out to obscure, not reveal the true causes of the financial crisis. Without addressing the root cause of the financial crisis, reform is destined to be both ineffective and costly. But if your goal is a power grab—to pass "reform" not for the purpose of preventing a future crisis but strictly to accomplish a government takeover of the financial sector—it's sheer genius. As Mr. Emanuel has famously said, "never let a crisis go to waste."

WE ARE AT A CROSSROADS

Take a look at Figure 12.1. If it does not scare you, take a second look. It shows percent job losses and recoveries for all 11 of the post-WWII recessions—1948, 1953, 1958, 1960, 1969, 1974, 1980, 1981, 1990, 2001, and 2007. All 10 of the concluded recessions—in terms of job losses and recoveries—are roughly symmetrical. We lost jobs for roughly the same number of months that we gained jobs, and the decline and recovery are of roughly equal steepness. But there is a clear categorization possible—the first eight recessions are similar to one another but different from the last two (concluded) recessions, which themselves are similar to one another.

The first eight are much briefer both in the decline and recovery periods than are the two modern recessions. Of the first eight recessions, the shortest lived was nine months long (from onset to recovery in the job market), while the longest was 26 months from onset to jobs recovery. The job loss and recovery curves are steep on the decline and steep on the recovery—they are "V" shaped. The two modern recessions (leaving the current recession out)—1990 and 2001—have much flatter job loss/recovery curves. The long, flat, shallow job loss/recovery curve started with the 1990 recession (only 1.5 percent job losses but 31 months from onset to recovery) and

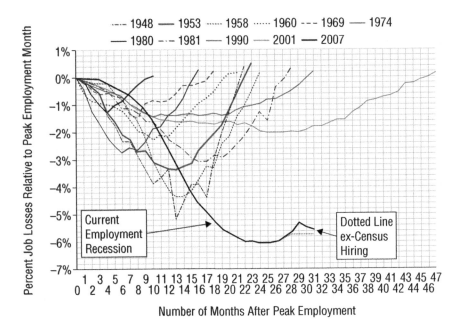

FIGURE 12.1 Percent Job Losses Relative to Peak Employment Month in Post WWII Recessions

Source: www.businessinsider.com/chart-of-the-day-percent-job-lossess-in-post -wwii-recessions-2010-8.

became undeniable in the 2001 recession, which peaked at about 2 percent job losses yet took a staggering 47 months—nearly four years—from onset until prerecession employment rates were regained.

What does this mean for the current (2007) recession and why the flattening of the percent job loss curve in the modern recessions?

Let's start by looking at the ratio of the national debt to gross domestic product ("GDP") during this same post-WWII period. As seen in Figure 12.2, national debt rose dramatically as FDR was leaving office and peaked during the Truman presidency.

This precipitous rise in our national debt undeniably resulted from the vast costs of financing our wartime efforts. At its peak in 1945, our national debt was 120 percent of our GDP. The 1948 recession was the worst recession (save possibly for the current recession—we don't know yet), with job losses peaking at more than 5 percentage points off the prerecession unemployment rate, but the lost jobs were regained quickly—in about 9 months. From 1945 to 1981—a period of three and a half decades—our national debt was on the decline, falling from 120 percent of GDP to about 35

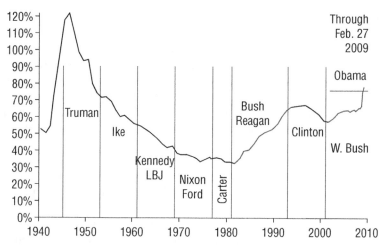

FIGURE 12.2 The National Debt as a Percent of GDP
Note: Data through 2007 is from Bush's whitehouse.gov.
Source: zFacts.com.

percent of GDP. *Thus all eight of the earlier recessions occurred during a period when national debt was falling as a percentage of GDP.*

In 1980 our national debt started to rise. With the exception of a slight dip during the Clinton terms (due to a sharply rising GDP during that period), national debt as a percentage of GDP rose from roughly 35 percent to 75 percent by the end of the Bush terms. With the two trillion of debt added by Obama in his first year alone, the national debt at the end of 2009 stood at $12.340 trillion against a 2009 GDP of roughly $14.35 trillion. Our national debt therefore stood at 86 percent of GDP.

For those who prefer to look at the publicly held portion of our national debt—reasoning that debt we owe to ourselves is not really debt at all—consider these sobering facts. Prior to the TARP funding that began with Secretary Paulson during the waning days of the Bush administration, our public debt stood at about $5.4 trillion in early August 2010. It had taken 232 years—1776 to 2008—to build up $5.4 trillion in public debt. That means we accumulated public debt an average of $1 trillion every 43 1/3 years for the first 232 years of our existence.

Between August 1, 2008 and August 1, 2010, we added an astonishing $3.4 trillion of additional public debt—by August 1, 2010, our public debt stood at $8.8 trillion. So, in the two-year period August 1, 2010 through August 1, 2010, we added public debt at the mind-numbing rate of $1 trillion every 7 months—more than 70 times our historical rate. This debt trajectory is nothing less than apocalyptic.

Our national debt, of course, follows our government spending habits—particularly our deficit spending—the more we deficit spend, the more we must go into debt to finance that spending. Thus, in periods when our national debt is falling as a percentage of GDP, the private sector—large and small businesses alike—are optimistic and invest in business expansion and opening new businesses as we begin to emerge from the recession (in terms of GDP growth, which always precedes the jobs recovery). That's why the first eight post-WWII recessions were so short-lived.

In the eight earlier recessions, the private sector invested in business expansions and openings, created jobs in the process, and in a relatively few months (at most 12), we had recovered to our prerecession employment rate. This makes sense. When business owners consider an investment, they weigh risks and rewards. The business owner alone bears all the risk. If the new business or the business expansion does not work out, the business owner's capital investment is gone. But if the business owner is successful, he or she has an ever-present partner with whom to share the profits—Uncle Sam. Thus, when faced with the *prospect* of high rates of *future* taxation, the business owner sees himself as bearing all the potential losses but keeping only a part of the potential gains. It is not so important where the marginal tax rates are at the moment. What is important is where the business owner thinks they are headed.

It is thus not surprising that when our national debt was falling, business owners were optimistic about business prospects. They figured tax rates would (hopefully) decline in the future, and that they could hold onto an increased share of their gains were they lucky enough to have them (not losses). They invested. On the other hand, during a period of rising national debt, business owners are pessimistic. They see a tax trap—no way out but raising taxes. And so they reason—why take the risk? The business owner says to himself, "If I am lucky enough to make my new business or business expansion work out, I will keep only a fraction of the profits, but if things turn south, I alone will bear the losses; better in such times to keep my money in the bank."

For the past decade, our deficit (until President Obama took office) averaged about 2 percent of GDP and never exceeded 4 percent of GDP. President Obama more than tripled the deficit in his first year of office—taking the deficit to a stunning 13 percent of the GDP, and his 2010 budget shows an even larger $1.6 trillion deficit.

But what about the neo-Keynesians—those who insist that government must spend in times of recession in order to create the private sector demand lost through the recession—that it is only through fiscal stimulus that we can recover jobs? Government spending does indeed create some *temporary* jobs, just not nearly as many as are lost through an intimidated (and crowded out) private sector afraid or unable to invest in business expansions and start-ups due to the prospect of future tax increases and fiscal uncertainty and lack of available credit.

We see the jobs created by an infrastructure project—say, the construction of a new bridge. We can drive by the bridge and see the workers with our own eyes. We see living proof that the fiscal stimulus has created jobs. What we do not see are the many more jobs never created or lost due to a pessimistic private sector—business owners who see the bridge and wonder how much of their future profits they will have to give up to pay for it. To compound matters, the jobs lost to an intimidated private sector are permanent, while the jobs gained through fiscal stimulus are only temporary. As a result, when the stimulus funds run out, we are only left with job losses and economic contraction (or more anemic growth than would have occurred absent the fiscal stimulus).

Though the debate over whether to use Keynesian stimulus or across-the-board tax cuts to stimulate job creation has raged for 80 years (thanks to political contamination of the science of economics), the jury, no objective person can deny, came in long ago. Keynesian stimulus does not work. Consider the following evidence compiled in large part by the Heritage Foundation:

- During the 1930s FDR doubled federal spending; yet unemployment remained above a punishing 20 percent for more than a decade, until WWII forced the government to abandon stimulus spending.
- Japan passed 10 stimulus bills over 8 years (building the largest national debt in the industrialized world); yet its economy remained stagnant.
- Tax rates were slashed dramatically during the 1920s, dropping from over 70 percent to less than 25 percent. What happened? GDP grew, more were employed, and personal income tax revenues increased substantially during the 1920s, despite the reduction in rates. Revenues rose from $719 million in 1921 to $1,164 million in 1928, an increase of more than 61 percent
- President Hoover dramatically increased tax rates in the 1930s and President Roosevelt compounded the damage by pushing marginal tax rates to more than 90 percent. Seeing that high tax rates were hindering the economy, President Kennedy implemented across-the-board tax rate reductions that reduced the top tax rate from more than 90 percent down to 70 percent. What happened? GDP and jobs grew and tax revenues climbed from $94 billion in 1961 to $153 billion in 1968, an increase of 62 percent (33 percent after adjusting for inflation). According to President John F. Kennedy: "Our true choice is not

between tax reduction, on the one hand, and the avoidance of large Federal deficits on the other. It is increasingly clear that no matter what party is in power, so long as our national security needs keep rising, an economy hampered by restrictive tax rates will never produce enough revenues to balance our budget just as it will never produce enough jobs or enough profits. . . . In short, it is a paradoxical truth that tax rates are too high today and tax revenues are too low and the soundest way to raise the revenues in the long run is to cut the rates now."

- Thanks to "bracket creep," the inflation of the 1970s pushed millions of taxpayers into higher tax brackets even though their inflation-adjusted incomes were not rising. To help offset this tax increase and also to improve incentives to work, save, and invest, President Reagan proposed sweeping tax rate reductions during the 1980s. What happened? GDP and jobs grew and total tax revenues climbed by 99.4 percent during the 1980s. Income tax revenues climbed dramatically, increasing by more than 54 percent by 1989 (28 percent after adjusting for inflation).

- In 2001, President Bush attempted to stimulate jobs through tax rebates (not tax reductions)—the equivalent of spending—but the economy did not respond until two years later, when he implemented across-the-board tax reductions.

- In 2009, Obama ran the greatest Keynesian experiment in history—spending a stunning $1.4 trillion in excess of Treasury receipts, yet instead of getting the 3.3 million in net jobs he promised us, we lost nearly 4 million jobs net during his first year in office (a 7.3 million job swing).

Now go back to Figure 12.1 and try to project in your mind's eye the completed shallow job loss/recovery curve (like the ones for the 1990 and 2001 recessions) based upon the first half (or part) of the 2007 recession. You run off the chart, don't you? In order to project the modern flat job loss/recovery curve out of the 2007 recession curve to date, we will need a good 60 months, maybe longer, until we recover to our prerecession employment rates.

This, regrettably, makes all the sense in the world, as business owners refuse to invest in business expansions and openings due to the tax trap lying over the horizon. The fact that "spreads" have dropped—that the interest rates investors are willing to accept has gone down—does not assure us that business investment will occur. That metric only deals with the *supply* of capital. But in addition to the supply of capital, we also are short *demand* for borrowing (because business owners have been intimidated into not investing by the prospect of rising tax rates).

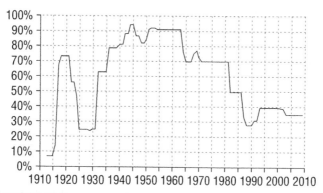

FIGURE 12.3   Marginal U.S. Tax Rates

Current marginal tax rates alone do not drive business investment, rather it is the trend or at least the perceived trend of where the rates are headed that drive investment. In times of a falling national debt (as a percentage of GDP), the business owner perceives the prospect of lower taxes in the future. This encourages investment. As Figure 12.3 demonstrates, for the same 35-year period during which our national debt as a function of GDP fell, our top marginal rates, though very high at the outset, were trending down as one would expect during a period of declining national debt. (Marginal rates did continue to trend down during the Reagan–Bush I years even as national debt rose.)

To compound matters, our profligate spending worsens federal creditworthiness and devalues the dollar. Some argue that the devalued dollar fosters domestic business expansion as it gives U.S. exporters a pricing edge against foreign competition. But this is as false an argument as Keynesian spending. Just as the lack of job creation in the private sector overtakes job creation by the government sector in times of deficit spending, so too the exportation of capital to foreign countries—which means the exportation of jobs—overtakes the minor temporary job gains from temporary rises in exports. Business owners in a time of a devaluing dollar prefer to earn their profits in non-dollar-denominated currencies (so they may repatriate their non-dollar-denominated future profits against a future devalued dollar), and so they build their plants (and buy businesses) overseas.

And, if all that were not bad enough, our entitlement programs—Social Security, Medicare, and Medicaid—independently threaten to bankrupt us. The costs of those entitlement programs, coupled with the cost of interest on our national debt, are projected to exceed 21 percent of GDP in 2075 by the Congressional Budget Office. In other words, we will one day spend as much on those entitlement programs as we spend now on all budgeted costs. Said differently, we are committed to a course of combined federal spending approaching 50 percent of GDP.

A CRUCIAL MOMENT . . .

Today, we have even more at stake than just a "super-recession"—five to six years of real double-digit unemployment rates. Today, we are faced with national debt levels that are so high, they threaten our ability to borrow from foreigners (and domestic investors), thereby threatening our ability to roll (refinance) our existing national debt (never mind financing new deficits).

Worse, the sovereign debt crisis is now upon us in Europe and at home—in the form of state insolvencies principally due to unfunded public pension plans. Greece found itself unable to finance its national debt, and Portugal and Spain are not far behind. Once those eurozone countries, loaded with socialist-style national debt, go bankrupt, the euro will crash and America (and its insolvent states) will be among the next dominoes to fall. Sooner rather than later, investors will not lend America (or its insolvent states) money.

President Obama has escalated spending to an unprecedented 24 percent of GDP. Yet historically Treasury receipts have averaged about 19 percent of GDP for over a half century (and government spending has averaged just over 20 percent). That 5 percent (of GDP) excess spending amounts to $700 billion per year. We need to lop a good trillion dollars off the Obama budget and phase down our entitlement programs to reverse course. We must live within our means. If we do, the private sector will respond with robust job creation. Americans will get back to work, and when the economy starts growing again in earnest, we can begin to work off our mountain of debt.

We are at a crucial crossroads. Either we get serious about cutting our spending—and I am not talking about "freezing" 17 percent of our budget a year from now—or we eventually will go down the tubes, like Greece. The situation is binary: cut or die. We need to get really serious about fiscal responsibility.

CHAPTER 13

Assessing Blame
for the Financial Crisis

Ignorance more frequently begets confidence than does knowledge.

—Charles Darwin

Assessing blame for the financial crisis is not as complicated as it is made out to be. Far more complex is the task of concealing the true causes and politicizing the process of fault attribution.

The financial contagion that set off the financial crisis was subprime (and Alt-A) mortgages. Trillions of dollars were loaned to homebuyers who put little or no money down on homes they purchased, and to existing homeowners who used their appreciating homes like ATM machines by taking ever larger cash-out refinancing loans. In both cases, the borrowers lacked the income and other assets necessary to repay those loans.

Given the success of the RMBS market, Wall Street began bundling up commercial real estate mortgage loans to back collateralized debt obligations. Thanks to a robust CMBS market, commercial real estate owners found themselves awash in money. Whole-loan lenders were forced to lend to second-tier commercial properties as CMBS loans pushed rates lower. Cap rates were driven to new lows and CRE prices skyrocketed. A widespread failure to appreciate risk in both residential and commercial real estate permeated the marketplace.

WHO'S TO BLAME?

In 2007, the housing bubble started to lose some air, thanks in part to synthetic CDOs, like Goldman Sach's much maligned ABACUS fund, which allowed some prescient investors to bet against the subprime mortgages, or at least hedge against their long positions. Synthetic CDOs effectively mitigated what would otherwise have been an even worse financial catastrophe.

By signaling to investors worldwide that risk levels had risen and by siphoning off the capital of long investors into synthetic instruments not involving the making of more real mortgage loans, synthetic CDOs and the credit default swaps on which they were based arrested (or at least slowed) the otherwise unchecked growth of the housing bubble. But the U.S. bubble had grown too large, too fast. The soft landing the long investors were looking for did not materialize.

While many institutions acted as enablers, facilitators, spreaders, and intensifiers of the subprime mortgage contagion, without the bad mortgage loans having been made in the first place, there would have been no housing bubble and with no bubble there would have been no crisis. Typhoid Mary would not have been a problem absent the typhoid bacterium.

The bad mortgage loans were made because congressmen, senators, and other politicians—mostly Democrats and a few Republicans[1]—commanded that they be made, and because Fannie and Freddie gave them the ability to carry out these wishes. On a policy level, the "democratization of credit"—making sure residential mortgage money found its way into the hands of the "underserved"—is the real culprit. Money must be loaned to those who can pay it back regardless of race, or where they live.

In the end, Congress imposed an outright quota compelling Fannie and Freddie to devote 50 percent of the cheap, implicitly guaranteed funds they borrowed and then spent in the secondary market on subprime and Alt A mortgage loans.

In 1992, a tiny agency known as the Office of Federal Housing Enterprise Oversight was formed to oversee Fannie and Freddie. In late 2004, Armando Falcon, Jr., the director of OFHEO, released a bombshell report charging then-Fannie CEO Franklin Raines with falsifying documents and cooking the books of Fannie in order to line his own pockets with millions in bonus money. In an April 7, 2005, article, the *Washington Post*, describing Falcon's report, said: "Fannie Mae employees falsified signatures on accounting transactions that helped the company meet earnings targets for 1998, a 'manipulation' that triggered multimillion-dollar bonuses for top executives. . . . Armando Falcon Jr., director of the Office of Federal Housing Enterprise Oversight, said the entries were related to the movement of $200 million in expenses from 1998 to later periods."

In a 2004 House hearing held after Falcon leveled his charges, Falcon and a handful of brave Republican congressmen—Ed Royce (R-CA), Chris

Shays (R-CT), and Richard Baker (R-LA)—were shouted down and vilified by Democratic congressmen, who insisted that neither Fannie nor Freddie had done anything wrong and that they must be allowed to continue their good work of democratizing credit.

In a stunning display of either ignorance or deceit—take your pick—then-Fannie CEO Franklin Raines described the mortgages (and RMBS) Fannie bought as "riskless," arguing that unlike other banks and other financial companies, there was no need to regulate Fannie or to compel it to hold significant capital reserves against future losses. In an equally stunning display of racism, one African American congressman, Lacy Clay, accused Falcon (a white man) of engaging in a "political lynching" of Raines (also an African American).

Here are some excerpts from that 2004 House hearing.[2] Note: I have put my comments to each congressperson's comments in italics below their statements.

Congresswoman Maxine Waters (D-CA): "Through nearly a dozen hearings where, frankly, we were trying to fix something that wasn't broke, Mr. Chairman, we do not have a crisis at Freddie Mac, and particularly at Fannie Mae, under the outstanding leadership of Mr. Frank Raines."

My Response: Congress was trying to "fix something that was not broke [sic]"? Imagine the financial devastation that would have been averted had Congressman Waters allowed Falcon to do his job.

Congressman Gregory Meeks (D-NY):[3] "As well as the fact that I'm just pissed off at OFHEO, because if it wasn't for you, I don't think that we'd be here in the first place, and now the problem that we have and that we're faced with is: maybe some individuals who wanted to do away with GSEs in the first place, you've given them an excuse to try to have this forum so that we can talk about it and maybe change the, uh, the direction and the mission of what the GSEs had, which they've done a tremendous job. There's been nothing that was indicated that's wrong, you know, with Fannie Mae! Freddie Mac has come up on its own. And the question that then presents is the competence that—that—that—that your agency uh, uh, with reference to, uh, uh, deciding and regulating these GSEs. Uh, and so, uh, I wish I could sit here and say that I'm not upset with you, but I am very upset because, you know, what you do is give—you know, maybe giving any reason to, as Mr. Gonzales said, to give someone a heart surgery when they really don't need it."

My Response: Falcon was trying to "change the direction and mission" of the GSEs? Really, I thought he was just doing his job as a regulator and reporting a financial fraud by Raines. Imagine what Congressman Meeks would have said if the man Falcon had accused of wrongdoing had been the head of Goldman Sachs instead of a GSE executives giving away mortgage money to minority borrowers.

Congressman Lacy Clay (D-MO): "This hearing is about the political lynching of Franklin Raines."

My Response: A white regulator reports a fraud by a black CEO and that makes OFHEO's report a "political lynching"? What a disgrace. Clay should have been thrown out of office for that brazenly racist remark.

Congressman Ed Royce (R-CA): "There is a very simple solution. Congress must create a new regulator with powers at least equal to those of other financial regulators, such as the OCC or Federal Reserve."

Congressman Chris Shays (R-CT): "And you have about 3 percent of your portfolio set aside. If a bank gets below 4 percent, they are in deep trouble. So I just want you to explain to me why I shouldn't be satisfied with 3 percent?"

Raines: "Because banks don't—there aren't any banks who only have multifamily and single-family loans. These assets are so riskless that their capital for holding them should be under 2 percent."

My Response: Thanks to his cooking Fannie's books, Raines was able to pay himself over $91 million from 1998 to 2004. His share of the settlement paid out on a civil lawsuit over the frauds he presided over while at Fannie Mae was less than $25 million. That means Raines netted $66 million for seven years of employment. That's over $9 million per year for buying "riskless" securities with taxpayer-guaranteed money. Not bad work if you can get it. Raines was contacted, according to a July 16, 2008, Washington Post article, by President Obama for advice on housing.

And from an earlier Senate Banking Committee hearing held on Oct. 16, 2003:

Senator Charles Schumer (D-NY): "And my worry is that we're using the recent safety and soundness concerns, particularly with Freddie, and with a poor regulator, as a straw man to curtail Fannie and Freddie's mission. And I don't think there is any doubt that there are some in the administration who don't believe in Fannie and Freddie altogether, say let the private sector do it. That would be sort of an ideological position."

My Response: Senator Schumer is another mission protector. "Safety and soundness concerns" were being used as excuses by heartless Republicans ("some in the administration") to stop the good work of Fannie and Freddie. Falcon was a "poor regulator" and hence his report should be disregarded. It would be nice if New York's senior senator admitted he was wrong and that Congress and Fannie and Freddie were the principal causes of the financial crisis. Maybe then financial reform would include some mention of Fannie and Freddie.

Raines: But more importantly, banks are in a far more risky business than we are.

My Response: There we go again. Raines was in a risk-free line of work. The banks were not. Go after them.

And from a Senate Banking Committee hearing held on Feb. 24–25, 2004:

Senator Thomas Carper (D-DEL): "What is the wrong that we're trying to right here? What is the potential harm that we're trying to avert?"

My Response: What wrong were we trying to right? Umm, how about sparing the world a global financial crisis and saving the taxpayers trillions of dollars?

Federal Reserve Chairman Alan Greenspan: "Well, I think that that is a very good question, senator. What we're trying to avert is we have in our financial system right now two very large and growing financial institutions which are very effective and are essentially capable of gaining market shares in a very major market to a large extent as a consequence of what is perceived to be a subsidy that prevents the markets from adjusting appropriately, prevents competition and the normal adjustment processes that we see on a day-by-day basis from functioning in a way that creates stability. . . . And so what we have is a structure here in which a very rapidly growing organization, holding assets and financing them by subsidized debt, is growing in a manner which really does not in and of itself contribute to either home ownership or necessarily liquidity or other aspects of the financial markets. . . ."

My Response: So it wasn't that Greenspan didn't see the housing bubble, it's really just that there's simply no way for the average human being to ever understand what the man is saying.

Senator Richard Shelby (R-AL): "[T]he federal government has [an] ambiguous relationship with the GSEs. And how do we actually get rid of that ambiguity is a complicated, tricky thing. I don't know how we do it. . . . I mean, you've alluded to it a little bit, but how do we define the relationship? It's important, is it not?"

Greenspan: "Yes. Of all the issues that have been discussed today, I think that is the most difficult one. Because you cannot have, in a rational government or a rational society, two fundamentally different views as to what will happen under a certain event. Because it invites crisis, and it invites instability."

My Response: Still not sure what he is saying, but he did say "instability," so it sounds as if he was issuing a warning.

Sen. Christopher Dodd (D-Conn): "I just briefly will say, Mr. Chairman, obviously, like most of us here, this is one of the great success stories of all time. And we don't want to lose sight of that and [what] has been pointed out by all of our witnesses here, obviously, the 70 percent of Americans who own their own homes today, in no small measure, due because of the work that's been done here. And that shouldn't be lost in this debate and discussion."

My Response: That's right, Mr. Dodd, Fannie and Freddie's role in the "debate and discussion" should not be "lost." And yes, you and other liberals used Fannie and Freddie to drive U.S. homeownership rates to an impossibly high near 70 percent level in late 2005. My question is: How come Dodd "lost" sight of the role of the GSEs in the "debate and the discussion" about financial reform when he proposed his financial reform bill, which somehow forgot to mention them?

And from a Senate Banking Committee hearing, held on April 6, 2005:

Senator Schumer: "I'll lay my marker down right now, Mr. Chairman. I think Fannie and Freddie need some changes, but I don't think they need dramatic restructuring in terms of their mission, in terms of their role in the secondary mortgage market, et cetera. Change some of the accounting and regulatory issues, yes, but don't undo Fannie and Freddie."

My Response: Unfortunately, Senator Schumer, the "marker" you laid down was that of the American taxpayers.

And from a Senate Banking Committee hearing held on June 15, 2006:

Schumer: "I think a lot of people are being opportunistic, . . . throwing out the baby with the bathwater, saying, 'Let's dramatically restructure Fannie and Freddie,' when that is not what's called for as a result of what's happened here."

My Response: Only a member of the liberal left could describe trying to spare the world a global financial crisis and saving American taxpayers trillions of dollars as "opportunistic."

Senator Chuck Hagel (R-Neb.): "Mr. Chairman, what we're dealing with is an astounding failure of management and board responsibility, driven clearly by self interest and greed. And when we reference this issue in the context of—the best we can say is, 'It's no Enron.' Now, that's a hell of a high standard."

And finally, the whopper of all time from the one and only Barney Frank on September 25, 2003:

Barney Frank: "I do think I do not want the same kind of focus on safety and soundness that we have in OCC [Office of the Comptroller of the Currency] and OTS [Office of Thrift Supervision]. I want to roll the dice a little bit more in this situation towards subsidized housing." And in July 2008, just two months before then Secretary of the Treasury Henry Paulson seized Fannie and Freddie due to their imminent insolvency, Frank said "they are fundamentally sound, not in danger of going under."

My Response: You rolled the dice Mr. Frank, and the taxpayers lost.

WALL STREET

Given the cheap subsidized rates at which the GSEs could borrow the trillions of dollars they spent in the secondary mortgage markets, and given the congressionally mandated quota compelling them to spend that money buying subprime mortgage loans, it is no wonder that Wall Street investment banks responded by securitizing the very subprime loans Congress (through its control of the GSEs) demanded. It is likewise no wonder that loan originators responded to the demands of the Wall Street securitizers by originating those same subprime loans.

In this way Wall Street facilitated and enabled the subprime mortgage crises. But in the end Wall Street and the banks did what Congress through the GSEs paid them to do—originate, bundle up, and securitize subprime mortgage loans. The democratization of mortgage credit was in full swing.

There is no question that Wall Street and the loan originators were guilty of underwriting some frauds and shortcuts. Though it is no excuse, it is fair to say that Wall Street and the banks were part of a feeding frenzy set off by the GSEs, who chummed the financial waters acting under a congressional mandate. Had they been required to retain risk on the loans they originated and securitized, the crisis would have been far less severe.

But what about private-label residential mortgage-backed securities? In 2007 much of the private-label RMBS—the RMBS not backed by the GSEs—were nonetheless bought up by Fannie and Freddie in the secondary market. During this time period, private-label RMBS represented 56 percent of Fannie's RMBS book and 54 percent of Freddie's RMBS book.[4] In this way, the GSEs drove the home mortgage market—either directly in the case of agency-backed RMBS or indirectly through their purchases of private-label RMBS. In consequence, there is simply no way to deny that the financial crisis was the direct and proximate result of the acts of an economically illiterate and irresponsible Congress and the GSEs Congress controlled.

THE FED, THE RATERS, AND THE APPRAISERS

Besides the GSEs, Wall Street, and the mortgage originators, the Greenspan Fed deserves some of the blame, as it was Greenspan's monetary policies that created the liquidity without which the housing bubble would not have grown so large. But really, how far can we blame Greenspan? He printed the money but he did not lend it out to bad credits—Congress and the GSEs did (or they supplied the demand for such loans in the secondary market, which amounts to the same thing). Mr. Greenspan cautioned Congress about Fannie and Freddie, but his warnings went either unheeded or not understood. At worst, his crime was in not seeing and stopping the bubble at an earlier stage. Said differently, Greenspan's real crime is having done less to save us from the incompetence of Congress.

Other culprits who have escaped relatively unscathed are the rating agencies—Moody's, Standard & Poor's, and Fitch Ratings. The federally protected cartel of raters was slow to downgrade subprime RMBS, but when the ship was sinking, mass downgrades swiftly occurred. This is how Paulson and Company made a quick billion on Goldman Sach's now infamous ABACUS synthetic CDO.

Also, real estate appraisers, controlled by mortgage lenders, were complicit in giving overly optimistic appraisals, justifying the supposed safety of mortgage loans to be securitized.

THE MAINSTREAM MEDIA

As long as we are giving credit where credit is due, let us not forget that the mainstream liberal media played an Oscar-worthy supporting role in the financial crisis. Without the propaganda campaign waged by the liberal mainstream media, the public would have better understood congressional fault in the crisis, and lawmakers would have lost their political will to continue on the path of financial destruction at an earlier time.

A Google search at the time of the writing of this book for "financial crisis and Wall Street" yielded 7,420,000 returns in .23 seconds. Conversely, a Google search for "financial crisis and Fannie or Freddie" yielded 720,000 returns—about one-tenth as many. That's a pretty odd result given that GSEs are primarily responsible for the crisis, but entirely consistent with the absurd notion that Senator Dodd's financial reform bill nowhere even mentions the GSEs.

To take just one example of how blatantly one-sided (and wrong) the liberal mainstream media are about the financial crisis, its causes and effects, consider the case of Faisal Shahzad, the bungling Pakistani-born Times Square dud-building bomber. Did you know that he was just a poor victim of a JP Morgan Chase foreclosure?

In a CNN segment aired in the wake of Shahzad's bungled terrorist attack, anchor Jim Acosta said: "If it can be confirmed that his house has been foreclosed in recent years. I mean, one would have to imagine that brought a lot of pressure and a lot of heartache on that family." CNN co-host Kiran Chetry followed by remarking: "Yeah, she said July of 2009 they left and then shortly after that they changed the locks on the home."[5]

Lest anyone think that these insightful remarks are the independent thoughts of the anchors speaking them and not those of the media company that employs them, recall that Chetry, a former co-host of *Fox and Friends*, was released by Fox and picked up by CNN in 2007. (Also recall that these anchors read off teleprompters just like our president.)

Mainstream media's gold standard for printed liberalism, the *New York Times*, had this to say about the Shahzad-foreclosure connection: "The recession had taken a toll on [the Shahzads], I guess," [one of their wedding guests] wrote in an e-mail message [presumably to the *Times* reporter] from Pakistan. He said that their money worries became apparent in 2008 or 2009 and that Mr. Shahzad "'lost his way during the financial problems.' JPMorgan Chase has since moved to foreclose on the Shelton house, which the couple had abandoned in a hurry, leaving behind clothes and toys."

Not content to report merely the facts concerning Shahzad's financial woes, however obviously irrelevant to his acts of terrorism, the *Times* news article (this was not published as an editorial) went on to speculate about how financial stresses wreaked by heartless banks had driven Shahzad to attempted mass murder: "Mr. Shahzad, now 30, appeared to be *tracing a familiar arc* of frustration, increasing religiosity and, finally, violence" (emphasis mine).

The implication from the *Times* "news" article is clear: This regrettable and avoidable process—financial stress giving birth to terrorism—traces "a familiar arc" likely to be repeated in the future.

Washington Post blogger Ezra Klein had this to say: "The hearts of men are opaque, and motives are complex. But it's a reminder that foreclosures generate an enormous amount of misery and anxiety and depression *that can tip people into all sorts of dangerous behaviors* that don't make headlines but do ruin lives. And for all that we've done to save the financial sector, we've not done nearly enough to help struggling homeowners" (emphasis mine).[6]

It must have been a severe blow to these astute mainstream media reporters that neither Mr. Shahzad's first mortgage, held by JP Morgan Chase, nor his piggybank home equity line, held by Wachovia, had been part of the reference pool of mortgages used by Goldman Sachs in their ABACUS fund—the investment vehicle that led to the SEC's bringing civil fraud charges against the giant Wall Street investment bank in April 2010.

There was no blaming Goldman Sachs for the bungled Times Square terrorist plot. But that does not mean the liberal mainstream media could not blame the banking community for Shahzad's terrorist acts.

The subliminal mainstream media message is not hard to discern: It is critical that we conclude and pass financial reform immediately. If these banks are allowed to continue their predatory lending processes unchecked, who knows what further terrorist acts might unfold? Financial reform kills two birds with one stone. We prevent future financial panics and as an added bonus stop terrorism at its source: foreclosures.

According to the liberal mainstream media, we'll just never be financially or physically safe and secure unless and until Democrats have a firm grip over the financial sector and Fannie Mae and Freddie Mac are allowed to continue their good work democratizing credit.

Had the Shahzads only been able to refinance, Lord only knows what model citizens they might be today. (Never mind that they likely would have been able to keep up with their 30-year fixed mortgage had Mr. Shahzad not quit his job and spent his life savings running back and forth to Pakistan to attend terrorist training camp.)

But getting back to the teary-eyed context, are the taxpayers losing a few hundred billion dollars more by funding new mortgage loans to the disadvantaged really such a big price to pay for the safety of our citizens?

Maybe, with the good help of the mainstream media, President Obama will propose funding Fannie and Freddie's future financial needs out of our defense budget and get those pesky losses off the discretionary budget.

At its core, the policy that brought U.S. homeowner rates from below 50 percent prior to World War II to nearly 70 percent brought about the U.S. housing bubble. Politicians favoring the vote-getting policy used the Community Reinvestment Act to create the supply of mortgage loans necessary to push homeownership rates, and congressional control of the GSEs to create the demand via the trillions of dollars they spent in the secondary mortgage market purchasing the CRA-mandated subprime loans needed to fulfill their congressionally imposed quotas.

High home ownership rates are associated with structurally high unemployment rates. Some European countries, notably Greece, Spain, Portugal, and Ireland have home ownership rates of 80 percent or higher, along with their fiscal problems and high unemployment rates. A high homeownership rate decreases the mobility of a country's workforce, creating unnecessary frictional resistance to the labor market adapting quickly and efficiently to regional fluctuations in labor demand.

Pushing homeownership rates itself is part of a broader social agenda—wealth equalization or "economic justice." President Lyndon Johnson's building of the "Great Society" in the early 1960s was predicated on the so-called "root cause" theory, that unequal wealth distribution was the cause of most crime and most of society's ills.

In January 2010, *City Journal* contributing editor Heather MacDonald wrote in the *Wall Street Journal* that the recent recession had "undercut one of the most destructive social theories that came out of the 1960's: the idea that the root cause of crime lies in income inequality and social justice." Ms. MacDonald made the case that, because violent crime rates had dropped throughout 2009, as we were losing millions of jobs and suffering through the most severe recession since the Great Depression, the "root cause" theory had been debunked.

While some liberals will doubtless make the case that rising mortgage fraud revalidates the "root cause" theory, I would argue that the uptick in widespread mortgage fraud cases and the advent of systematic fraudulent adverse possession cases—together let's call them "housing fraud" cases—do not revalidate the "root cause" theory but rather, to the contrary, prove its antithesis.

In June 2010, U.S. Attorney General Eric Holder announced that nearly 500 arrests were made in "Operation Stolen Dream," a massive multiagency crackdown on mortgage fraud. Mortgage fraud is now rampant across the 50 states—it's occurring on a scale never before witnessed. With the help of hundreds of FBI agents, Holder brought charges against 1,215 defendants, calling it the "largest collective law enforcement effort ever brought to bear on mortgage fraud."

In a different crackdown, Florida law enforcement officials announced in June 2010 several arrests in widespread cases of "squatter-fraud" in Broward and Palm Beach counties—hundreds of fraudulent adverse possession claims were filed against vacant homes. The homeowner victims, many current on their mortgages and desperately trying either to rent or sell their homes, found that their locks had been changed and that tenants had been moved into their homes without their knowledge.

The vacant houses were rented out by individuals who, based on Florida's adverse possession law, claimed the properties had been abandoned and that they would become the legal owners by reason of their "occupancy" of the vacant homes. Adverse possession allows someone eventually to take legal ownership of property if he pays the taxes, occupies, maintains, and improves the land for a period of years—seven in Florida. The law, which dates back to sixteenth-century England, is designed to prevent abandoned properties from sitting idle without anyone paying taxes, and historically it was used mainly to reclaim abandoned farmland or settle boundary disputes, such as where a fence or building encroaches on a neighbor's land. The squatter-fraud cases are not limited to South Florida—they have been reported in other parts of Florida and elsewhere across the country.

Does the recent widespread incidence of mortgage fraud on an unprecedented national scale, and the invention of an altogether new crime—systematic fraudulent adverse possession filings—put the "root cause" theory back on track?

With half of all American "taxpayers" paying no taxes, and the U.S. government buying or insuring virtually every mortgage loan now being made, some Americans just don't see housing fraud as a crime with a victim—at least not one worth worrying about. Instead, they see it as a way of getting their "fair share" of the hundreds of billions of taxpayer funds being handed out by the federal government. So far, $148 billion of taxpayer funds have been paid to Fannie Mae and Freddie Mac, which, together with the Federal Housing Administration, are making or insuring nearly all mortgage loans now being made.

So stealing mortgage money or a vacant house mortgaged to the hilt is really just another way of getting to the bailout money. These folks believe the taxpayer funds will only end up in the hands of some less deserving bailout beneficiary absent their "intervention." And even if the perpetrators of this new brand of housing fraud think they are stealing from banks and not the taxpayers, the message coming from both our leaders and their supporters in the mainstream liberal media is clear—the bankers, not our politicians, are to blame.

That message only emboldens people to commit housing fraud. Following the arrest of one of the Florida squatters, his attorney said, "The banks are letting these properties go down the tubes. . . . Here's a guy trying to help out, and he ends up in jail."

And housing fraud is not the only problem. A *Wall Street Journal* blogger recently wrote, "Trying to rip off the TARP program is like, well, going for the collective front pocket of the nation in an attempt to pull out some change." Even tax credits (payable as checks) are fair game: According to recent data, 19,000 taxpayers who filed for the first-time homebuyer's tax credit had not bought a home, and 74,000 credit claimers were not first-time homebuyers. And we also recently learned that nearly 1,300 prison inmates, including 241 serving life sentences, stole millions of dollars from the government by fraudulently filing for first-time homebuyer's tax credits.

As if the moral hazard created by our bailout mania were not enough temptation, Robin-Hoodism against the public fisc is made even easier to rationalize given that the new American royalty—the elite members of the political class—are brazenly corrupt. Though the examples are legion, consider just these two: Former House Ways and Means Committee Chairman Charles Rangel—in charge of writing tax laws—failed to report income from renting his Caribbean villa and other sources. Senator Chris Dodd, chairman of the Senate Banking Committee—the man in charge of writing the laws that regulate our banks—got six below market mortgage loans from Countrywide Financial as part of a special VIP loan program set up by its then chairman, Angelo Mozilo, just for lawmakers.

The moral hazard presented by our bailout mania, the brazen corruption of our politicians, and the relentless propaganda war that Obama and his minions have waged against big business since he took office, form a complex of powerful behavior-altering pressures, which, as we speak, are shifting the moral tectonic plates undergirding our society. The perpetrators of housing fraud don't see themselves as committing a crime. After all, raiding the public fisc and stealing from fat cat bankers are what our leaders do every day. And our political leaders are certainly no more deserving of a handout than are the perpetrators of housing fraud.

Tellingly, many workaday folks see nothing wrong with what the housing fraud perpetrators are doing—after all, they could not pull off these legally complex crimes without a host of willing accessories: attorneys, appraisers, and title insurers in the case of mortgage fraud; locksmiths, attorneys, contractors, and renters, in the case of fraudulent adverse possession cases. Ms. MacDonald was right—the drop in violent crime rates in 2009 disproved the "root cause" theory. But she did not go nearly far enough. In fact, while income inequality and social injustice never caused any crime, our response to the theory that it did—redistributing wealth—has caused crime by providing both opportunity and motive. That is what we are seeing now.

Here is my scorecard for those at fault for the housing crisis:

Congress, past administrations, the GSEs and the liberal mainstream media:	70%
Wall Street and mortgage loan originators:	15%
Rating agencies:	10%
Greenspan fed:	5%

COMMERCIAL REAL ESTATE LOANS

Responsibility for the commercial real estate crisis must be assessed differently. There, the GSEs played a minor direct role by funding CMBS loans to the multifamily sector, and a more significant indirect role by acting as the catalysts that imploded the CRE bubble by setting off a global financial crisis. However, in the case of the CRE bubble, more fault lies with private-sector loan originators and securitizers, who underwrote risky and speculative loans, often betting on a future "repositioned property value" and deploying reserve funds to bridge the owner to that future nirvana. Rating agencies get an "assist" for the ridiculously optimistic ratings they placed on these loans. Of course, the Greenspan Fed cannot escape blame altogether for its liquidity injections and failure to see and stop the CRE bubble.

CHAPTER 14

The Centerpiece for Real Reform

As $1.4 trillion of commercial real debt comes due over the five-year period of 2010 to 2014, several trends will emerge. CRE lenders who seek to put off taking loan impairments will come under increasing pressure. Many will prefer to sell their notes and collateral as "loans to own" to opportunistic real estate owner operators—frequently real estate private equity firms and publicly traded REITS—who will then commence or continue the foreclosure process.

Mezzanine UCC foreclosure sales, where available, will become the preferred enforcement mechanism due to their ease, speed, and low cost structure. Where borrower workouts occur, they will frequently be forced into short-term extensions where additional equity is posted, and restricted or no net cash flow is leaked to the borrower or underwater junior lenders.

Where extensions occur and junior lenders are deprived of cash flow, or where one lender in a multilender debt stack seeks to take over the property from the borrower and wipe out junior lenders, tranche warfare will be waged.

All this will play out over the next five years, much of it in our courts. Fortunes will be made and lost. Regrettably, due to delays in residential foreclosures brought about by Obama's policies, much of the CRE losses will occur simultaneously with a double dip in housing. This will place our banks, particularly our regional banks, with high concentrations of CRE exposure, often to lower tier whole-loan collateral, under increasing and sometimes insurmountable financial pressure.

Given the $3.4 trillion accumulation of U.S. public debt between mid-2008 and mid-2010, it remains to be seen whether our politicians will demonstrate the political will to bail out the hundreds more banks that will inevitably fail as residential and commercial real estate foreclosures peak in unison.

The centerpiece in any real financial reform must address the four key troublemakers:

1. The failed policy underlying the housing bubble—pushing home owner-ship rates through a federal affordable home ownership mandate
2. Fannie and Freddie
3. The Federal Housing Administration
4. The Community Reinvestment Act

FANNIE AND FREDDIE

Any serious financial reform package must address Fannie and Freddie front and center; but given the Democrats' role in the crisis and their having used the GSEs as the principal tool to press their affordable home ownership mandate and push U.S. homeownership rates to over 69 percent, is it really surprising that the Dodd bill does not even mention Fannie or Freddie, or that Senator McCain's proposed amendment (dealing with Fannie and Freddie) was voted down?

Fannie and Freddie should be wound down and shuttered, so that the taxpayer bleeding is arrested. There is no reason for the U.S. government to be subsidizing home ownership over any other commodity, let alone making (by buying in the secondary market or insuring), as it is now, nearly 100 percent of all U.S. home mortgage loans.

Democrats have nationalized residential mortgage lending. What they have accomplished is no less than this: They have used the vast borrowing power of the United States to crowd private banking out of the $11 trillion U.S. home mortgage market so that currently virtually all home mortgage lending is controlled by three wholly owned, cash-hemorrhaging subsidiaries of the Democratic Party—Fannie, Freddie, and the Federal Housing Administration.

Democrats argue that the GSEs cannot be shuttered—that if they were, our fragile housing recovery would derail. This is akin to a drug pusher saying to one of his "customers"—you can't get off the stuff now, you're hooked. Having pushed trillions of dollars of subprime mortgage money (borrowed on the backs of the U.S. taxpayers) to millions of noncreditworthy borrowers incapable of repaying their mortgage loans—the greatest failed social engineering experiment in U.S. history—supporters of the GSEs now claim the market cannot withstand a withdrawal of this "life support."

One mortgage analyst, Howard Glaser, while being interviewed alongside me by CNBC's Larry Kudlow, likened the federal support of the mortgage market to the Vietnam War, arguing that we are too fearful to "pull out." But I think that analogy is more helpful for the differences it highlights. Forty years ago we were afraid to pull out of Vietnam because we were warned that if we did, the Communists would take over. Today, we are afraid to "pull out" of the mortgage market because we are warned that if we do, the "Communists"—really European-style Socialists—will lose control.

The notion that the federal government withdrawing its support of the mortgage market is not true or at a minimum is a gross overstatement. In any event the day of reckoning cannot be put off forever—the sooner we deal with it the better off we will be.

Really, the issue for GSE supporters is the continued democratization of credit—the making of mortgage loans to the "underserved"—not a potential derailing of the housing recovery. When the Fed ended its massive purchases of RMBS on March 30, 2010, many predicted that the supply of mortgage loans would dry up and that with that reduced supply, mortgage rates would spike. But neither calamity occurred. Rate-hungry investors stepped in to fill the void. Comfortable that tougher underwriting standards and the 30 percent drop in housing prices made RMBS safe, investors flocked to RMBS. Said differently, while the Fed "crowded out" private investors when it was making massive RMBS purchases, when it withdrew from the RMBS market, and made room for private investors, they stepped back in. Free-market capitalism worked as it always does (and government subsidies fail, as they always do).

The empirical evidence does not support the Chicken Littles who cry "the sky is falling" whenever the subject of Fannie and Freddie comes up. Beyond the demonstrated appetite of private investors for the new generation of safer RMBS, there is reason to believe that a cessation of government subsidies to the housing sector will actually enhance the prospects for a recovery in housing in the long term (not to mention the economy at large).

In Canada, for example, there is no Fannie or Freddie buying mortgage loans in the secondary market, and Canada's housing market is vastly outperforming that of the United States. In Canada, private banks typically require 20 percent down payments and our default rates are 21 times theirs. While the Canadian government does offer mortgage insurance to low down payment borrowers (akin to FHA) insurance, unsecured loans represent a small percentage of the overall loan market. With all that said, Canada's home ownership rate is 68 percent to our 66 percent.

In contrast, in the United States, thanks to Congressional mandates compelling the GSEs to buy subprime mortgage loans to the underserved, the federal government has effectively crowded out all private investors and banks from the mortgage market.

Thanks to the First Time Homebuyer's Tax Credit, first-time homebuyers have accounted for about 42 percent of the market in 2009 and 2010. That means that other buyers currently comprise the remaining 58 percent of homebuyers. While there is no doubt that President Obama's policies have subsidized the first-time homebuyer, the question that must be asked is this: Have those same policies scared away buyers?

Many experienced homebuyers have pushed off their purchase decisions, despite attractive home prices, for fear that once the unsustainable federal subsidies are withdrawn, as they inevitably must be, a new and lower floor in housing prices will be made. These buyers—fearful that they are standing on the hangman's trap door and not a firm floor—refuse to buy until the subsidies expire. No one knows how much pent-up demand is out there (or how much pent up supply there is) and how much of either will be unleashed by ending U.S. housing subsidies.

The gradual and orderly dissolution of the GSEs, therefore, will be felt more in terms of the mix of buyers than in the dreaded "bottom falling out." And even if the markets demand a further price correction, it cannot be avoided. In any event, the GSEs are not sustainable in the long term. While some first time homebuyer activity undoubtedly will be lost by virtue of the orderly winding down of the GSEs, some of that lost demand is likely to be made up by enhanced demand from more experienced buyers. These second- and third-time homebuyers are able to make bigger down payments, and in consequence are more likely to be served by private investors in an unsubsidized mortgage market.

What is really at stake is not the housing recovery, but rather the Democratic effort to maintain the unsustainable near 70 percent level to which they have pushed U.S. homeownership rates via the democratization of mortgage credit achieved through Fannie and Freddie—the very failed policy that got us in trouble in the first place.

Because Obama's reaction has been so slanted toward the lower end of the housing market, his policies have created a narrow and illusory recovery in housing. We need a broad-based, self-supporting recovery in housing spread among all price levels. And that can happen only if and when the federal government stops crowding out unsubsidized, private mortgage lending.

This is not to say that there is no more downside to housing following an initial leveling off beginning at the end of 2009 and moving into 2010. While approximately 6.4 million foreclosures were initiated in 2007, 2008, and 2009,[1] only 2.2 million people were removed from their homes during that three-year period.[2] There is a substantial backlog in the mortgage foreclosure pipeline. Even if not one more foreclosure action were commenced after 2009, there would still be approximately 4 million foreclosed homes hitting the market just from the backlog in foreclosures filed through the end of 2009.

Couple the foreclosure backlog with the fact that one in four American homeowners is underwater—the amount owed on the mortgage is greater than the value of the home—and it is easy to see that we can expect millions more foreclosures to be filed in 2010 and beyond, especially given the stubborn unemployment rate, which remains for all practical purposes, taking into account the underemployed and those who have given up looking for a job, around 17 percent.

I expect that over the three-year period 2010–2012, we will see 7–10 million more people lose their homes as a result of foreclosures or short sales. The organic rate of home turnover in the United States (with a population of about 310 million) seems to be on the order of 5 to 5.5 million sales per year—that is, in normal times 15 to 16.5 million homeowners over a three-year period would voluntarily list their homes for sale, as divorces, deaths, births, job changes, retirements, children moving out, and the like induce people to change their housing.

In normal times the housing market would move to a price point low enough to attract the 15 to 16.5 million buyers during this three-year period needed in order to absorb that voluntarily listed inventory. But in the three-year period 2010–2012, an additional 7 to 10 million foreclosed homes likely will hit the market. While some of those might have been voluntarily listed for sale even absent a foreclosure, it is likely that the great majority of foreclosures represent forced sales, which otherwise would not have occurred (absent the foreclosure process). Said differently, the market will have to move to a price point sufficient to attract two additional buyers (10 million) for every three buyers (15 million) it needs to attract in normal times. To compound matters, it is likely that there is pent-up supply—homeowners who are still current on their mortgages and who would like to relocate or downsize but have thus far resisted doing so in the hopes of waiting for a "better market." Eventually these people will give up waiting and list their homes for sale.

Prices will have to move down to absorb the additional "shadow" inventory represented by the foreclosed homes. Currently, the existing home inventory is about 3.6 million, which we are told represents an eight-month supply. But the current shadow inventory by my calculations is 4.2 million, making the real effective inventory more like a 17-month supply. This means prices will move down, at least in foreclosure-rich regions.

This additional price downside cannot be averted. It can only be put off. And putting off the day of reckoning will only make things even worse. As it now stands, President Obama's efforts to delay the final day of reckoning on housing has moved the final housing market correction so that it will coincide with an enormous uptick in commercial real estate foreclosures, the European debt crisis, and state insolvencies, thus generating a heightened prospect of systemic risk to the banking sector.

But is housing finding an unsubsidized true economic bottom really a bad thing? As it stands, thanks to Obama's mortgage modification efforts—failures though they've been—millions of underwater homeowners continue to support uncollectible mortgage debts (beyond the values of their homes) or they and their banks wait in the hopes of getting a bailout—subsidized mortgage modifications. If the market clearing processes were allowed to work, these people would lose their homes (in which they have no equity anyway) and would then rent or possibly purchase another home at a current market price at vastly reduced interest rates. In other words, once the market clearing processes are allowed to work, tens of millions of Americans would reduce their housing costs by 20 to 40 percent. Their savings would then be spent in other sectors of the economy—a recurring negative cut stimulus.

The sensible approach for Fannie and Freddie is to develop a plan for their orderly and gradual wind-down and dissolution—and then to stick to the plan. The GSE purchases in the secondary market and securitization of home mortgages should be wound down to zero over the next three years. At the end of that period the GSEs should be dissolved and their portfolios gradually sold.

In order to accomplish the crucial goal of winding down and ultimately dissolving the GSEs, lawmakers need to abandon the failed policy of using subsidized affordable home loans to push U.S. homeownership rates. In the last analysis, it was that toxic policy that spawned the crisis and that policy must be abandoned. Government (state and local, not federal) should concern itself with decent and safe housing—not with whether citizens own or rent their shelter. Our failed homeownership policy has benefited no one but mortgage loan securitizers, originators, brokers, and some politicians (for example, Barack Obama, Chris Dodd, and Barney Frank).

The intended beneficiaries—underserved minorities—have had their life savings vaporized by this failed policy, as the homes they were permitted to buy courtesy of government subsidies were lost through foreclosures. In many cases, these people struggled for years to keep up with mortgage payments, sacrificing in other areas of their lives—like spending money on their children's educations—in order to pay the lenders who ultimately took over (or will take over) ownership of their homes. Even worse, thanks to Obama's mortgage modification efforts, some people will continue to have an unsustainable portion of their household income sapped by mortgage payments as they continue to pay modified mortgage loans, which exceed their homes' value. Homeowners with no equity are, economically speaking, nothing but (subsidized) renters, whether or not their name appears in the deed records.

In many instances, housing conditions have deteriorated as a result of this failed policy, too. People struggling to pay their mortgage loans do not keep up with repairs and maintenance of their home and grounds. They are far better off as renters from professional landlords who have the means to maintain safe and decent housing.

The subsidizers—the half of the taxpayers who pay tax—were left holding the bag, as they continue to fund the GSEs massive losses—$145 billion and counting. So in the end, who really benefited from this policy?

Fannie and Freddie also account for the vast majority of mortgage loans made on multifamily rental properties. This too must be stopped. Why should the American taxpayers be making hundred million dollar–plus loans to wealthy real estate investors? How does this advance any legitimate public goal? In the end, all this practice will do is crowd out the private banking sector and cause a bubble in multifamily housing. Why push the prices in that sector?

THE FEDERAL HOUSING ADMINISTRATION

FHA Commissioner David Stevens is drinking from the liberal Kool-Aid punch bowl and has no idea of the staggering risk levels to which he is exposing U.S. taxpayers. He is just another zombie-adherent to our failed policy of pushing affordable home mortgages and U.S. homeownership rates to unsustainable (and dangerous) levels.

In 2006, the FHA insured just 3 percent of home mortgages. Today it insures more than 10 times that amount—nearly one of every three home mortgages now being made is insured by the FHA. Together with Fannie and Freddie, the FHA is putting the risk for the entire U.S. home mortgage market—nearly an $11 trillion market—on the backs of the American taxpayers.

How did the FHA multiply its market share by tenfold in the past three years? Simple; while private lenders, in response to the bursting of the housing bubble and the subprime (and now prime) mortgage crisis, have toughened up underwriting standards, the FHA has stubbornly refused to touch the most basic of underwriting standards—the down payment requirement.

Private lenders now require 10 percent to 20 percent minimum down payments. But a strapped homebuyer can still get the FHA to insure a mortgage with as little as 3.5 percent down. But when you take into account that the FHA allows sellers to pay up to 6 percent of the buyer's closing costs, the FHA guidelines really allow federal mortgage insurance for loans exceeding 100 percent of the price.

Residential brokerage commissions in the United States run 5 to 6 percent of the total price. That means that a homebuyer investing about half (or a little more) of what the broker makes as a commission can buy a home and get the U.S. government to insure the mortgage. It's not hard beating the competition—private mortgage insurers—when you have the U.S. taxpayers behind you.

In March 2010, Commissioner Stevens told Congress he wanted to increase the FHA insurance premium from 1.75 percent to 2.25 percent as a method of increasing the FHA's dwindling capital reserves. But adding $10 per month to the cost of the monthly payment for the median-priced home is no solution. Stevens also proposed that the level of closing costs a seller can pay—a gimmick used to inflate a home's price and thereby justify an even bigger mortgage—be reduced from 6 percent to 3 percent.

That half measure is likewise worthless. We need to minimize future defaults on FHA insured mortgages, not increase the FHA's premium income or limit the amount of allowable gimmickry in pricing, and the only way to minimize future defaults on FHA-insured mortgages is to demand much more substantial down payments.

Commissioner Stevens also said he will require increased down payments of 10 percent from borrowers with FICO scores below 580. But for some perspective, consider that Fannie and Freddie are now requiring FICO scores ranging from 750 to 760.

As default rates have increased on FHA-insured mortgages, the FHA's capital reserves have dwindled to about one-quarter of the congressionally mandated minimums. As of September 30, 2009, the FHA's capital reserves stood at $3.6 billion, just .53 percent of the value of the mortgages it insures, down 72 percent from a year earlier. While the FHA can tap other funds besides its capital reserve account, if the capital reserve fund falls below zero, the FHA can get funded directly from the Treasury without having to ask Congress for more money.

At the end of February 2010, the "seriously delinquent" rate for FHA-insured mortgages spiked to 7.5 percent, up from 6.2 percent a year earlier. But in some cities, FHA default rates are far higher. According to HUD, at the end of 2009, FHA default rates were at 18 percent in Punta Gorda, Florida; 15.6 percent in Flint, Michigan; 15.1 percent in Fort Meyers–Cape Coral, Florida; and 15 percent in Elkart–Goshen, Indiana. The FHA continues to insure far more than its national average of nearly one in three mortgages in many distressed housing markets.

Apart from insuring one in every three mortgage loans taken out to buy homes, the FHA also now insures one in five refinancings. Realizing that, via FHA insurance, he can accomplish a massive redistribution of wealth without the vote of a single member of Congress, President Obama recently announced that he will use FHA insurance to enable homeowners who are underwater but still current on their mortgages to refinance them.

Obama is allowing upper-income homeowners (owing mortgage balances up to $729,750) to refinance, by paying their banks if they reduce the principal balance to 97.5 percent of the home's value and payments to "affordable" levels—31 percent of the homeowners' income. For homeowners who owe second-mortgage loans, the balance need only be reduced to 115 percent of the home's value.

Thanks to the FHA, subprime mortgage lending is alive and well. And thanks to President Obama's latest program, private mortgage investors will be able to pick the riskiest of their not-yet-defaulted underwater loans, and get them off their books and onto the FHA's books, making the inevitable taxpayer bailout of the FHA come even sooner.

Because the FHA can demand funds from the Treasury without congressional approval once its dwindling capital reserve fund falls below zero, President Obama and Commissioner Stevens have an "express lane" for bailing out the FHA. President Obama also has an "express lane" for funding Fannie and Freddie via the conservatorship Secretary Paulson instituted in September 2008 and the elimination of the $400 billion cap on GSE bailout money the White House implemented on Christmas Day, 2009. While Obama, Stevens, and GSE executives may think they are fulfilling the "American Dream" for the newly minted subprime borrowers, for the rest of us, they are just continuing an "American Nightmare."

Before leaving the subject of the GSEs and the FHA, a word on executive compensation in the public and private sectors is in order. President Obama gave a nice Christmas present in 2009 to Fannie CEO Mike Williams and his Freddie Mac counterpart—$6 million in year-end bonuses. All told, Obama approved $42 million in year-end bonuses for the top 12 GSE executives in 2009, even while his pay czar, Kenneth Feinberg, was on the warpath looking to cut executive compensation in private-sector financial institutions.

Conversely, Barack Obama's annual salary is $400,000 and the salary of FHA Commissioner David Stevens is below $200,000. Why should the CEOs of Fannie and Freddie be paid a multiple of the president's salary? Why should they get a dime more than FHA Commissioner Stevens?

Only because of the pulp fiction that the GSEs are still "private" companies is this ridiculous charade continued. The GSEs are arms of the U.S. government and their executives should receive government-salary ratings like any other public officials. Exactly how much talent is needed to make mortgage loans with taxpayer money and lose $10 billion a quarter?

REPEAL THE COMMUNITY REINVESTMENT ACT

In 1977, Congress passed and President Carter signed into law the Community Reinvestment Act (CRA). The ostensible purpose of the CRA was to reduce alleged discriminatory credit practices by banks and other lenders against low-income neighborhoods, a practice known as redlining.

The CRA was supposed to put an end to redlining by requiring the appropriate federal financial supervisory agencies to "encourage" regulated financial institutions to meet the credit needs of the local communities in which they are chartered, consistent with safe and sound underwriting practices. To enforce this vague statutory objective, federal regulatory agencies were directed to examine banking institutions for CRA compliance and take this information into consideration when approving applications for mergers, acquisitions, and opening and closing new bank branches.

In 1989, George H.W. Bush signed into law the Financial Institutions Reform Recovery and Enforcement Act (FIRREA), which in part amended the CRA's provisions concerning regulatory reporting of banks' CRA compliance efforts. The additional disclosure mandated by FIRREA greatly enhanced the ability of affordable housing advocacy groups like ACORN to perform quantitative analysis of banks' loans to "underserved areas" and thereby significantly impacted bank lending policies.

In 1992, the Federal Housing Enterprises Financial Safety and Soundness Act was enacted. This act furthered the CRA anti-redlining mandate by compelling Fannie and Freddie to devote a specified percentage of their purchases on the secondary mortgage market to affordable housing loans. In 2000, then-HUD commissioner Andrew Cuomo urged Fannie and Freddie to reach the goal of committing 50 percent of their assets to serving low- and moderate-income families.

U.S. Attorney General Janet Reno, a Clinton appointee, unleashed the staggering power of that office against the banking industry by bringing multiple lawsuits against banks for alleged CRA noncompliance. Her remarks at a March 20, 1998 luncheon sponsored by the National Community Reinvestment Coalition, a public advocacy group, sent chills down the spines of bankers nationwide. They also knew better than to resist her demands for affordable housing loans. They knew that absent their coming to heel, they would face lawsuits or worse, have their mergers and acquisitions blocked.

Here are some of Ms. Reno's remarks at the 1998 NCRC convention:

Access to credit is the lifeblood of economic opportunity. With credit, homes can be bought, businesses started, neighborhoods rebuilt, and communities revitalized. . . .

The Community Reinvestment Act has played a critical part in ensuring that lending institutions put some of their capital into underserved areas, especially the inner cities and in minority neighborhoods.

The new Community Reinvestment Act regulations enable lenders to develop customized strategic plans for meeting their obligations under the Act. . . . In this way you are not only helping to rebuild your communities, but you are showing bankers how to be responsible corporate citizens. . . . (Applause.)

It has been my experience in these five years in office that most bankers want to be good and responsible corporate citizens, or they're willing to be if they're nudged in the right direction by vocal, knowledgeable, constructive groups such as the NCRC members and by Justice Department lawyers who care and want to do the right thing.

And I discovered . . . in talking to bankers, that it is better to educate first and then litigate later only if necessary. But you got to be prepared to litigate, and I am prepared to litigate when it's going to be necessary. (Applause.)

In these efforts we continually stress that fair lending laws do not require lenders to make bad loans. They require simply that people be treated equally. . . .

We want to see equal credit being offered by banks because it is the right thing to do, because the law requires it, because it is good business, because people accept it.

You've noted that since the inception of our fair lending initiative in 1992 the Department has filed and settled 13 major fair lending lawsuits. We are going to continue these efforts . . . in every way that we possibly can. We will continue to focus on discrimination in underwriting, the process of evaluating the qualifications of credit applicants. This was the issue in our suits against Shawmut in Boston, Northern Trust Company in Chicago, and First National Bank of Donna Anna in New Mexico.

We have also focused on the problem of redlining by lenders and insurance companies. This past August we reached an agreement with Allbank of New York. We alleged that the bank had carved out and refused to make loans in urban minority enclaves within the bank's lending areas in Connecticut and Westchester

County, New York. The settlement with Allbank requires it to make $55 million in loans at below-market rate in the areas previously redlined. (Applause.) . . .

Pricing discrimination has also been a problem. Minorities have been charged higher interest rates and fees for loans. Several of the Department of Justice minorities have been charged higher interest rates and fees for loans. Several of the Department of Justices have been involved in this type of discrimination. . . .

New reporting under the Community Reinvestment Act provides aggregate data on small business loans by census tracts for some banks. This helps us get an idea of how much credit is flowing to communities with differing economic and demographic characteristics. But the data are not sufficient to determine whether there is unlawful discrimination against minorities in small business lending. The data tell very little about the recipients of the loans and nothing at all about applicants who are denied, information that is essential to determining whether illegal discrimination is preventing some potential borrowers from obtaining credit.

In fact, right now lenders are prohibited by the Federal Reserve Regulation B from inquiring about the race, color, sex, religion, or national origin of an applicant for a nonmortgage loan. The intent of this prohibition on collection in Regulation B was to prohibit the discriminatory use of such data, and that intent was laudatory. But we now know from our experience with home mortgage data that this information has been critical to ferreting out discrimination.

Requiring banks to collect this data has not led to the discriminatory or improper use of the data. Just the opposite is true. We have been able to use the information in numerous lawsuits to combat discrimination, and you have been able to use this data in monitoring lenders' fair lending performance.

We believe that changing Regulation B to permit creditors to collect such information would greatly assist the Department's efforts to investigate business lending discrimination. The Department of Justice, along with the Comptroller of the Currency, the Office of Thrift Supervision, and the Treasury Department, urge the Federal Reserve to consider making this change in its regulatory review of Regulation B. (Applause.)

And, as I think you know, just this month the Fed issued its notice of proposed rulemaking and is soliciting comments on this proposal. I know from your reaction that you're going to join in supporting this effort to change Regulation B, and we hope the lending industry will support it as well.

The additional data will allow institutions to monitor their own performance and give regulators the tools needed to identify problems and work to solve them. The lending institutions are not being asked to make bad loans. They will now have information that can enable them to make more good loans, and I think they will join us.

There is still much work for all of us to do in advancing fair lending enforcement. Although many of us act independently, our efforts are in reality intertwined. The NCRC has done an extraordinary job and I commend you for your splendid efforts to revitalize communities. We are committed to working with you to achieve our common objectives. . . .

And you can say all there is to say about economic justice much better than I can say it. But let us all speak loudly and clearly for justice, not just for the rich, not just for the adults, but justice for all Americans—economic justice, the justice that gives them the opportunity to go to school and get a good education, the justice that enables them to compete for jobs, the justice that brings community together in one whole strong effort to serve all its people.[3]

Imagine how these words—coming from the lips of the most powerful federal law enforcement officer in the country—sounded to the banking community?

The CRA in Reno's hands was the stick; the trillions in funding provided by the GSEs to buy subprime loans to the underserved was the carrot. Together they got the job done—trillions of dollars were lent to nonunderwritable credit.

Federal lawmakers and regulators should make up their minds—are the bankers and Wall Street investment bankers greedy or are they bigoted? They can't be both.

It is self-evident that financial institutions will take a profit wherever it can be made. If loans to minority borrowers bear an interest rate commensurate with the risks associated with making the loans, then the loans will be made. If our government uses all its might and taxpayer dollars to force lending at "nondiscriminatory rates" to no-skin-in-the game subprime borrowers, we create and inject a financial contagion. Credit should extended to people of all races when it is safe and sound to do so and not otherwise. The CRA should be repealed.

CHAPTER 15

Other Areas Requiring Reform

Other areas in need of financial reform include:

- Raising capital reserves for banks and lowering leverage limits for investment banks
- Instituting across-the-board risk retention requirements for both residential and commercial real estate loans
- Compensation reform for residential and commercial real estate loan originators
- Putting credit default swaps and interest rate swaps and caps under control of a regulated clearinghouse
- Finally breaking the control of residential and commercial real estate lenders over appraisers
- Using our tried and true bankruptcy laws instead of creating an altogether new and dangerous class of "too big to fail" rules
- Expanding whistleblower laws to cover political malfeasance
- Slashing federal spending and adopting across-the-board tax cuts
- Reforming immigration policy to bring a new wave of educated immigrant homebuyers.

CAPITAL RESERVE REQUIREMENTS AND LEVERAGE LIMITS

While the Savings and Loan Crisis of the early 1990s was in large part spawned by thinly capitalized real estate developers who overleveraged construction projects, the current crisis was exacerbated by the leverage ratios and thin capitalization of lenders.

In the period leading up to the current crisis, investment banks were vastly overleveraged and banks were undercapitalized. As a result, some of the largest banks and investment banking firms were unable to withstand drops in the prices of collateral securing loans (houses) without taxpayer bailouts.

An investment banking firm with a 30:1 leverage ratio is wiped out by a 3.3 percent drop in the value of the assets collateralizing its loans. So far, housing prices have dropped by roughly 10 times that amount. The same is true of undercapitalized banks. They were unable to withstand (without a taxpayer bailout) the drop in housing prices. As a result of overleverage and undercapitalization, Bear Stearns and Lehman failed, Merrill Lynch was forced upon the Bank of America, and all of our major banks needed to be bailed out.

We need to limit leverage ratios at investment banking firms to 15 to 1 and to require tougher capital reserves at commercial banks. That, instead of restricting consumer and small business credit, by regulating fees, will mitigate the risk of a future crisis without unreasonably stunting future growth.

COMPENSATION REFORM AND RISK RETENTION

Loan originators at our banks and mortgage lenders were given bonuses based on loan origination volume, rather than on profits to lenders from making loans that got repaid. These loan officers were economically incentivized to enlarge principal amounts even if the loans were not repaid. This flawed compensation practice affected not only home mortgage loans but commercial real estate loans.

In the case of CRE loans, originators who stood to make hundreds of thousands if not millions of dollars in bonuses tied strictly to the volume of loans they originated built massive "interest reserves" into their loans in order to justify bloated loans far in excess of 100 percent of the underlying collateral value.

Real estate developers acquiring or refinancing CRE assets would present a "repositioning story" to the lender. An aging office building would receive a shiny new glass curtain wall replacing its tired old façade, modern elevators, and a refurbished lobby; or an apartment complex would receive an upgraded amenity package and modernized building systems. Once these improvements were put into place, the owner would be able to charge much higher rents.

Loan originators in collaboration with borrowers "modeled" a future fantasy—an office building or apartment complex with substantially higher rents and net income than currently existed. That model would predict how long it would take to reach financial nirvana and then an interest reserve would be established to "bridge the borrower" to the "modeled outcome" on the theory that once the modeled nirvana were reached, the loan would then be self-supporting by the "repositioned property."

In other words, CRE lenders loaned to a future predicted value—far in excess of current value—and funded interest reserves knowing the borrower had no way of paying the interest on the bloated debt out of the present net income generated by the property. Loan originators, desperate to earn their loan-principal based bonuses, advanced loans so large they could not be supported by the mortgaged property and then loaned the borrower many years' worth of interest, knowing that, in the best of all worlds, it would take the owner years to attain the rents necessary to support the loan. In many CRE loans it was not uncommon to incorporate interest reserves designed to last a half a decade.

These interest-reserve CRE loans have an analogue in the residential space—negative amortization loans. In "neg-am" loans, home mortgage lenders were able to make loans to borrowers who could not afford them by adding to principal the portion of interest payments the borrowers could not afford to pay currently. In both cases—the interest reserve CRE loan and the "neg-am" home mortgage loan—the lender was betting on an inflated future value of its collateral.

And what did lenders get in return for these massive risks? Usually, a loan based on a small spread above the London Interbank Offered Rate. It is easy to see why loan officers compensated based on how much principal they pushed out the door—with no regard for whether the loans were ever repaid—made such risky loans for such a minimal return; but why would the lenders themselves take such massive risks for so little return?

The answer is simple: They didn't. The CRE loan originators worked for lenders—commercial banks and investment banking firms—which did not keep the loans they originated. Within weeks of making the loans, the loans were securitized and sold. They were off the books of the originating lender and on the books of CMBS bondholders.

In one case in which I was involved, a major foreign bank was contemplating a multi-hundred-million-dollar cash-out refinancing of a large CRE asset. At the time of the refinancing, a tenant lawsuit was pending, which sought to reduce rents by a large margin. I was the lead counsel representing the owner in defending the tenant lawsuit but did not represent the owner in the refinancing transaction.

The owner's counsel on the refinancing transaction disclosed to the bank's law firm, a major international law firm employing hundreds of lawyers, the pendency of the tenant lawsuit. That firm responded by asking the owner's transactional counsel to ask me if I would render an opinion that the "likely outcome" of the suit was that the owner would prevail—that the rents would not be reduced.

I was asked to participate in a conference call involving many lawyers representing both the lender and the borrower. On the call, the bank's lead counsel asked me to render the "likely outcome" opinion. I was fuming mad at this idiotic request. How could I possibly predict the final outcome of a lawsuit? More important, though, what was the real point of such an opinion, assuming I was foolish enough to render it? If I had said that it was my opinion that ownership would win the lawsuit, and I proved to be wrong, what then? My malpractice insurance limits were a fraction of the loan amount. The only point of the opinion was to create political cover for the bank so that it could make the loan and then securitize it, passing the risk of the tenant lawsuit onto the CMBS bondholders.

I adamantly refused and in fact lambasted the bank counsel for having the temerity to even ask for such an opinion. I gave them the pleadings in the case and told them to read them, form their own opinion, and issue their own "likely outcome" opinion to their bank client. A few weeks later the loan closed anyway. If the suit were lost, the loan would be vastly underwater.

I have no doubt that the bank's law firm disclosed the lawsuit to the bank without any "likely outcome" opinion. So why was the loan made anyway? Because the bank stood to make vast origination fees and knew it would be able to securitize the loan and quickly shed the enormous risk presented by the lawsuit.

The broken compensation policies of our commercial banks and investment banking firms—based as they are on loan origination volume and not loan repayments—are themselves a function of another broken structure—the lack of risk retention by loan originators.

In the version of the financial reform bill just passed by the Senate as of the writing of this book, a provision requiring lenders to retain a portion of the risk embodied in their loans was watered down by an amendment added on the Senate floor, exempting from the risk retention requirement supposedly less risky fixed-rate fully amortizing home loans. We have heard this line before. Recall that discredited Fannie Mae CEO Franklin Raines described Fannie's mortgages as "riskless" at the House hearing considering charges that he cooked Fannie's books in order to line his own pockets with millions in bonus money.

There are no riskless mortgages. This is just the banking lobbyists having gotten to the bill's proponent, Chris Dodd, and other senators, in time. Again, this is hardly a surprise. Mr. Dodd, we know, took multiple sweetheart loans—really bribes—from former Countrywide CEO Angelo Mozilo. When the regulated regulate the regulators, real reform is unlikely.

Loan origination should carry with it risk retention. If it did, risky loans would be originated far less often and loan officer compensation policies would be based on loan repayments, not loan originations. While risk retention would undoubtedly have the effect of slowing loan origination, isn't that the point? Bubble prevention is a better course than bubble detection.

DERIVATIVES

The much maligned derivatives—credit default swaps—and synthetic collateralized debt obligations, like those involved in Goldman's ABACUS deal, actually helped let some air out of the housing bubble before it burst. Without these securities the financial crisis would have been much worse.

Credit default swaps are a legitimate method of off-loading risk to those better equipped to handle it. They are a form of insurance. The spreads paid by credit default swap buyers act like smoke detectors. When they widen, that means credit default issuers think there is default risk in the covered securities. Outlawing smoke detectors is not a good way to prevent fires.

Likewise, synthetic CDOs mitigated the adverse effects of the housing bubble. Investors like IDB Industriebank and ACA, the long investors in Goldman's ABACUS deal, would have made their long bets anyway even in the absence of Goldman's creation of a synthetic CDO. And absent a synthetic CDO, the billion dollars they invested would have resulted in a billion dollars worth of additional subprime mortgages being advanced. By creating synthetic CDOs, Wall Street enabled investors to bet the long side of the housing market without further inflating the bubble. Some of the "air" that otherwise would have further inflated the housing bubble was harmlessly expelled "outside the bubble" by virtue of ABACUS and other synthetic CDOs created by Wall Street investment banking firms.

That said, the interconnectedness of credit default swap issuers, investment banks, commercial banks, loan originators, and CMBS and RMBS investors, means that the entire financial system is placed at risk for defaults by CDS issuers. As a result, regulation decreasing the likelihood of these CDS issuer defaults would tend to mitigate systemic risk. But care must be taken that the effect of the regulation is not simply to push the underwriting of CDS offshore. Were that to happen, we would simply shrink the U.S. economy, lose jobs, and not reduce systemic risk.

One appropriate measure would be to capture CDS transactions now written over the counter into an organized clearinghouse with clear rules on capital reserves and membership responsibility for defaults. CDS issuers should not have the Federal Discount Window accessible to them, as this tends to socialize risk. But preventing commercial banks from derivative underwriting will only further weaken our banks by depriving them of a large profit center, which will end up only reducing their capital reserves—thereby increasing rather than decreasing systemic risk—and the derivatives will end up getting underwritten anyway by offshore financial institutions.

A critical exception, however, should be created for commercial hedgers. Mandatory requirements that derivatives trade through a clearinghouse instead of over the counter will expose contract buyers to the capital or margin requirements imposed by the clearinghouse. While this may be appropriate for financial institutions that buy interest rate and credit default swaps, it would be a tragic mistake to impose those costs on farmers, electricity producers, and airlines, for example. When they hedge against fluctuations in the price of crops, electricity, and fuel, they are not engaging in financial speculation—just the reverse; they are protecting themselves against market gyrations. Increasing these commercial hedging costs will only hurt consumers and cost us jobs.

CREDIT RATING AGENCIES AND APPRAISERS

Credit rating agencies were seriously delinquent in downgrading both subprime mortgage-backed RMBS and CMBS. When the housing bubble started to deflate, the credit rating agencies began *en masse* downgrades. These failures contributed significantly to the financial crisis.

Many politicians blame the rating agency compensation system, and that is how the financial reform law seeks to deal with the rating agency failures. Claiming that by offering securitizers leniency in their ratings they competed for ratings assignments, the Dodd bill shifts the rating agency selection process to a new regulatory body (just what we need, another regulatory body to round out our already bloated federal government), whose SEC-appointed commissioners will pick and choose which rater gets to rate which MBS.

This is no solution. All that we can expect from this "reform" is a shift from free-market to crony capitalism, a subject Dodd knows all too well. After all, the chairman of the Senate Banking Committee thought it fitting to take six sweetheart loans from one of the banks he was in charge of regulating, Countrywide Financial, under the "Friends of Angelo" VIP loan program.

I am not quite sure what benefits will go to the federal rater-pickers from the soon-to-be created "Friends of Standard & Poor's" program, but I am confident they will not make the anointed any poorer. Why on earth would anyone expect the commission that ignored the plaintive cries of Madoff-whistleblower Harry Markopolos for years on end—failing during all that time to expose the too-cozy relationship between Madoff and his feeder funds—to fix the too-cozy relationship between raters and securitizers?

A better fix would be to open up the universe of raters and allow the free market to go to work. By creating and protecting a small oligopoly of rating agencies, our lawmakers have paved the way for the protected cartel of raters to offer lenient ratings, and thus have once again demonstrated their economic illiteracy.

Were the marketplace opened up to free competition, new rating agencies would emerge. Soon enough, only those raters whose honest ratings proved analytically sound would carry any real weight among investors. Securitizers would be forced to use those raters whose ratings investors valued in order to sell their MBS. The free market, if it were allowed to operate, would end the rater problem.

The rating agency problem, like so many others, is just more governmental Munchausen by proxy—government, having infected us with a problem of its own creation (the rating agency cartel), rushes in to solve the problem with a nonsolution, which of course involves more regulation, increases the size of our already bloated government, and puts regulators in line to receive the benefits of crony capitalism.

Another helpful step would be to trim the legal protections now offered rating agencies. While they should not be made into insurers, the law should imply a duty of loyalty running from the rating agencies to the investors who rely on their ratings. The agencies should not be accountable for failing to predict adverse credit events; but they should be held accountable for selling out—for intentionally giving rosier than deserved ratings in order to line their own pockets with fees.

Besides lenient rating agencies, lenient appraisers contributed to the subprime mortgage process. Banks wanted a cut of appraisal fees charged to borrowers and formed or controlled appraisal companies to whom they assigned the appraisal work emanating from their home loans. Countrywide Financial owned and controlled Landsafe and a Wells Fargo parent company owned and controlled Rels Valuation. Washington Mutual was alleged to have exerted excessive control over First American's EAppraiseIT.

New York Attorney General Andrew Cuomo took action against Washington Mutual with regard to bank-controlled appraisals. That effort spawned the Home Valuation Code of Conduct. The HVCC attempts to erect a firewall between banks and appraisers by inserting appraisal management companies as middlemen between the appraisers and the banks.

But the HVCC allows banks to own stakes in the appraisal management companies, which get varying shares of the appraisal fees. The end result is that the banks have not been removed from the process.

Bank control and the pressure they can and do exert over appraisers resulted in two different wrongs—appraisals were inflated and consumers were ripped off with excessive fees for fraudulent appraisals. Recall that given the securitization of residential mortgage loans, originating banks have nothing to lose by overlending based on inflated appraisals, since the excessive loans are sold and off their balance sheets before the defaults occur.

A similar appraisal problem arises in the context of commercial real estate loans. Although the CRE loan originators do not control the CRE appraisers, the pressure they can exert frequently results in inflated appraisals.

The real solution lies in requiring loan originators—both residential and commercial—to retain risk on all loans they originate. If that were done, the weed would be pulled out by the root. Without an incentive to loan excessive principal sums based on inflated appraisals—because in that instance the loans would not get paid back in full—the appraisal problem would come to a quick end.

Of course, that's exactly what the Dodd–Frank financial reform bill failed to do, as the banking lobbyists pressured Dodd into amending his bill from the floor of the Senate to exclude fixed-rate self-amortizing residential mortgage loans from the risk retention requirements. The floor amendment was served up by the banking lobby as appropriate because they argued the fixed-rate self-amortizing mortgages are low risk.

But if that were true, then what's the problem with holding onto a small piece of the resultant RMBS? The back-story here is that with FHA Commissioner David Stevens running amok insuring one in three mortgages (up from 1 in 30 a few years back) based on a 3.5 percent down payment requirement, the FHA is minting subprime 2.0. The banks are only too happy to comply, and with a U.S. taxpayer guarantee, these new subprime loans make for great securitization vehicles. Why gum up the works by making the loan originators retain risk?

A better answer would be to say that on any loan obtaining FHA insurance, the originator must retain a participation in the loan—say 5 to 10 percent of the loan—and that that participation *not* be protected by FHA insurance even though the remaining 90 to 95 percent of the loan is. That would kill two birds with one stone—it would ensure quality loans were underwritten based on valid appraisals and limit the taxpayer's exposure on FHA-insured loans. Of course, that's not in the Dodd-Frank law.

TOO BIG TO FAIL

These four little words are going to cost hundreds of billions of dollars. Putting our lawmakers in charge of deciding when an institution is too big to fail and to bail it out on the taxpayers' backs if in their infinite wisdom they deem that prudent, is lunacy.

The Greek crisis is instructive. Was Greece too "big" to fail, or was it simply too "interconnected" to be allowed to fail? Greece's gross domestic product is running at about $200 billion. For some perspective, California's gross domestic product is about $1.85 trillion, and New York's gross domestic product is over $1.1 trillion. In fact, more than half the 50 states, in 2008, had an economy larger than Greece's is today. And New York, Boston, Atlanta, Houston, Miami, Philadelphia, San Francisco, and Washington, D.C all have economies larger than Greece's.

Greece was not too big to fail; it was too interconnected to be allowed to fail. The bailout of Greece was really a bailout of the German and French banks that imprudently bought Greek bonds. Instead of asking whether Greece is too big to fail, Europeans should ask themselves this: Is there any reason German and French banks should be held harmless from doing what bondholders and mortgage lenders all over the world are doing—restructuring their obligations, giving debtors breaks, or resorting to collateral?

The so-called systemic risks presented by the failure of a too-big-to-fail financial institution can and should be mitigated by increased capital reserve requirements, more stringent leverage limits on investment banks, clearinghouses for derivatives, and as a last resort, good old-fashioned bankruptcy. No financial institution is too big to fail.

More to the point, no country's taxpayers can afford an unending line of bailouts. By not allowing the creditors of the failed institution to take the hit they signed on for when they extended credit to the institution that later failed, we socialize private risks and doom the overall economy.

EXPANDING WHISTLEBLOWER LAWS

On March 2, 1863, Congress passed the False Claims Act in an effort to encourage through financial rewards the disclosure of frauds against the U.S. government. The act was spawned by various financial frauds perpetrated against the federal government, then engaged in the Civil War effort, including the sale to the United States of mules in ill health.

The False Claims Act, also known as the Whistleblower Law, allows a person who has original information concerning a fraud being perpetrated against the federal government to bring what is called a *qui tam* proceeding in his or her own name as "relator" for the benefit of the United States.

The *qui tam* action is filed under seal, but a copy is sent to the Justice Department. If the Justice Department believes the claim has merit, it takes over the prosecution of the claim. If the United States is successful in obtaining a recovery on the claim, the relator is paid a significant percentage of the recovery and damages are trebled. In this way an employee of a defense contractor who is aware of a fraud being perpetrated by his or her employer against the government has ample economic incentive to blow the whistle on the employer.

Where members of our legislative, executive, and even judicial branches are involved in fraudulent conduct, there is not necessarily a cognizable financial fraud perpetrated against the United States. For example, Angelo Mozilo, the former CEO of Countrywide Financial, engaged in a systematic effort to bribe, through sweetheart loans not available in the free market, lawmakers and other government and GSE officials in a patent attempt to curry favor with these politicians and GSE executives.

Under Countrywide's "Friends of Angelo" loan program, Senator Dodd received a $75,000 reduction in mortgage payments at below-market rates on his Washington, D.C. and Connecticut homes. Clinton Jones III, senior counsel of the House Financial Services Subcommittee on Housing and Community Opportunity, was singled out for special treatment. Jones became state director for federal residential-mortgage bundler Freddie Mac and was thereafter hired to serve on the House Financial Services Committee. Alphonso Jackson, acting secretary of the Department of Housing and Urban Development, received a discounted mortgage loan for himself and sought one for his daughter. In 2003, using VIP loans for nearly $1 million apiece, Franklin Raines, the since disgraced Fannie Mae CEO, twice refinanced his seven-bedroom home. (See Chapter 1.)

In 2001, Dodd used his access to President Clinton to get Clinton to issue a presidential pardon to Dodd's friend, Edward Downe, who had pleaded guilty to criminal securities law violations.

The next year, Dodd, who owned a house on 10 acres in Ireland together with Downe's business partner, William Kessinger, miraculously managed to purchase Kessinger's two-thirds' stake in the Irish estate for a fraction of its market value.

Access to a sitting president can be lucrative.

The Whistleblower Law can and should be expanded to reward both uninvolved lawmakers and private citizens if they blow the whistle on this sort of disgraceful self-dealing. Our regulators breach the public trust when they take bribes from those they are supposed to be regulating. Such actions should result in severe penalties to the bribe-accepting lawmakers including impeachment, salary clawbacks, and pension and health care plan terminations and reductions, instead of our current policy—nothing. Senator Dodd was the proponent of the financial reform bill; but how can he speak to how the behaviors of others should be reformed? He should work on his own behavior first and come back to us when he has got that down.

THE NEXT BUBBLE: BIG GOVERNMENT

In a May 20, 2010, op-ed appearing in *Investor's Business Daily* Newt Gingrich and Dan Varroney warned us that bloated government is the next big bubble. They are right.

The U.S. national debt (public and U.S. government held) is over $13 trillion; the publicly held portion of the national debt as of August 1, 2010, was $8.8 trillion; $3.4 trillion of public debt has been added since TARP began. Far worse, though, are our unfunded entitlement liabilities for Social Security, Medicare, and prescription drugs. These unfunded liabilities total a mind-bending $109 trillion. Together, our national debt and unfunded entitlement liabilities come to nearly $400,000 per citizen (not per taxpayer). The United States, the greatest borrower in the world, is insolvent.

In 2010, President Obama spent nearly 25 percent of U.S. gross domestic product. But when one adds in state and local spending (including sales and real estate taxes), total government spending is more like half of all U.S. economic output (depending on the state). No economy can withstand such a high level of economic output being siphoned off by punitive taxation for too long. Much of this government spending, of course, is being financed with borrowed dollars. The Congressional Budget Office estimates that in 2011 the federal deficit will be 10.3 percent. That's not that far from the Greek deficit, which is estimated to be 13.6 percent. CBO estimates that the portion of our national debt held by the public will more than double from 40 percent in 2008 to 90 percent by 2020.

Most of our state governments are insolvent with California leading the charge. The states are going broker because public sector unions are bribing "management"—elected officials—with millions in campaign contributions. We cannot afford to go on granting our police, firefighters, and teachers gigantic defined benefit pensions (versus the defined contribution pensions more popular in the private sector) based on a huge percentage of their last few years' work including overtime.

Career politicians who have never run a business, never refrained from paying themselves in order to make a payroll, or ever really created a single job in their lives may think they can tax the private sector into oblivion—and equalize wealth no matter what the losses are in terms of overall prosperity (aggregate economic output)—but they can't.

Back in 1993, Hoover Institute scholar and economist W. Kurt Hauser published a paper making a remarkable assertion: Federal tax revenues since World War II have always been equal to approximately 19.5 percent of GDP, regardless of wide fluctuations in the top marginal tax rate. Said in reverse, individual and corporate taxpayers somehow always find a way of not paying more than 20 percent of gross economic output to the federal government. Whether that's done by tax cheating, the economy going underground (which is what happened in Greece), or by clever tax avoidance techniques, the empirical data over many decades reveal what is now known as "Hauser's Law" because of its inviolate nature.

The *Wall Street Journal,* on a few occasions since Hauser's observations were made, has printed a simple chart depicting Hauser's Law, the most recent version of which appears in Figure 15.1.

As can be seen, since 1929, the dotted 20 percent line has never been crossed. No matter how high the highest marginal tax bracket

Federal tax receipts (left scale in billions of dollars) will always fall short of 20% of GDP (bottom scale in trillions of dollars), 1929-2009

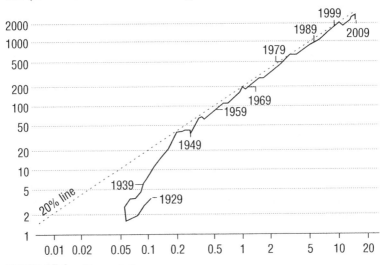

FIGURE 15.1   Hauser's Law

Note on Data: Calendar-year gross domestic product and current receipts of the federal government (Bureau of Economic Analysis). These data derive from the national income accounting (NIA) system, which is different from the cash-based system used by the Congressional Budget Office and the Office of Managemenand Budget.

has been, this line is never breached. Einstein taught us that matter can approach but never reach the speed of light, and Hauser taught us that the federal tax receipts can approach but never reach 20 percent of gross domestic product.

What this means is that unless federal spending is brought below the Hausian limit (20 percent), federal spending will of necessity be funded out of borrowed funds. But deficit spending cannot go on forever. Obviously the public debt will eventually reach proportions not tolerable to the lending community and it will stop lending.

Sooner or later the massive federal spending will stop—the only question is will it stop before it's too late for the United States to recover. Tragically, profligate federal spending and the prospect of the vastly increased taxes that must necessarily follow, far from stimulating the economy, ensure economic stagnation.

As the private sector is crowded out and punitively taxed into abandoning or deferring expansion plans, job growth is stultified. And of course jobs are exactly what we need to break the vicious negative feedback loop in which we now find ourselves. People lose their jobs, can't find new ones, and go into default on their home mortgages. That triggers bank losses, reductions of capital reserves, less bank lending, and more bank failures. And that in turn triggers lower rents and higher vacancy rates at apartment buildings (people without jobs can't pay rent), office buildings (job growth directly affects office vacancy and rental rates as each office worker takes up about 200 square feet), and retail projects (as retailers depend on consumers). With businesses hurt by the weakened consumer and restricted credit, more businesses fail and we see more job losses.

The problem of stagnant job growth caused by profligate spending and taxation is particularly pernicious in the current recession because now, unlike prior recessions, nearly half of the 8 million unemployed have been unemployed for a long time. The long-term unemployed eventually burn through their savings or simply give up hope, and mortgage defaults follow.

The only way to break this tragic negative feedback loop is to slash government spending, disenfranchise public unions—and cut marginal tax rates across the board. Doing that would unleash the formidable power of free-market capitalism. Businesses would prosper and the job growth engine would begin firing on all cylinders.

Another step that could help us unload the millions of "extra" homes our failed housing policies resulted in our building—we now have 19 million vacant housing units—would be to modify immigration policy to allow more homebuyers into the country. Granting visas to PhDs and other highly educated immigrants like engineers would help absorb our excess housing inventory.

TAXATION WITHOUT REPRESENTATION

On July 4, 1776, when our Founding Fathers signed the Declaration of Independence, they explained to the world the justifications for their actions. The oppressions of King George were so numerous and so punitive, revolution was their only course. In listing their grievances, the signers of the Declaration had this to say about the king's expansion of government and taxation: "He has erected a multitude of New Offices, and sent hither swarms of Officers to harass our people and eat out their substance."

The similarities of the present situation to the circumstances leading to our War of Independence do not end there. Cries of "taxation without representation!" led to the iconic Boston Tea Party, which now bears the name of a newly emerging and powerful grassroots movement.

While it is easy to say that in the present day all voters get a vote and therefore there is no taxation without representation, the statement rings hollow, because nearly half of all American taxpayers pay no tax whatsoever (or get checks in a disguised welfare/redistribution system). Those tax-filers are entirely disconnected from bearing any responsibility for our federal government and in consequence have no earthly reason to vote for politicians who seek to restrain federal spending.

Worse, with so many tax-filers freeloading, there is little political profit in trying to get voted in by the real taxpayers. In the end, the real job of a politician is to get reelected, and the easiest path to reelection is to promise more spending to benefit the freeloaders.

So there really is taxation without representation, as any politician in favor of big government who captures even the even the smallest percentage of the real taxpayers is bound to get elected when he or she adds on 100 percent of the votes of the freeloaders. This has prompted some to propose that we grant an exception to the one man, one vote principle (this is not contained in the U.S. Constitution anyway) by granting voting rights that reflect tax burdens.

In an April 20, 2010, op-ed article appearing in *Investor's Business Daily*, Walter Williams, economics professor at George Mason University, proposed that each citizen get one vote plus one additional vote for every $20,000 of federal tax he or she pays. It would be fascinating to see how many adherents the neo-Keynesians would lose upon the passage of law making that fundamental change to our voting rights.

However it is done, we must break the spend-and-tax mentality and the conspiracy between politicians and public unions. Perhaps we should grant Wall Street–style bonuses to all federal lawmakers for delivering a balanced budget. We could give everyone in the Oval Office and every senator and congressman a million dollar bonus if the budget is balanced, and we would save hundreds of billions of dollars.

When that good work is done we must slash marginal rates across the board. With those steps taken, ironically, federal revenues will increase; but instead of regrowing government, we must amortize our vast debts in order to restore growth and prosperity. We must not let well-intentioned but misguided notions of social justice destroy our country and economy.

As Winston Churchill said more than a half century ago, "the inherent vice of capitalism is the unequal sharing of blessings; the inherent virtue of socialism is the equal sharing of miseries."

Notes

CHAPTER 1   The Housing Bubble

1. See United States Bureau of Economic Analysis Report, "GDP and the Economy, Advance Estimates for the Third Quarter of 2009," www.bea.gov/scb/pdf/ 2009/11%20November/1109_gdpecon.pdf.
2. See www.nytimes.com/2008/09/15/business/15lehman.html.
3. See Congressional Reseach Service Report for Congress dated Septermber 15, 2008, http://fpc.state.gov/documents/organization/110097.pdf.
4. www.census.gov/hhes/www/housing/census/historic/owner.html. In the United States, the homeownership rate is set forth in the Housing Vacancy Survey by the U.S. Census Bureau. It is determined by dividing the owner-occupied units by the total number of occupied units.
5. The Servicemen's Readjustment Act of 1944. See U.S. Department of Veterans Affairs, www.gibill.va.gov/GI_Bill_Info/history.html. "Millions . . . took advantage of the GI Bill's home loan guaranty. From 1944 to 1952, VA backed nearly 2.4 million home loans for World War II veterans." U.S. Department of Veterans Affairs, www.gibill.va.gov/GI_Bill_Info/history.html.
6. Until 1986, all loan interest was deductible for federal income tax purposes. The 1986 Tax Reform Act, however, limited the interest deduction for individual taxpayers, making home mortgage interest deductible. See www .investopedia.com/articles/pf/06/MortIntTaxDeduct.asp?viewed=1.
7. When initially chartered in 1938 Fannie Mae was a wholly owned government corporation. In 1954, Fannie Mae became partly owned by private shareholders and partly owned by the federal government. In 1968, with an amendment to Title III of the National Housing Act (12 USC 1716 et seq.), Fannie Mae was split into two agencies, Ginnie Mae, a wholly owned government corporation, and Fannie Mae, a stockholder-owned corporation. In 1970, Congress authorized Fannie to buy and sell conventional loans, in addition to FHA and VA loans. Congress created the Federal Home Loan Mortgage Corporation, now named Freddie Mac, through Title III of the Emergency Home Finance Act of 1970 (12 USC 1451 et seq.), originally to provide a secondary market in which savings and loans could sell the mortgages they originated, but now Freddie Mac buys mortgages from commercial banks, mortgage bankers, and others as well.
8. Dan Immergluck, *Foreclosed: High-Risk Lending, Deregulation and the Undermining of America's Mortgage Market* (Ithaca, NY: Cornell University Press, 2009), pp.89–92.

9. The U.S. Department of Veterans Affairs (VA) issues government-backed mortgage insurance on home mortgages issued to veterans. The VA provides guarantees for a specified percentage of the mortgages. Ginnie Mae (GNMA) securitizes the loans and guarantees timely payment of interest and principal. *Legislative History of VA Program*, Department of Veterans Affairs. A separate government agency, Ginnie Mae, issues the actual government insurance through Ginnie Mae mortgage-backed securities.

10. In fact, the 3.5 percent down payment requirement was only brought up to that level in 2009. In 2008, it was at 3 percent. The Housing and Economic Recovery Act of 2008, FHA Modernization Act of 2008 (Section 2113) took effect January 1, 2009.

11. Immergluck, *Foreclosed: High-Risk Lending*.

12. www.opensecrets.org/news/2008/07/top-senate-recipients-of-fanni.htm.

13. www.acorn.org; www.huduser.org/Periodicals/ushmc/spring97/summary.html.

14. The quoted remarks of Kennedy, Humphrey, and Voegeli appeared in a June 28, 2010, *Investor's Business Daily* op-ed piece by syndicated columnist George F. Will.

15. William D. Cohan, *House of Cards: A Tale of Hubris and Wretched Excess on Wall Street*, (New York, NY: Doubleday, 2009), pp. 296–297.

16. Chevy Chase settled the alleged violation of the Fair Housing Act and Equal Credit Opportunity Act claim by agreeing to open three mortgage offices in majority African American neighborhoods in the Washington, D.C. metropolitan area and one bank branch in the Anacostia section of D.C., and to fund $140 million in discounted loans for residents in those communities. Department of Justice, press release dated August 22, 1994.

17. In addition to the $1 million to compensate minority borrowers, Shawmut was forced to set aside $85 million to make below market rate loans for the privileged applicants. "The Economics of Discrimination," speech delivered by Llewellyn H. Rockwell, Jr. to Georgia State University School of Law in Atlanta, April 1994. "The Fed later reversed its disapproval after Shawmut settled the case for approximately $1 million to compensate black and Hispanic applicants turned down for mortgages by the bank, and acted to take further steps to prevent future discrimination." Vern McKinley, "Community Reinvestment Act: Ensuring Credit Adequacy or Enforcing Credit Allocation?" *Regulation* 4 (1994).

18. www.consumer-guides.info/housing/Home_Ownership/.

19. http://thomas.loc.gov/cgi-bin/bdquery/z?d110:HR01852:@@@P.

20. http://online.wsj.com/article/SB121279970984353993.html. *Wall Street Journal*, June 7, 2008.

21. www.politico.com/news/stories/1009/28673.html.

22. http://brokencontrollers.com/forums/obama-s-million-dollar-men-franklin-raines-and-tim-howard-t25580.php.

23. Sowell, *Housing Boom and Bust*, (New York, NY: Basic Books, 2009), p. 38.

24. Id., p. 39.

25. Id.

26. Id.

27. An option ARM is a variation on adjustable-rate mortgage loans (where the interest rate on the note adjusts periodically in response to changes in an index) with borrowers offered options on how large a payment they will make. The options include interest-only, which covers the interest that accrues but does not amortize the loan, and a payment for less than the interest owed that results in a growing loan balance or "negative amortization." Option ARM loans were issued under a variety of names, including Pick-A-Payment, Cash Flow Option Loan, Pay Option ARM, and 1 Month Option ARM. The low initial payment entices some borrowers into buying higher-cost homes than they would have otherwise and to rely on housing price appreciation and refinancing at a future date before the loan rate adjusts. Although this type of loan worked as a legitimate way for wealthy people with lumpy income streams to manage their cash flows, they are dangerous when sold to consumers who are unlikely to be able to repay the loan should interest rates rise or housing prices fall.

28. Bob Secter and Andrew Lajac, "Rahm Emanuel's Stint at Mortgage Giant," *Chicago Tribune*, March 26, 2009, www.chicagotribune.com/news/politics/obama/chi-rahm-emanuel-profit-26-mar26,0,5682373.story.

29. See also http://abcnews.go.com/Blotter/story?id=6201900&page=1, www.sec.gov/news/press/2007/2007-05.htm, and http://articles.latimes.com/2009/mar/26/nation/na-emanuel-freddie26.

30. Id.

31. See testimony of former Fannie Mae Chief Credit Officer Ed Pinto when he appeared before the House Financial Services Committee on September 16, 2009, www.house.gov/apps/list/hearing/financialsvcs_dem/pinto_testimony.pdf.

CHAPTER 2   The Bubble Implodes

1. Alt-A (Alternative A paper) mortgage risks falls between prime and subprime, but is closer to prime, also known as alternative-documentation loans. The lack of a standard lender definition leads to variability, and the underwriting and credit quality of Alt-A pools can vary. The Alt-A product is primarily credit-score driven, as its borrowers don't have proof of income from traditional employment. The lack of income verification and documentation of assets associated with traditional, fully documented loans provided mortgage originators and borrowers with the opportunity to claim higher than actual income and assets levels in order to qualify for larger loan amounts, known as "liar loans."

2. Paul Moulo and Matthew Padilla, *Chain of Blame: How Wall Street Caused the Mortgage and Credit Crisis* (New York, NY: John Wiley & Sons, 2008).

3. Robert J. Shiller, *Irrational Exuberance*, 2nd ed. (Hoboken, NJ: Princeton University Press, 2005), and Robert J. Shiller, The Subprime Solution: *How Today's Global Financial Crisis Happened, and What to Do About It* (Hoboken, NJ: Princeton University Press, 2008).

4. A FICO score is a credit score derived from the credit model developed by Fair Isaac Corporation. The FICO score, which has a range of 300–850, is the best-known credit score in the United States and is calculated by all three of the major credit bureaus from reported information. A higher FICO score indicates better credit, and a FICO score below 620 is considered poor. The most important factor in determining a FICO score is past payment punctuality. The percentage of credit limit used is another critical parameter in the FICO score models, with a penalty for using too much of available credit. These two factors are given a total weight of around two-thirds in determining the typical individual's FICO score. Other major FICO score variables include length of credit history and types of credit used. Bankruptcy, foreclosure, court judgments, and tax liens receive a strong FICO score penalty, especially when they are recent.

5. MAI is a real estate appraiser credential standing for Member of the Appraisal Institute.

6. Fannie had 10 consecutive quarters of losses totaling $136.8 billion. Fannie lost $132.7 billion in the last three years: 2009, 2008, and 2007 losses were $72 billion, $58.7, and $2.1 billion, respectively. Freddie reported 10 consecutive quarters of losses totaling $75.4 billion, and three consecutive years of losses totaling $74.8 billion. The 2009, 2008, and 2007 losses were $21.6 billion, $50.1 billion, and $3.1 billion, respectively. In aggregate, that's $212.2 billion for the last 10 quarters and $207.5 billion in the last three years.

7. Actual decline from from the peak was 28.3 percent. Peak level for the National Index was 189.93 at 2006Q2 vs. 136.09 at 2009Q4. For descriptions and definitions of the index see: www.standardandpoors.com/servlet/ BlobServer?blobheadername3=MDT-Type&blobcol=urldata&blobtable=M ungoBlobs&blobheadervalue2=inline%3B+filename%3DMethdology_SP_CS _Home_Price_Indices_Web.pdf&blobheadername2=Content-Disp osition&blobheadervalue1=application%2Fpdf&blobkey=id &blobheadername1=content-type&blobwhere=1243624745188& blobheadervalue3=UTF-8. The 10-City Composite is a subset of the 20-City Composite. The 10-City Composite is comprised of the Boston, Denver, Las Vegas, Los Angeles, Miami, San Diego, San Francisco, and Washington, D.C. MSAs and the Chicago Metropolitan and New York City Areas. The 20-City Composite is made up of the areas in the 10-City plus 10 additional MSAs: Atlanta, Charlotte, Cleveland, Dallas, Detroit, Minneapolis, Phoenix, Portland, Seattle, and Tampa.

8. www.foxnews.com/story/0,2933,432173,00.html. Interview of Barney Frank by Bill O'Reilly, July 14, 2008. Frank also walked off the set of CNBC. For a video clip of Barney Frank ending the CNBC interview, see: www.breitbart .tv/?p=359093.

9. Sowell, *Housing Boom and Bust*, p. 55.

10. Id.

11. http://financialservices.house.gov/archive_membership.html. Frank has served on the House Banking Committee since becoming a congressman in 1981

and became the ranking Democrat in 2003. He became the chair of the committee, now called the House Financial Services Committee, in January 2007.

12. Bureau of Labor Statistics, Gallup, www.gallup.com/poll/126272/Underemployment-February-Par-January.aspx.

13. A total of 861,664 families lost their homes to foreclosure in 2008, according to RealtyTrac. There were more than 3.1 million foreclosure filings issued during 2008, which means that one of every 54 households received a notice that year. On Jan. 14, 2010, RealtyTrac® (www.realtytrac.com) released its Year-End 2009 Foreclosure Market Report, which shows a total of 3,957,643 foreclosure filings; default notices, scheduled foreclosure auctions, and bank repossessions—were reported on 2,824,674 U.S. properties in 2009, a 21 percent increase in total properties from 2008 and a 120 percent increase in total properties from 2007. www.realtytrac.com/contentmanagement/pressrelease.aspx?channelid=9&itemid=8333. On Jan. 15, 2009, RealtyTrac® released its 2008 U.S. Foreclosure Market Report, which shows a total of 3,157,806 foreclosure filings; default notices, auction sale notices, and bank repossessions—were reported on 2,330,483 U.S. properties during the year, an 81 percent increase in total properties from 2007 and a 225 percent increase in total properties from 2006. www.realtytrac.com/contentmanagement/pressrelease.aspx?channelid=9&itemid=5681.

14. www2.tbo.com/content/2009/apr/28/sp-record-number-of-homes-vacant/news-money/.

15. www.msnbc.msn/id/24988315/.

16. www.census.gov/hhes/www/housing/hvs/qtr409/files/q409press.pdf. As of September 2009, First American CoreLogic estimated there was a 1.7 million-unit pending supply of residential housing inventory, up from 1.1 million a year earlier. Pending supply, sometimes referred to as "shadow" inventory, estimates real estate owned (REO) by banks and mortgage companies as a result of foreclosures and other actions, such as deeds in lieu, as well as real estate that is at least 90 days delinquent. Normally, shadow inventory would not be included in the official measures of unsold inventory. At the current sales rate, the pending supply is 3.3 months, up from 2.4 months a year ago. The months' supply measures how quickly the inventory will run off given the current sales rate. The visible supply of unsold inventory was 3.8 million units in September 2009, down from 4.7 million a year earlier. The visible inventory measures the unsold inventory of new and existing homes that are currently on the market. The visible months' supply fell to 7.8 months in September 2009, down from 10.1 months a year earlier. The total unsold inventory (which combines the visible and pending supply) was 5.5 million units in September 2009, down from 5.7 million a year ago. The total months' supply was 11.1 months, down from 12.7 a year earlier. This indicates that while the visible months' supply has decreased and is beginning to approach more normal levels, adding the pending supply reveals there is still quite a bit of inventory that will impact the housing market for the next few years, especially in the context of the current increase in home sales, which is in

part due to artificially low interest rates and the homebuyer tax credit. www.reedconstructiondata.com/news/2010/01/u.s.-inventory-of-unsold -new-homes-isnt-getting-much-better/.

17. http://blogs.abcnews.com/george/2009/11/bush-i-went-against-my-freemarket -instincts.html. The former president made the remarks November 12, 2009, at the unveiling of the George W. Bush Presidential Center at Southern Methodist University. "I went against my free-market instincts and approved a temporary government intervention to unfreeze the credit markets so that we could avoid a major global depression," Bush said.

18. Alaska, Arizona, California, Connecticut, Florida, Idaho, Minnesota, North Carolina, North Dakota, Texas, Utah, Washington. www.loansafe.org/forum/ foreclosure-laws/4130-recourse-v-non-recourse-states.html.

19. OneWest Bank FSB, which acquired the deposits and the majority of assets of IndyMac Federal Bank, FSB from the FDIC, did not receive TARP funds, but the FDIC agreed to share in future losses.

20. See www.washingtonpost.com/wp-dyn/content/article/2009/11/25/AR200911 2504186.html. *Indymac Bank FSB v. Yano-Horoski* (2009 NY Slip Op 52333 (U)). decided November 19, 2009. www.nycourts.gov/reporte/3dseries/2009/ 2009_52333.htm. See also www.businessinsider.com/judge-slams-indymac -cancels-defendants-mortgage-2009-11 and www.washingtonpost.com/wp-dyn/ content/article/2009/11/25/AR2009112504186.html.

21. HR 3648 passed in the House of Representatives March 5, 2009, by a vote of 234–191.

22. http://online.wsj.com/article/SB1000142405274870447150457444307247935 6040.html. *Wall Street Journal*, October 14, 2009, "MBS, R.I.P.?" p. A22.

23. See www.nypost.com/p/news/opinion/opedcolumnists/mortgage_madness_ 4eBKDKDuKBSxKJH2ZG0U2J

24. www.treas.gov/tic/mfh.txt.

25. U.S. Department of the Treasury, http://financialstability.gov/docs/HAMP/ 12242009/Fannie.pdf. http://financialstability.gov/docs/HAMP/12242009/ Freddie.pdf

26. Speaking to the *Wall Street Journal* on November 16, 2008, Rahm Emanuel said, "You never want a serious crisis to go to waste. And what I mean by that is an opportunity to do things you think you could not do before."

CHAPTER 3 Capital Markets Supporting U.S. Commercial Real Estate

1. JP Morgan Asset Management.
2. CMBS: commercial mortgage-backed securities.
3. Second mortgages remain popular in residential lending. Home equity lines of credit—or HELOCs as they are called—and home equity loans are secured by second mortgages.
4. "LTV" stands for loan-to-value.

CHAPTER 4   CRE Values and Loan Defaults

1. Congressional Oversight Panel (COP) Report, p. 7.
2. Id., at 2.
3. Id., at 2.
4. Id., at 2.
5. LIBOR refers to the London Interbank Offered Rate.
6. COP Report, p. 72, footnote 246, citing the written testimony of Jon Greenlee, associate director of the Federal Reserve's Division of Bank Supervision and Regulation.
7. Id., at 22 (figure 4).

CHAPTER 5   Putting Off the Day of Reckoning

1. These options are also impacted by FASB pronouncements which were either just becoming effective in 2009 or going to become effective in the first quarter of 2010. FAS 166, *Transfers and Servicing,* eliminates qualified special purpose entities (QSPEs); also, FAS 167 changes the approach for valuable interest enterprises (VIEs). In addition to AS 157-4, FSP FAS 115-2 and FAS 124-2 dealt with OTTI write-downs and gave some relief in the first quarter by letting the lenders bifurcate the loss between the income statement (credit loss) and OCI (other factors).
2. The FASB no longer uses pronouncements. Effective July 1, 2009, the FASB established the Codification as the source of authoritative generally accepted accounting principles (GAAP) for companies to use in the preparation of financial statements. SEC rules and interpretive releases are also authoritative GAAP for SEC registrants. The guidance contained in the Codification supersedes all existing non-SEC accounting and reporting standards. The references have not been changed for the Codification because of historical context.
3. FASB ASC 320-10 (FSP FAS 115-2 and FAS 124-2) states that an OTTI write-down of debt securities, where fair value is below amortized cost, is triggered in circumstances where (1) an entity has the intent to sell a security, (2) it is more likely than not that the entity will be required to sell the security before recovery of its amortized cost basis, or (3) the entity does not expect to recover the entire amortized cost basis of the security. If an entity intends to sell a security or if it is more likely than not that the entity will be required to sell the security before recovery, an OTTI write-down is recognized in earnings equal to the entire difference between the security's amortized cost basis and its fair value. If an entity does not intend to sell the security or it is more likely than not that it will not be required to sell the security before recovery, the OTTI write-down is separated into an amount representing the credit loss, which is recognized in earnings, and the amount related to all other factors, which is recognized in OCI. The new accounting requirements for recording OTTI on debt securities were effective for second quarter 2009; however, as permitted under the pronouncement, companies were allowed to early adopt on January 1, 2009.

4. FAS 166 modifies certain guidance contained in FASB ASC 860, *Transfers and Servicing*. This standard eliminates the concept of qualifying special-purpose entities (QSPEs) and provides additional criteria transferors must use to evaluate transfers of financial assets. To determine if a transfer is to be accounted for as a sale, the transferor must assess whether all of the entities included in its consolidated financial statements have surrendered control of the assets. A transferor must consider all arrangements or agreements made or contemplated at the time of transfer before reaching a conclusion on whether control has been relinquished. FAS 166 addresses the situation in which a portion of financial asset is transferred. In such instances, the transfer can only be accounted for as a sale when the transferred portion is considered to be a participating interest. FAS 166 also requires that any assets or liabilities retained from a transfer accounted for as a sale be initially recognized at fair value. This standard was effective for most companies as of January 1, 2010, with adoption applied prospectively for transfers that occur on and after the effective date.

5. FAS 167 amends several key consolidation provision related to variable-interest entities (VIEs), which are included in FASB ASC 810, *Consolidation*. First, the scope of FAS 167 includes entities that are currently designated as qualified special purpose entities (QSPEs). Second, FAS 167 changes the approach companies use to identify the VIEs for which they are deemed to be the primary beneficiary and are required to consolidate. Under existing rules, the primary beneficiary is the entity that absorbs the majority of a VIE's losses and receives the majority of the VIE's returns. The guidance in FAS 167 identifies a VIE's primary beneficiary as the entity that has the power to direct the VIE's significant activities and has an obligation to absorb losses or the right to receive benefits that could be potentially significant to the VIE. Third, FAS 167 requires companies to continually reassess whether they are the primary beneficiary of a VIE. Existing rules only require companies to reconsider primary beneficiary conclusions when certain triggering events have occurred. FAS 167 is effective for most companies as of January 1, 2010, and applies to all current QSPEs and VIEs, and VIEs created after the effective date.

6. The business judgment rule "bars judicial inquiry into actions of corporate directors taken in good faith and in the exercise of honest judgment in the lawful and legitimate furtherance of corporate purposes. Questions of policy of management, expediency of contracts or action, adequacy of consideration, lawful appropriation of corporate funds to advance corporate interests, are left solely to their honest and unselfish decision, for their powers therein are without limitation and free from restraint, and the exercise of them for the common and general interests of the corporation may not be questioned, although the results show that what they did was unwise or inexpedient." *Auerbach v. Bennett*, 47 N.Y.2d 619, 629, 393 N.E.2d 994, 1000, 419 N.Y.S.2d 920, 926 (N.Y. 1979), *citing Pollitz v. Wabash R.R. Co.*, 207 N.Y. 113, 100 N.E. 721 (N.Y. 1912).

7. www.forbes.com/2009/04/02/accounting-fasb-banking-busienss-wall-street-fasb.html

CHAPTER 6   Tranche Warfare

1. This does not amount to a final determination by Justice Lowe that the allegations of collusion were proved.
2. In addition, CRE lenders, particularly in the case of securitized loans, usually took the additional precaution of requiring the borrower to have "independent managers" whose votes were required, under the organizational documents governing the borrower entities, in order to file a bankruptcy petition. This precaution as well was taken by the ESH lenders. Because equity interests are pledged to secure mezzanine loans, non-recourse carve-out guarantors find themselves no longer in control of the borrower entity following a mezzanine lender's UCC foreclosure sale. Many non-recourse carve out guaranties do not distinguish between a bankruptcy petition filed at the behest of the non-recourse guarantor and those filed by a mezzanine lender who took over the borrower. Thus some non-recourse carve-out guarantors may one day find themselves in the unenviable position of taking on liability (at least in theory) due to a bankruptcy filed by a foreclosing mezzanine lender.

CHAPTER 7   Loans to Own and Chilling the Bid

1. COP Report, p. 3.
2. Section 489 of the New York Judiciary Law.

CHAPTER 8   Funding Cessations and Extension Fights

1. 2009 WL 3790441 (4th Dep't Nov. 13, 2009).

CHAPTER 9   Bankruptcy Considerations

1. www.ggp.com/Company/Pressreleases.aspx?mode=view&prid=451
2. In Re General Growth Properties, Inc. et al., 409 B.R. 43 (S.D.N.Y. 2009)
3. August 11, 2009, Decision, p. 17.
4. There is a debate as to whether a director's duty shifts to creditors prior to a business entity becoming insolvent. Hence some courts have triggered the shift when a company enters the "zone of insolvency," meaning the period during which a business may be approaching the point at which it becomes insolvent.
5. Id. at p. 40.
6. Richard Parkus, *Commercial Real Estate at the Precipice* (Commercial Real Estate Outlook Q1 2009, Deutsche Bank).
7. COP Report, page 2.
8. In *Blue Hill Office Park LLC v. J.P. Morgan Chase Bank*, 477 F. Supp. 2d 366 (D. Mass. 2007), the federal district court held that a commercial mortgage lender was entitled to enforce a "springing guaranty" against the borrower's principals where such guaranty sprung to life based on typical carve-outs from the nonrecourse provisions, such as fraud and waste. In *F.D.I.C. v.*

Prince George Corp. 58 F.3d 1041 (4th Cir. 1995), the Fourth Circuit, applying Texas and South Carolina state law, held that springing guarantees are valid and do not violate any public policy. In *LaSalle Bank, N.A. v. Mobile Hotel Properties, LLC, et al.*, 367 F.Supp.2d 1022 (E.D. La. 2004), the District Court held a guarantor liable under a springing guaranty for the full deficiency claim for failure to maintain its single-purpose entity status. *See also CSFB 2001-CP-4 Princeton Park Corporate Center, LLC v. SB Rental I., LLC*, 980 A.2d 1,7 (N.J. Super. Ct. 2009) (finding that springing recourse guarantee was valid and enforceable under New Jersey law and stating that having "freely and knowingly negotiated for the benefit of avoiding recourse liability generally, and agreeing to the burden of full recourse liability in certain specified circumstances, defendants may not now escape the consequences of their bargain").

9. Id. at 621.
10. Id. at 11.
11. Id.
12. In Re Extended Stay, Inc. et al., 418 B.R. 49, 60 (S.D.N.Y. 2009)

CHAPTER 10 Multifamily Market

1. www.costar.com/News/Article.aspx?id=57A497448DB5B02048AAB449236CDC75
2. http://community.nasdaq.com/News/2010-03/Freddie-Rolls-Out-Mezzanine-Program.aspx
3. www.nmhc.org/Content/ServeContent.cfm?ContentItemID=1162
4. Gunnar Myrdal, "Opening Address to the Council of International Building Research in Copenhagen," *Dagens Nyheter* (Swedish newspaper), August 25, 1965, p. 12; cited in Sven Rydenfelt, "The Rise, Fall and Revival of Swedish Rent Control," in *Rent Control: Myths and Realities*, Walter Block and Edgar Olsen, eds. (Vancouver: The Fraser Institute, 1981), p. 224.
5. Assar Lindbeck, *The Political Economy of the New Left* (New York: Harper and Row, 1972); cited in Sven Rydenfelt, "The Rise, Fall and Revival of Swedish Rent Control," pp. 213, 230.
6. www.nytimes.com/2008/07/11/nyregion/11rangel.html?pagewanted=1&_r=1
7. www.nypost.com/p/news/regional/item_2o6e4Oyrrsdsn8f60PRBFM
8. *Roberts v. Tishman Speyer Properties, L.P.*, 13 N.Y.3d 270, 890 N.Y.S.2d 388 (2009).
9. www.wikipedia.org/wiki/Peter_Cooper_Village (footnote 14)*
10. *NY Times*, July 29, 1947.
11. See New York Emergency Tenant's Protection Act of 1974.
12. Section 26-504(c) of the Rent Stabilization Law.
13. See RSL §§ 26-504.1 and 26-504.2(a). The $250,000 annual income threshold was later reduced to $175,000. 1997 N.Y. Sess. Laws 218 (McKinney) (L. 1997, ch. 116).
14. *Roberts v. Tishman Speyer*. 13 N.Y.3d 270, 285 (2009).

15. See Private Housing Finance Law § 100, et seq.
16. The Court of Appeals also cited to some ambiguous statements, I think taken out of context, in the legislative record of the debate over the Luxury Decontrol Law. Regardless, there was no reason to look to the record, since the statute is clear on its face.

CHAPTER 11   Governmental Actions Caused the Affordable Housing Crisis

1. www.nantucketlandbank.org/index.php
2. Id.
3. www.nantucket-ma.gov/Pages/NantucketMA_Conversation/index
4. www.mass.gov/dfwele/dfw/nhesp/nhesp.htm
5. www.mass.gov/dfwele/dfw/nhesp/land_protection/twnrpts/nantucket_care _habitats.pdf

CHAPTER 13   Assessing Blame for the Financial Crisis

1. For example, George W. Bush fell prey to the politically irresistible lure of democratizing mortgage credit when on December 16, 2003, he signed into law the American Dream Downpayment Act.
2. The C-Span footage of this hearing may be viewed at www.youtube.com/ watch?v=_MGT_cSi7Rs. I urge readers to watch this breathtaking footage.
3. Thanks to the good work of some investigative reporters at the *New York Post*, Meeks and New York State Senator Malcolm Smith became the subject of a federal probe into a charity they helped establish for Hurricane Katrina victims. According to the *Post*, only $1,392 of the funds collected ever made their way into the hands of Katrina victims.
4. www.usc.edu/schools/sppd/lusk/research/pdf/wp_2009-1001.pdf (p. 23).
5. www.realclearpolitics.com/video/2010/05/04/cnn_foreclosure_brought _pressure_and_heartache_on_ny_car_bomb_terrorist.html
6. www.voices.washingtonpost.com/ezra-klein/2010/05/the_economic_crisis _meets_terr.html

CHAPTER 14   The Centerpiece for Real Reform

1. There were 1.3 million foreclosure filings in 2007; 2.3 million filings in 2008; and 2.8 million filings in 2009.
2. In 2007, 404,000 people lost their homes to foreclosures; 850,000 lost their homes in 2008; and 980,000 lost their homes in 2009.
3. www.justice.gov/archive/ag/speeches/1998/0320_agcom.htm

About the Author

STEPHEN B. MEISTER, founding partner of Meister, Seelig & Fein, LLP, a 45-attorney commercial law firm with offices in New York, Los Angeles, Boston, and East Brunswick, New Jersey, represents real estate investment trusts, real estate private equity firms, hedge funds, banks, and real estate developers and investors. Well known throughout New York City for the powerful deal making presence he brings to high-stakes negotiations, he is also nationally recognized for the trial skills he brings to bear in CRE debt stack and intercreditor disputes, complex lender liability cases, mortgage and mezzanine equity collateral foreclosures, affordable housing cases, mandamus proceedings against state and municipal agencies, contract disputes, business tort actions, legal malpractice, and brokerage commission claims. Mr. Meister appears regularly on Fox Business News and CNBC, and writes an op-ed column for the *New York Post,* which is picked up and reprinted by numerous web sites. Mr. Meister is often quoted or featured in the *Wall Street Journal, New York Times, New York Post, Crain's New York Business, Real Estate Weekly, The Real Deal,* and other business journals and daily newspapers around the country. An accomplished pilot, Mr. Meister splits his time between his homes in Mill Neck, NY, and Nantucket, MA. He is married to Melissa A. Meister and has three children, Jason, Jessica, and Micaela.

Index

Printed and bound by CPI Group (UK) Ltd, Croydon, CR0 4YY

16/04/2025